Diggers at War

Diggers at War
Accounts of Australians During
the Great War in the Middle East,
at Gallipoli and on the Western Front

"Over There" With the Australians
by R. Hugh Knyvett

★

Over the Top With the
Third Australian Division
by G. P. Cuttriss

LEONAUR

Diggers at War: Accounts of Australians During the Great War in the Middle East, at Gallipoli and on the Western Front

"Over There" With the Australians
by R. Hugh Knyvett

Over the Top With the Third Australian Division
by G. P. Cuttriss

Leonaur is an imprint of Oakpast Ltd

Text in this form and material original to this edition
copyright © 2008 Oakpast Ltd

ISBN: 978-1-84677-562-8 (hardcover)
ISBN: 978-1-84677-561-1 (softcover)

http://www.leonaur.com

Publisher's Notes

The opinions expressed in this book are those of the author and are not necessarily those of the publisher.

Contents

"Over There" With the Australians 7
Over the Top With the Third Australian Division 233

"Over There" with the Australians

by R. Hugh Knyvett

Contents

"Over There" with the Australians	7
Bill-Jim's Christmas	11
Mainly About Scouts	13
The Call Reaches Some Far-Out Australians	21
An All-British Ship	25
Human Snowballs	29
Training-Camp Life	36
Concentrated for Embarkation	43
Many Weeks at Sea	52
The Land of Sand and Sweat	63
Heliopolis	65
The Desert	68
Picketing in Cairo	71
Nipper	78
The Adventure of Youth	85
The Landing That Could Not Succeed—But Did	88
Holding On and Nibbling	94
The Evacuation	99
Ships That Pass …	103
Ferry Post and the Suez Canal Defences	111
First Days In France …	118
The Battle of Fleurbaix …	124
Days and Nights of Strafe	134
The Village of Sleep	143
The Somme	151
The Army's Pair of Eyes	160
Nights in No Man's Land	166
Spy-Hunting	174

Bapaume and "a Blighty"	179
In France	187
In London	193
The Hospital-Ship	198
In Australia	204
Using an Irishman's Nerve	208
The Right Infantry Weapons	213
The Forcing-House of Bestiality	216
The Psychology of Fear	219
The Splendour of the Present Opportunity	222
Not a Fight for Race but for Right	225
Keeping Faith With the Dead	228
But a Short Time to Live	231

Bill-Jim's Christmas

(Bill-Jim is Australia's name for her soldier)

Here where I sit, mucked-up with Flanders mud,
Wrapped-round with clothes to keep the Winter out,
Ate-up wi' pests a bloke don't care to name
To ears polite,
I'm glad I'm here all right;
A man must fight for freedom and his blood
Against this German rout
An' do his bit,
An' not go growlin' while he's doin' it:
The cove as can't stand cowardice or shame
Must play the game.

Here's Christmas, though, with cold sleet swirlin' down ...
God! gimme Christmas day in Sydney town!
I long to see the flowers in Martin Place,
To meet the girl I write to face to face,
To hold her close and teach
What in this Hell I'm learning—that a man
Is only half a man without his girl,
That sure as grass is green and God's above
A chap's real happiness,
If he's no churl,
Is home and folks and girl,
And all the comforts that come in with love!

There is a thrill in war, as all must own,
The tramplin' onward rush,

The shriek o' shrapnel and the followin' hush,
The bosker crunch o' bayonet on bone,
The warmth of the dim dug-out at the end,
The talkin' over things, as friend to friend,
And through it all the blessed certainty
As this war's working out for you an' me
As we would have it work.

Fritz maybe, and the Turk
Feel that way, too,
The same as me an' you,
And dream o' victory at last, although
The silly cows don't know,
Because they ain't been born and bred clean-free,
Like you and me.
But this is Christmas, and I'm feeling blue,
An' lonely, too.

I want to see one little girl's sly pout
(There's lots of other coves as feels like this)
That holds you off and still invites a kiss.
I want to get out from this smash and wreck
Just for today,
And feel a pair of arms slip round me neck
In that one girl's own way.
I want to hear the splendid roar and shout
O' breakers comin' in on Bondi Beach,
While she, with her old scrappy costume on,
Walks by my side, an' looks into my face,
An' makes creation one big pleasure-place
Where golden sand basks in that golden weather—
Yes! her an' me together!
I do me bit,
An' make no fuss of it;
But for today I somehow want to be
At home, just her an' me.

(From the Sydney *Sunday Times*)

Introduction
Mainly About Scouts

I am a scout; nature, inclination, and fate put me into that branch of army service. In trying to tell Australia's story I have of necessity enlarged on the work of the scouts, not because theirs is more important than other branches of the service, nor they braver than their comrades of other units. Nor do I want it to be thought that we undergo greater danger than machine-gunners, grenadiers, light trench-mortar men, or other specialists. But, frankly, I don't know much about any other man's job but my own, and less than I ought to about that. To introduce you to the spirit, action, and ideals of the Australian army I have to intrude my own personality, and if in the following pages "what I did" comes out rather strongly, please remember I am but "one of the boys," and have done not nearly as good work as ten thousand more.

I rejoice though that I was a scout, and would not exchange my experiences with any, not even with an adventurer from the pages of B. O. P.[1] Romance bathes the very name, the finger-tips tingle as they write it, and there was not infrequently enough interesting work to make one even forget to be afraid. Very happy were those days when I lived just across the road from Fritz, for we held dominion over No Man's Land, and I was given complete freedom in planning and executing my tiny stunts. The general said: "It is not much use training specialists if you interfere with them," so as long as we did our job we were given a free hand.

The deepest lines are graven on my memory from those days, not by the thrilling experiences—"th' hairbreadth 'scapes"—but by the fellowship of the men I knew. An American general said to

1. *Boys Own Paper.*

me recently that scouts were born, not made. It may be so, but it is surprising what opposite types of men became our best scouts. There were two without equal: one, city-bred, a college graduate; the other a *bushie*, writing his name with difficulty.

Ray Wilson was a nervous, highly strung sort of fellow, almost a girl in his sensitiveness. In fact, at the first there were several who called him Rachel, but they soon dropped it, for he was a lovable chap, and disarmed his enemies with his good nature. He had taken his arts course, but was studying music when he enlisted, and he must have been the true artist, for though the boys were prejudiced against the mandolin as being a *sissy* instrument, when he played they would sit around in silence for hours. What makes real friendship between men? You may know and like and respect a fellow for years, and that is as far as it goes, when, suddenly, one day something happens—a curtain is pulled aside and you go "ben"[2] with him for a second—afterward you are *friends*, before you were merely friendly acquaintances.

Ray and I became friends in this wise. We were out together scouting preparatory to a raid, and were seeking a supposed new listening post of the enemy. There had been a very heavy bombardment of the German trenches all day, and it was only held up for three-quarters of an hour to let us do our job. The newstale earth turned up by the shells extended fifty yards in No Man's Land. (Only earth that has been blown on by the wind is fresh over there. Don't, if you have a weak stomach, ever turn up any earth; though there may not be rotting flesh, other gases are imprisoned in the soil.) This night the wind was strong, and the smell of warm blood mingled with the phosphorous odour of high explosive, and there was that other sweet-sticky-sickly smell that is the strongest scent of a recent battle-field. It was a vile, unwholesome job, and we were glad that our time was limited to three-quarters of an hour, when our artillery would re-open fire. I got a fearful start on looking at my companion's face in the light of a white star-shell; it might have belonged to one of the corpses lying near, with the lips drawn back, the eyes fixed, and the complexion ghastly. He replied to my signal that he was all right, but

---

2. "Ben" was the living-room of a Scotch cottage where only intimate friends were admitted. Ian Maclaren says of a very good man: "He was far ben wi God."

a nasty suspicion crept into my mind—his teeth had chattered so much as to make him unable to answer a question of mine just before we left the trench, but one took no notice of a thing like that, for stage fright was common enough to all of us before a job actually started. But could he be depended on? was the fear that was now haunting me.

Presently some Germans came out of their trench. We counted eight of them as they crawled down inside their broken wire. We cautiously followed them, expecting that they were going out to the suspected listening post, but they went about fifty yards, and then lay down just in front of their own parapet. After about twenty minutes they returned the way they came, and I have no doubt reported that they had been over to our wire and there were no Australian patrols out.

This had taken up most of our time, and I showed Wilson that we had only ten minutes left, and that we had better get back so as not to cut it too fine. I was rather surprised when he objected, spelling out Morse on my hand that we had come out to find the listening post, and we had not searched up to the right. The Germans were evidently getting suspicious of the silence, and to our consternation suddenly put down a heavy barrage in No Man's Land, not more than thirty yards behind us. There was no getting through it, and we grabbed each other's hand, and only the pressure was needed to signal the one word *trapped*. When the shelling commenced we had instinctively made for a drain about four feet deep that ran across No Man's Land, and sat up in about six inches of water. Had we remained on top the light from the shells would have revealed us only too plainly, being behind us. I was afraid to look at my wristwatch, and when I did pluck up sufficient courage to do so, I might have saved myself the trouble, as the opening shell from our batteries at the same moment proclaimed that the time was up. As we huddled down, sitting in the icy water, we realized that the objective of our own guns was less than ten yards from us, and we could only hope and pray that no more wire-cutting was going to be done that night. Once, when we were covered with the returning debris, we instinctively threw our arms round each other. When we shook ourselves free, what was my amazement to find my companion shaking with—

laughter. There was now no need for silence, a shout could hardly be heard a few yards away. He called to me: "Did you ever do the Blondin act before, because we are walking a razor-edge right now. We're between the devil and the 'deep sea,' anyway, and I think myself the 'deep sea' will get us."

As I looked at him something happened, and I felt light-hearted as though miles from danger—all fear of death was taken away. What did it matter if we were killed?—it was a strange sense of security in a rather tight place.

After a short while our bombardment ceased. We learned afterward that word was sent back to the artillery that we were still out. As the *boche* fire also stopped soon afterward, we were able to scurry back and surprise our friends with our safe appearance.

After this experience Ray Wilson and I were closer than brothers—than twin brothers. It was only a common danger shared, such an ordinary thing in trench life, but there was something that was not on the surface, and though I was his officer, our friendship knew no barrier. I went mad for a while when his body was found—mutilated—after he had been missing three days. Don't talk of not hating to a man whose friend has been foully murdered! What if he had been yours?

A very different man was Dan Macarthy, a typical outbacker. All the schooling he ever got was from an itinerant teacher who would stay for a week at the house, correct and set tasks, returning three months later for another week. This system was adopted by the government for the sparsely settled districts not able to support a teacher, as a means of assisting the parents in teaching their children themselves. But Dan's parents could neither read nor write, and what healthy youngster, with all *out-of-doors* around him, would study by himself. Dan read with difficulty and wrote with greater, but I have met few better-educated men. His eyesight was marvellous, and I don't think that he ever forgot an incident, however slight. After a route march our scouts have to write down everything they saw, not omitting the very smallest detail. For example, if we pass through a village they have to give an estimate by examining the stores, how many troops it could support, and so on. No other list was ever as large as Dan's. He saw and remembered everything. He had received his training as a child looking for horses in a paddock so large that if you did not know where to look you might search for a week. Out there in the country of the black-tracker powers of observation are abnormally developed—lives depend on it, as when in a drought the watercourses dry up, and only the signs written on the ground indicate to him who can read them where the life-saving fluid may be found. Dan was a wonderful scout, a true and loyal friend, but he had absolutely no sense of ownership. He thought that whatever another man possessed he had a right to; but, on the other hand, anyone else had an equal right to appropriate anything of his (Dan's). He never put forward any theory about it, but would just help himself to anything he wanted, not troubling to hide it, and he never made any fuss if someone picked up something of his that was not in use. I never saw such a practical example of communism.

At first, there were a number of rows about it, but after a while if any of the boys missed anything they would go and hunt through Dan's kit for it. The only time he made a fuss at losing anything was when one of his mates for a lark took his rosary. He soon discovered, by shrewd questioning, who it was, and there was a fight that landed them both in the guard-tent. The boys forbore to tease him about his inconsistency when he said: "It was mother's. She brought it from Ireland."

Dan was still scouting when I was sent out well-punctured, and I doubt if there are any who have accounted for more of the Potsdam swine single-handed. His score was known to be over a hundred when I left. If I can get back again, may I have Dan in my squad! These two are but types of the boys I lived with so long, and got to love so well. Few of my early comrades are left on the earth; but we are not separated even from those who have *gone west*, and the war has given to me, in time and eternity, many real friends.

The following pages are not a history of the Australians. I have no means of collecting and checking data, but they are an attempt to show the true nature of the Australian soldier, and sent out with the hope that they will remind some, in this great American democracy, of the contribution made by the freemen who live across the ocean of peace from you to *make the world safe for democracy*.

I also have the hope that the stories of personal experience will make real to you some of the men whose bodies have been for three years part of that human rampart that has kept your homes from desolation, and your daughters from violation, and that you will speed in sending them succour as though the barrier had broken and the bestial Hun were even now, with lust dominant, smashing at your own door.

PART 1

The Call to Arms

Chapter 1

The Call Reaches Some Far-Out Australians

Just where the white man's continent pushes the tip of its horn among the eastern lands there is a black man's land half as large as Mexico that is administered by the government of Australia. New Guinea has all the romance and lure of unexplored regions. It is a country of nature's wonders, a treasure-chest with the lid yet to be raised by some intrepid discoverer. There are tree-climbing fish, and pygmy men, mountains higher and rivers greater than any yet discovered. To the north of Australia's slice of this wonderland the Kaiser was squeezing a hunk of the same island in his mailed fist.

The contrast between the administration of these two portions of the same land forms the best answer to the question: *What shall be done with Germany's colonies?*

In German New Guinea there have always been more soldiers than civilians, cannibalism is rife, and life and property are insecure outside the immediate limits of the barracks. In British New Guinea or Papua there has never been a single soldier and cannibalism is abolished. A white woman, Beatrice Grimshaw, travelled through the greater part of it unprotected and unmolested.

The following story told of Sir William Macgregor, the first administrator, shows the way of Britishers in governing native races. He one day marched into a village where five hundred warriors were assembled for a head-hunting expedition. Sir William, then Doctor Macgregor, had with him two white men and twelve native police. He strode into the centre of these blood-thirsting savages, grasped the chief by the scruff of the neck, kicked him around the circle of his warriors, demanded an immediate apology and the payment of a fine for the transgression of the Great White Mother's orders for peace—the bluff worked, as it always does.

Australia has now added the late German colony Hermanlohe, or German New Guinea, to the southern portion, making an Australian crown colony of about two hundred and fifty thousand square miles. This was taken by a force of Australian troops conveyed in Australian ships. I was not fortunate enough to be a member of the expedition, but the ultimatum issued to the German commandant resulted in the Australian flag flying over the governor's residence at Rabaul within a few hours of the appearance of the Australian ships.

It was soon evident to the Australians that this was intended to be a German naval station and military post of great importance. Enough munitions, and accommodation for troops were there to show that it was to be the jumping-off place for an attack on Australia. Such armament could never have been meant merely to impel *Kultur* on the poor, harmless blacks with their blowpipes and bows and arrows.

Every Australian is determined that these of nature's children shall not come again within reach of German brutality, but that they shall know fair play and good government such as the British race everywhere gives to the "nigger," having a sense of responsibility toward him that the men of this breed cannot escape. It would almost seem that the Almighty has laid the black man's burden on the shoulders of the Briton, as he was the first to abolish slavery, and no other people govern coloured peoples for the sole benefit of the governed.

In every British colony other nations can trade on equal terms, and millions of pounds sterling are squeezed from the British public every year to provide for the well-being of native peoples, worshipping strange deities and jabbering a gibberish that would sound to an American like a gramophone-shop gone crazy! While other nations make their colonies *pay* for the protection they give them, the British people pay very heavily for the privilege (?) of sheltering and civilizing these far-flung, strange peoples. No true friend of the black man can consider the possibility of handing him back to the cruelty of Teutonic forced *Kultur*.

The most heartless of Japanese gardeners could never twist and torture a plant into freak beauty more surely than the German system of government would compress the governed into a sham civilization. Australia would fight again sooner than that a German establishment should offend our sense of justice and menace our peace near our northern shores.

The western half of New Guinea (and the least known) belongs to Holland, and it was in the waters of this coast that the Australians whose story I am telling were living and working when the tocsin of war sounded. These sons of empire were registered under a Dutch name with their charter to work there from the Dutch Government, yet when they heard that men were needed for the Australian army, they dropped everything and hastened south to enlist. The long-obeyed calls of large profits and novel experiences, the lure of an adventurous life, were drowned by the bugle notes of the Australian call to arms.

These were young men who had left the shores of their native country, venturing farther out a-sea, ever seeking pearls of great price. They had once been engaged in pearl-fishing from the northernmost point of Australia—Thursday Island—that eastern and cosmopolitan village squatting on the soil of a continent sacred to the white races.

When the handful of white people holding this newest continent first flaunted their banner of "No Trespassers" in the face of the multicoloured millions of Asia, they declared their willingness to sweat and toil even under tropic skies, and develop their country without the aid of the cheap labour of the rice-eating, mat-sleeping, fast-breeding spawn of the man-burdened East. But this policy came well-nigh to being the death-blow to one little industry of the north, so far from the ken of the legislators in Sydney and Melbourne as to have almost escaped their recognizance.

The largest pearling-ground in the world is just to the north of this lovely *Southland*. It would seem as though the aesthetic oyster that lines its home with the tinting of heaven and has caught the *tears of angels*, petrifying them as permanent souvenirs, loves to make its home as near to this earthly paradise as the ocean will permit.

When the law decreed that only white labour must be employed on the fleets a number of the pearlers went north and became Dutch citizens, for from ports in the Dutch Indies they could work Australian waters up to the three-mile limit. But as soon as it was known that Australia needed *men*, that *we* were at war, then politics and profits could go hang: at heart they were all Australians and would not be behind any in offering their lives. It took but a few days to pay off the crews, send the Jap divers where they belonged, beach the schooners, and take the fastest steamer back *home*—then enlist, and away, with front seats for the biggest show on earth.

Chapter 2

An All-British Ship

We flew the Dutch flag, we were registered in a Dutch port, but every timber in that British-built ship creaked out a protest, and there paced the quarter-deck five registered Dutchmen who could not croak *"Gott-verdammter!"* if their lives depended on it, and who guzzled *rice taffle* in a very un-Dutch manner. Generally they forgot that they had sold their birthright. Ever their eyes turned southward, which was homeward, and only the mention of the Labour party brought to their minds the reason for leaving their native land. Each visit to port rubbed in the fact that they were now Dutchmen, as there were always blue papers to be signed and fresh taxes to be paid.

There was George Hym, who was a member of every learned society in England. The only letter of the alphabet he did not have after his name was "I," and that was because he did not happen to have been born in Indiana. Had that accident happened to him, even the Indiana Society would have given him a place at the speaker's table. He was the skipper of our fleet, had an extra master's certificate entitling him to command even the *Mauretania*. Many yarns were invented to explain his being with us. It was as if John D. should be found peddling hair-oil.

Some said he had murdered his grandmother-in-law and dare not pass the time of day with Mr. Murphy in blue. Others claimed that the crime was far greater—*the murder of a stately ship*—and that the marine underwriters would have paid handsomely for the knowledge of his whereabouts. At any rate, he never left the ship while in port, and he seemed to have no relatives.

There were times when the black cloud was upon him and our voices were hushed to whispers lest the vibration should cause it to break in fury on our own heads—then he would flog the crew with a wire hawser, and his language would cause the paint to blister on the deck. At other times the memory of his *mother* would steal over his spirit and in a sweet tenor he would croon the old-time hymns and the old ship would creak its loving accompaniment, and the unopened shell-fish would waft the incense heavenward.

We believed most of his ill temper was due to the foreign flag hanging at our stern that the Sydney-built ship was ever trying to hide beneath a wave. He had sailed every sea, with no other flag above him than the Union Jack, and felt maybe that even his misdeeds deserved not the covering of less bright colours. It was like a ringmaster fallen on hard times having to act the part of "clown." But needs must where necessity drives, and as his own country would have none of him, he was tolerant of the flag that hid him from the sleuths of British law.

But war came, and the chance to redeem himself. What washes so clean as blood—and many a stained escutcheon has in these times been cleansed and renewed—bathed in the hot blood poured out freely by the *sons of the line.* Whether the fleet was laid up or not, George was going! He might be over age, but no one could say what age he really was, and he was tougher than most men half his age. He left Queensland for Egypt with the Remount Unit in 1915, and is today in Jerusalem, with the British forces. Maybe he is treading the Via Dolorosa gazing at a place called Calvary, hoping that *One* will remember that he, too, had offered his life a ransom for past sins, which were many.

> *For ours shall be Jerusalem, the golden city blest,*
> *The happy home of which we've sung,*
> *In every land and every tongue,*
> *When there the pure white cross is hung,*
> *Great spirits shall have rest.*[1]

Prince Dressup was the dandy of the ship, a *swell guy* even at sea. His singlets were open-work, his moleskins were tailor-made, and his toe-nails were pedicured. The others wore only singlets and *pants,* but had the regulation costume been as in the Garden of Eden, his fig-leaf would have been the greenest and freshest there!

---

1. Mrs. A. H. Spicer, Chicago.

At one time he had been the best-dressed man in Sydney, giving the glad and glassy optic to every flapper whose clocked silk stockings caught his fancy. Some girl must have jilted him, and this was his revenge on the fluffy things, the choice of a life where none of them could feast their eyes on his immaculate masculine eligibility. Or, maybe, he was really in love, and some true woman had told him only to return to her when he had proved himself a man. If so, he had chosen the best forcing-school for real manhood that existed prior to the war. And there was real stuff in Prince Dressup; for, although there was distinction and style even in the way he opened shell-fish, he took his share of the dirty work, and when the time came he would not let another man take his place in the ranks of the fighters for Australia's freedom. He said, when we knew of the war, "that it would be rather good fun," and when he died on Gallipoli, the bullet that passed through his lungs had first of all come through the body of a comrade on his back.

Chum Shrimp's size was the joke of the ship—he must have weighed three hundred pounds. He could only pass through a door sideways, and the Binghis (natives of New Guinea), when they saw him, blamed him for a recent tidal wave, saying that he had fallen overboard. He was the most active man I have ever known, and on rough days would board the schooner by catching the *dinghee* boom with one hand as it dipped toward the launch, and swing himself hand over hand inboard. I never expected the schooner to complete the opposite roll until Chum was *playing plum* in the centre.

Chum's parentage was romantic—his father a government official and his mother an island princess—he himself being one of the whitest men I have ever been privileged to call friend. We never thought he would get into the army, for though he was as strong as any two of us, he would require the cloth of three men's suits for his uniform, and he would always have to be the blank file in a column of fours, as four of his size would spread across the street, and to *cover off* the four behind them would just march in the rear of their spinal columns, having a driveway between each of them.

He was determined to enlist, and a wise government solved the problem by making him quartermaster, thus insuring in the only way possible that Chum would have a sufficient supply of grub. This job was also right in his hands, because he possessed considerable business instinct; and you remember Lord Kitchener said of the quartermaster that he was the only man in the army whose salary he did not know!

The fifth Britisher of our crew will growl himself into your favour, being a well-bred British bulldog, looking down with pity on the tykes of mixed blood. Even before the war he showed his anti-German feelings by his treatment of a pet pig that we had on the schooner.

As I look back on it, our evening sport was a prophecy of what is today happening on the western front. Torres would stand growling and snapping at the porker, which would squeal and try to get away, but his hoofs could not grip the slippery deck, and though his feet were going so fast as to be blurred he would not be making an inch of progress. The Germans have been squealing and wanting to get away from the British bulldog but they do not know how to retire without collapse.

This pig had a habit of curling up among the anchor chains, and while we only used one anchor he escaped injury, but one rough day when both anchors were dropped simultaneously, piggy shot into the air with a broken back. The Germans have withstood the Allies so far, but now that America is with us, the back of the German resistance will soon be broken.

Of course Torres enlisted! In the beginning he was with Chum, and there was danger of his growing fat of body and soft of soul in the quartermaster's store, but he was rescued in time, and after months of exciting researches into canine history among the bones of the tombs of Egypt he earned renown at Armentières, as his body was found in No Man's Land with his head in the cold hand of a comrade to whom he had attached himself, and I believe his spirit has joined the deathless army of the unburied dead that watch over our patrols and inspire our sentries with the realization that on an Australian front No Man's Land has shrunk and our possession reaches right up to the enemy barbed wire.

CHAPTER 3

Human Snowballs

Way out back in the Never Never Land of Australia there lives a patriotic breed of humans who know little of the comforts of civilized life, whose homes are bare, where coin is rarely seen, but who have as red blood and as clean minds as any race on earth.

The little town of Muttaburra, for instance, has a population of two hundred, one-half of whom are eligible for military service.

They live in galvanized-iron humpies with dirt floors, newspaper-covered walls, sacking stretched across poles for beds, kerosene-boxes for chairs, and a table made from saplings. The water for household uses is delivered to the door by modern Dianas driving a team of goats at twenty-five cents per kerosene-tin, which is not so dear when you know that it has to be brought from a *billabong*[1] ten miles away.

Most of the men in such towns work as *rouseabouts* (handy men) on the surrounding sheep and cattle stations. At shearing-time the *gaffers* (grandfathers) and young boys get employment as pickers-up and rollers. Every shearer keeps three men at high speed attending to him. One picks up the fleece in such a manner as to spread it out on the table in one throw; another one pulls off the ends and rolls it so that the wool-classer can see at a glance the length of the wool and weight of the fleece; another, called the "sweeper," gathers into a basket the trimmings and odd pieces. These casual labourers and *rouseabouts* are paid ten dollars a week, while the shearer works on piece work, receiving six dollars for each hundred sheep shorn, and it is a slow man who does not average one hundred and fifty per day. All the shearing is done by machine, and in Western Queensland

1. *Billabong*—a water-hole in a dry river-course.

good shearers are in constant employment for ten months of the year. The shearers have a separate union from the *rouseabouts*, and there is a good deal of ill feeling between the two classes. When the shearers want a spell I have known them declare by a majority vote that the sheep were *wet*, though there had not been any rain for months! There is a law that says that shearers must not be asked to shear wet sheep, as it is supposed to give them a peculiar disease. The *rouseabouts* do not mind these *slow-down* strikes, as they get paid anyway, but the shearers are very bitter when these have a dispute with the boss and strike, for it cuts down their earnings, probably just when they wanted to finish the shed so as to get a *stand* at the commencement of shearing nearby.

When the war broke out the problem of the government was how to collect the volunteers from these outback towns for active service. It would cost from fifty to one hundred dollars per head in railway fare to bring them into camp.

The outbacker, however, solved the problem without waiting for the government to make up its mind. They just made up their swags and *humped the bluey*[2] for the coast. That is how the remarkable phenomenon of the human snowball marches commenced.

Simultaneously from inland towns in different parts of Australia men without the means of paying their transportation to Sydney or Melbourne simply started out to walk the three or four hundred miles from their homes to the nearest camp. In the beginning there would just be half a dozen or so, but as they reached the next township they would tell where they were bound, and more would join. Passing by boundary riders' and prospectors' huts, they would pick up here and there another red-blood who could not resist the chance of being in a real ding-dong fight. Many were grizzled and gray, but as hard as nails, and no one could *prove* that they were over the age for enlistment, for they themselves did not know how old they were!

> Said the squatter, 'Mike, you're crazy, they have soldier-men a-plenty!
> You're as grizzled as a badger, and you're sixty year or so!'
> 'But I haven't missed a scrap,' says I, 'since I was one-and-twenty,
> And shall I miss the biggest? You can bet your whiskers—No!!'[3]

---

2. *Humped the bluey*—tramped across country with blue blanket (or swag).
3. Robert W. Service.

From inland towns ... men without the means of paying their transportation ... started out to walk the three or four hundred miles ... to the nearest camp.

Presently the telegraph-wires got busy, and the defence department in Melbourne rubbed its eyes and sat up. As usual, the country was bigger than its rulers, and more men were coming in than could be coped with. The whole country was a catchment of patriotism—a huge river-basin—and these marching bands from the far-out country were the tributaries which fed the huge river of men which flowed from the State capitals to the concentration camps in Sydney and Melbourne. The leading newspapers soon were full of the story of these men from the bush who could not wait for the government to gather them in, and none should deny them the right to fight for their liberties.

Strange men these, as they tramped into a bush township, feet tied up in sacking, old felt hats on their heads, moleskins and shirt, *bluey*, or blue blanket, and *billy*, or quart canister, for boiling tea slung over their backs, all white from the dust of the road.

Old Tom Coghlan was there. He had lived in a boundary hut for twenty years, only seeing another human being once a month, when his rations were brought from the head station. His conversation for days, now that he was with companions, would be limited to two distinctive grunts, one meaning *yes*, the other *no*. But on the station he had been known to harangue for hours a jam-tin on a post, declaiming on the iniquities of a capitalist government. Those who heard him as they hid behind a gum-tree declared his language then was that of a college man. Probably he was the scion of some noble house—there are many of them out there in the land where no one cares about your past.

Here, too, was young Bill Squires, who had reached the age of twenty-one without having seen a parson, and asked a bush missionary who inquired if he knew Jesus Christ: "What kind of horse does he ride?"

Not much of an army, this band. They would not have impressed a drill-sergeant. To many even in those towns they were just a number of *sundowners*.[4] They would act the part, arriving as the sun was setting and, throwing their swags on the veranda of the hotel, lining up to the bar, eyeing the loungers there to see who would stand treat. Only the eye of God Almighty could see

---

4. *Sundowners*—tramps who arrive at a ranch at sundown expecting to be put up for the night.

that beneath the dust and rags there were hearts beating with love for country, and spirits exulting in the opportunity offering in the undertaking of a man-size job. Perhaps a Kitchener would have seen that the slouch was but habit and the nonchalance merely a cloak for enthusiasm, but even he would hardly have guessed that these were the men who would win on Gallipoli the praise of the greatest British generals, who called them "the greatest fighters in the world." Soon the news of these bands on the *wallaby*[5] at the call of country caught the imagination of the whole nation. Outback was *terra incognita* to the city-bred Australian, but that these men who were coming to offer their lives should walk into the city barefoot could not be thought of. The government was soon convinced that the weeks, and, in some cases, months that would be occupied in this long tramp need not be wasted. Military training could be given on the way, and they might arrive in camp finished soldiers.

So the snowball marches were at last recognized and controlled by the government. Whenever as many as fifty had been gathered together, instructors, boots, and uniforms were sent along, and the march partook of a military character. No longer were they *sundowners*; they *marched* into town at the end of the day, four abreast, in proper column of route, with a sergeant swinging his cane at the head, sometimes keeping step to the tune of mouth-organs. The uniforms were merely of blue dungaree with white calico hats, but they were serviceable, and all being dressed alike made them look somewhat soldierly. The sergeants always had an eye open for more recruits, and every town and station they passed through became a rallying-point for aspirants to the army.

Their coming was now heralded—local shire councillors gathered to greet them, streets were beflagged, dinners were given—always, at every opportunity, appeals were made for more recruits. Sometimes, to the embarrassment of many a bushman whose meetings with women had been few and far between, there were many girls who in their enthusiasm farewelled them with kisses, though one can hardly imagine even a shy bushman failing to appreciate these unaccustomed sweets!

The snowballs grew rapidly. Farmers let down their fences, and

---

5. *On the wallaby*—on the tramp.

they marched triumphantly through growing crops, each farmer vying with another to do honour to these men coming from the ends of the earth to deliver democracy.

> *They're fools, you say?*
> *Maybe you're right.*
> *They'll have no peace unless they fight.*
> *They've ceased to think; they only know*
> *They've got to go—yes, got to go!*[6]

By the time they reached the camp many of these groups had grown to regiments, and under names such as "Coo-ees," "Kangaroos," "Wallaroos," they marched through the streets of Sydney between cheering throngs to the tune of brass bands. Such was the intention, at any rate, but before they reached the railway station their military formation was broken up, and in their enthusiasm the people of the capital practically mobbed these *outbackers*, loading them, not merely with cigarettes and candy, but before night came there was many a bushman who had never seen a city before who carried a load of liquor that made even his well-seasoned head spin. The "chain lightning" of the bush was outclassed with the cinematograph whiskey of the city, that made its moving throngs and streets pass before his eyes like a kaleidoscope. A day or two in camp soon restored their balance. The training en route bore fruit; their commandant was so impressed that some of these regiments were equipped and officered, in a few weeks embarking for overseas.

Men from these regiments can be picked out today in London. If you see an Australian in a slouch-hat galloping his horse down Rotten Row, expecting "Algy" and "Gertrude" to give him a clear course, be sure it's a "Coo-ee!"

When some Australian sprawls in the Trocadero, inviting himself to table with the Earl of So-and-so, asking him to pass the butter, it's likely to be one of the Kangaroos.

These Australians have had no master in their lives but the pitiless drought; they respect not Kings, but they love a real man who knows not fear and is kind to a horse. Masefield said of them in Gallipoli: "They were in the pink of condition and gave a damn for no one!"

---

6. Robert W. Service.

There is a certain hospital in London provided by a certain grand lady for convalescent Australians. She is very kind, but rather inclined to treat the patients as *exhibits* and show them off to her *tony* friends. The Australians bore this meekly for some time, but one day it was announced that some high personages would be visitors. On their arrival they found every bed was placarded, such as this:

No. 1 Bed—This is a Military Cross Hero.
He bumped into a trench of Fritzes.
If he hides his face under the bedclothes,
it is because he is sensitive of his looks.

No. 2 Bed—Here lies a D.S.O. (Dirty Stop-Out).
He stopped out of the trenches as long as he could.
And now the old blighter must stop out for good.

The bushman is a real man under all circumstances, having no awe of authority, no hesitation in speaking his mind, but a great reverence for women and a real respect for a religion that does not savour of cant.

CHAPTER 4

Training-Camp Life

The town of Bendigo received a great increase of liveliness by having to accommodate four or five thousand soldiers.

It had known some lively times in the old gold days, but when its *yellow love* became thin, thousands of people went to other fields and the former flourishing city became a husk and as dull as only a declining mining city can become; but, as usually happens in old mining districts, when the gold gives out, the solid wealth of the soil in crop-growing capacity is developed, and Bendigo is prospering again through the labours of the tillers of the soil, if not by the delvings of its miners. Still, farmers have not the same habit of *blowing in their earnings* and are, admittedly, a little dull. There was a story that when the town council put a notice at the busy centre—*Walk Round Corners*—many of the farmers made sure of keeping the law by getting out of their vehicles and *leading* their horses round! The old-time miner was rather in the habit of smashing the unoffending lamp-post that barred his straight progress to the pub where his favourite brand of fire-water was on tap.

The Bendigoans will never forgive me for having failed to appreciate the fact that their Golden City was far ahead even of Melbourne. They would never believe that any one could make the mistake in regard to *their* city that an American did about an Australian seaport when he marvelled at our frankness in putting notice at the entrance to the harbour *Dead Slow*, and he never learned, after months of residence, that said notice was really a warning to shipping.

But at any rate the soldiers livened things up. They were gathered from many States—their day was just *one damn thing after another*—sometimes varied a bit with a right turn instead of left, and sometimes we would salute to the right instead of the left—but when night came, fun must be had somehow, and Bendigo had to supply it.

We all had some intelligence, so after spending a whole day in employment that forbade our using the smallest atom, we would seek during the night a *safety-valve*.

The camp was in the show-ground, which naturally divided the young animals in training into different sorts—the élite had the grand stand, horse-boxes were grabbed by the N. C. Os, prize-cattle stalls were clean enough, but some line of mental association must have caused the powers that be to allot the *pig-and-dog* section to the military police and their prey.

It was fun on the arrival of a fresh contingent who were told "they could take what accommodation was left in the grand stand, the remainder having to bunk in the animal stalls," to see them rush the lower tiers, appropriating their six-foot length by dumping their *blueys* upon it, but that same night they would be convinced of their mistake as the old hands, living above them, exhibited their joy at having dodged the guard, returning in the small hours, by walking on everyone possible on their way up top. Next morning there would be more applications for horse-and-cattle stalls, but the best ones would be gone, and they would have to be content to lie, six in a box, where a flooring-board was missing through which the rats would make their nightly explorations. But even this was better than the lower tiers of the grand stand, as the rats would not always wake you running across your face, but a husky in military boots stepping on it would rouse even the deadest in slumber. As he would step on about twenty others as well, the mutual recriminations would continue for hours, and as the real culprit would settle down in the dark into his own place without a word no one would know who it was. There would come from up above: "Shut up, there!"

"What the h—— are you makin' all that row about?" and the answer:

"So would you make a row if a b— b— elephant stepped on your face!"

"Go and bag your head! Anyway, there are two hundred men who didn't step on your face trying to go to sleep, and it will be reveille in an hour or so."

These grand-stand couches were bad places at the best of times. They may have been high and dry, but were open to every breeze that blew and were sheltered only on the side from which the rain never came. The Bendigo show committee must have faced them that way so that the sun and weather would be right in the eyes of the onlookers and prevent them seeing any *crook riding* or *running dead*, etc.

The first item on the day's programme was the "gargling parade." Meningitis had broken out in the camp and everyone had to gargle his throat first thing in the morning with salt water. We would be marched under our sergeant to each receive our half-pannikin of salt water at the A.M.C. tent. We would string out along the brick drain and then began the most horrible conglomeration of sounds that ever offended the ear. It was like the tuning up of some infernal orchestra. I don't know why it is, but it is surprising how few men can gargle "like a gentleman." For days I have not spoken to my best friend, who was most refined in other respects, but could not desist from spluttering and spraying the half dozen men nearest to him. We became friends again, but although we slept and messed together, I always took care never to be nearer than number ten from him at gargling parade. I never heard any complaints from the people at Bendigo about this early-morning discord, but I learn that no frogs have been heard in the neighbourhood since.

Our training at this camp was purely preliminary—we certainly formed fours seven billion times, and turned to the right fourteen billion, and saluted a post that represented an officer so often, that the rush of air caused by the quick movement of hands and heads had worn the edge off it.

We were so used to the sound of the sergeant-major's voice when he said, "The company will move to right in fours," that, when a grazing donkey happened to *hee-haw*, the whole company formed fours. Even then only about half the company discovered the mistake—there was mighty little difference in the tones, anyway!

For a man that has never previously had military training, the first few weeks in camp is the most humiliating and trying experience that could be inflicted on him. I am quite sure that were it a prison and a treadmill he could not hate it the more.

Here was I, never been under orders since I was breeched, and even before then getting my own way, suddenly finding myself with every movement I was to make laid down in regulations, with about a score of men round me all day to see that I carried them out correctly.

How I used to hate that camp band, when it played at reveille, I cursed it in full *blast* because it would wake me suddenly when I seemed to have only just lain down, and reviled it when it played softly because I would not hear it and some of the other boys would wake me only when they were fully dressed; and the last to fall in at roll-call were picked for cook's fatigue—peeling spuds and cleaning *dixies*! How I loathed those *dixies*! The more grease you got on your hands and clothes the more appeared to be left in the *dixie*! The outside was sooty, the inside was greasy, and after I had done my best, the sergeant cook would make remarks about my ancestors which had nothing to do with the question, and I could not resent them lest I be detailed for a whole week of infernal *dixie*-cleaning. Anyway, all his ancestors had ever dared to do in the presence of mine was to touch their forelock.

In those first weeks I think I would gladly have murdered every sergeant. It was "Number 10, hold your head up! Put your heels together!" or a sarcastic remark as to whether I knew what a button was for, when I happened to miss doing one up in my flurry to dress in time, so that I would not be at the bottom of the line and picked for fatigue.

It is not often realized what a purgatory the educated, independent man who enlists as a private has to go through before his spirit is tamed sufficiently to stand bossing, without resentment, by men socially and educationally inferior. There was a young officer who called me over one day and told me to clean his boots. I answered, "Clean them yourself!" and got three days C. C. (confinement to camp). This same officer took advantage of his rank on several other occasions and sought to humiliate me. He was a poor sort of a sport, and many months later when I was his equal in rank in France I punched his head, telling him I had waited eighteen months to do it. So you see, everything comes to those who wait.

As a matter of fact, it was only three weeks before I was made an acting sergeant, but I have great sympathy with the soft-handed rookie, for in those three weeks it seemed to me that it was an easy thing to die for one's country, but to train to be a soldier was about the worst kind of penal servitude a man could undergo.

When acting as sergeant I was boss of five stables, each containing eight men, who could only squeeze in the floor space by sleeping head to feet. These stables were only completely closed in on three sides, the entrance side being boarded up three feet high, except for the space of the doorway. There was no attempt to close up this opening, except after afternoon parade, when visitors would have arrived before our changing into reception-clothes was completed, and we would partially block it with our waterproof sheeting.

I must mention that in the early days we had no real uniforms, but used to parade in blue dungarees and white cloth hats. They certainly made the men look *uniform*, but *uniformly hideous*, and none of us would be seen in them by a pretty girl, for a king's ransom. As soon as afternoon parade was dismissed, we would dive for our quarters, and re-don our "civvies" until next parade. The "cocky" would be resplendent again in his soft collar and red tie, and the city clerk in starched collar and cuffs.

Sometimes, however, there was a variation in time between the watches of the sergeant-major on the parade-ground and the guard at the gate. Visitors would be let in too soon, and innocently curious dames would wonder what these rows of stables were for, and wandering in that direction, would suddenly beat a blushing retreat at the revelation of hundreds of young men getting into respectable clothes who had no other place in which to change. Even if you did put a blanket or W. P. sheet over the entrance, there were no tacks or nails, and it always fell down at the most awkward moments. However, the visitors soon got wise, and in about half an hour the boys who had callers would be proudly showing their friends, by the name above the feed-box, that the previous occupant of their quarters was the famous Highflyer, winner of scores of cups, etc.

There were a good lot of us there from other states, and *we* had no special callers, but there were always girls who came out to see a Sergeant Martin or some such name not on the rolls. "Couldn't we find him for you?" If we did happen to find a sergeant of that name, he would not happen to be the one she wanted, then we would offer to do the honours of the camp, and as she would not like the hamper brought for her friend to be wasted, an acquaintance was soon struck up. Some boys were too shy, but nearly all of us had visitors after we had been in camp a week or two.

The town had appointed a soldiers' entertainment committee, and they gave us a concert every night in the Y. M. C. A. tent. These were high-class shows, but most of us preferred to go into the town though we only had leave till six o'clock.

Some of us used to stay in town till midnight, trusting to our ingenuity in bluffing the guard. Many were the dodges used to gain entrance to the camp. Some townsboys could get passes till midnight about once a week, and instead of handing these to the guard, as they hurried past, they would substitute a piece of blank paper. If they got past it was good for another occasion, as the date was easily altered. If they were pulled up they would apologize profusely and hand up the right pass. Sometimes we would wait until there were a score of us, and while the sentry was examining the first pass the others would rush the gate. Rarely could more than one or two be identified, and the odds were in our favour.

Soon the guard was doubled, and only a small wicket was opened, where but one man could pass through at a time. Then we scraped holes under the galvanized-iron fence that surrounded the show-ground, concealing them carefully with bushes and watching out for the pickets who patrolled the outside of the camp.

I think I got my best training in scouting dodging these pickets. I have climbed trees, crawled into hollow logs, and played 'possum in gullies to escape them. Being caught meant not only several days in the guard-tent, but the loss of the chance of "stripes."

There was really not much excitement in the town and many of us just stayed late for the excitement of breaking the law without being caught. It was the outbreak of our personality after being mere cogs in a drill-machine all day. I never was guilty of returning except after hours, and I never was caught, even when extraordinary precautions were taken to get the delinquents. Sometimes a check-roll would be called, at some uncertain hour, but it was always a point of honour for the boys in camp to answer "present" for any absent mates.

Evidently I was destined to be a scout. From this camp I was drafted into the intelligence section for specialized training. That has been my work all the time overseas, and I never had harder work dodging Fritz's sentries than those pickets round Bendigo show-ground.

CHAPTER 5

Concentrated for Embarkation

One morning there was great excitement in the Bendigo camp. An announcement was made that members of rifle-clubs would be tried out on the range and all qualifying with ninety per cent of marks would be sent overseas in the earliest draft. All who had ever fired a gun, and some who hadn't, stepped forward for trial, but on the range the eligibles were found to be only fifty, of whom I was lucky enough to be one.

The next day we lined up for a final medical inspection. As we passed the doctor there were none to congratulate us, but we made allowances, knowing how sore the others were who had failed to qualify. We packed up our kits and marched to the train leaving a camp literally green with envy. We shouted good-bye, amazed at the good fortune that had chosen us to escape many months of deadly grind in the training-camp, and it seemed as we passed in single file through the old showground turnstile as if already we had left Australia behind, and in imagination our feet felt the roll of the ship that in our fancy was even now carrying us out on the Great Adventure; and our thoughts wafted farewells to mother or wife, as we bade them never fear but that we would show that their men were not unworthy of their regard.

Our spirits had not been so elated had we known that more weeks of camp life in Australia yet awaited us. Had we not thought that we were destined for immediate embarkation we might have been better disposed to appreciate Broadmeadows, but as it was it seemed to us about the last place made—and not yet finished.

As the days passed, our detestation of the place grew, but we soon found that our impatience of delay in embarking was shared by several thousand others who had gathered there from many States and been weeks trampling out the grass and raising the dust in those accursed fields till it choked them, when they had long before expected to be inhaling the ozone from the deck of some good ship that with every knot bore them nearer to the strife for liberty and a man's chance.

This camp was always seething with discontent, for with the delay was in every man's heart the haunting fear that the war might be over ere he got there, and none could think without dread of the possibility that we might have to endure the lowest depths of humiliation in returning home without having struck a blow.

On one occasion the impatience that was like a festering sore among the men of this camp nearly resulted in a show of mutiny. Oil was added to the flame of our discontent by the tactlessness of the camp adjutant. He will always be known to the men of those days as the "Puppy." His father was a commanding officer, and though he was only nineteen years of age and his voice was just breaking, he rode the "high-horse of authority" over those men as though they were schoolchildren. When his lady friends came to visit him he would order a special parade so that they might see him in command of "*his men*, doncherknow!" But his *high horse* nearly threw him one day when he gave the order, "Move to the right and fours, form fours!" and not a man moved. Blushing like a schoolgirl, he called the officers out for consultation and sent for the commandant. When, however, real men took command there was no further trouble, though the boys openly voiced their complaints—"that their leave was restricted for no reason—that they were on parade after hours—and why don't they send us away to fight, anyway? That's what we enlisted for."

The announcement that we would be sailing soon brought forth cheers and everyone was in good humour again. Only let us be sure that we were off to war, and we could stand even the Puppy's yelping.

But all the same, there were a couple more weeks of the mud and dust to be endured. I have been in sand-storms in the interior of Australia when the sun was blotted out and in Egypt when the Kamseen said to the mountain, "Be thou removed!" and it was removed in a single night some fifty miles away, but neither of these is worse than some of the dust-storms that blow over Melbourne, and at Broadmeadows we got their full force. We would march in from the parade-ground not being able to see the man in front of us, and in the light of the candles in our tents our very features were blotted out and nothing but eyes and teeth were visible, except that, perhaps, in some faces two small holes would suggest where the nose might be. It was only after a good deal of shaking that the place could be discerned where neck emerged from collar. There were some serious accidents in these dust-storms through men trying to bump buildings out of their way, and on one occasion two poor fellows were nearly killed in failing to give the *right-away* to a couple of sheets of galvanized iron. And when it rained, great snakes! Where was there ever mud like that! We certainly did a good deal in mixing the soil of those paddocks, for we would carry an acre of it from around the tents onto the drill-ground, where we would carefully scrape it off, and when we marched back we would bring another acre on our boots to form a hillock at our tent door. If there had been but an inch of rain we would lift up on the soles of our boots all the wet earth, uncovering a surface of dust to pepper our evening meal.

Large sums of money have been spent on this camp since those days and it is now a *nursery* for the recruits who have volunteered three years late and need the enticement of feather beds to induce them to leave mother. It has been thoroughly drained and terraced, and comfortable huts have been erected, but *we* simply rolled in blankets on bare Mother Earth and sheltered from sun and rain in tents that were supposed to be water-proof, and generally *were* unless you happened to touch them when wet. If you did accidentally happen to rub against the sides, there would be a stream of water pouring down on you all night. There was no escaping this, for there was not an inch of ground inside the tent that was not covered by man. In fact, with ten in a tent, one of us had to lie three-quarters outside, anyway, which was the chief reason why I was never last in. Dressing was a problem, for everyone must needs dress at the same time, and from the outside the tent must have looked something like a camel whose hump was constantly slipping. Perhaps that is why everyone used safety-razors after a while, for although our faces would frequently look as though they had been mixed up in barbed wire, there was really not much danger of cutting one's throat, for even though you received a forty-horsepower jolt at a critical moment, the razor-guard prevented your life being actually imperilled.

In this camp we received our uniforms and equipment, but it was only after a lot of exchanging had been done that our uniforms made us look soldierly. Oh, Lord! what caricatures many of us were after the first issue. There were practically no out-sizes in tunics, but plenty of the men were not merely out-size, but odd-sized. Some little fellows looked as if they were wearing father's coat, and there were others who looked as if they were wearing that of baby brother. Some had to turn back the cuffs two or three times, while others had at least a foot of wrist and forearm showing. But the breeches! Oh, my Aunt Sarah! Some were able to tuck the bottoms into their boots, while others had to wind puttees above their knees. There were men who couldn't bend comfortably, while others had room to carry a couch about with them. However, the orders were that we were to keep on exchanging until we got something like a fit, but as there were varieties in the quality of the cloth, there were those who preferred a misfit to poor material, so that there were always a number who looked like Charlie Chaplin.

New arrivals in camp were always called Marmalades, because they were distinguished by their relish for marmalade jam. After they had consumed over a ton of it and forgotten the taste of any other kind of jam then they looked at a tin of it with loathing, when they would be considered to have passed the recruit stage and be on a fair way to becoming soldiers.

Long before we got our uniforms we were issued greatcoats, hats, and boots. At this time the only other clothes we had were the blue dungarees and white cloth hats called fatigue dress. No self-respecting man would allow a lady friend to see him in this rig-out. Yet one must breathe the free air of liberty some time, and confinement to camp was a punishment for crime. So we compromised by strolling the city streets with our military hats and boots, with the army greatcoats seeking to hide the blue hideousness of our dungarees. Some of us sought to be unconscious of the foot or two of blue cloth showing beneath the greatcoat, and these were times when we envied the little chap enveloped in a greatcoat that hung down as low as his boots. We received at this time the nickname Keystone soldiers, some genial ass conceiving that we looked as funny as the Keystone police. These greatcoats were a bit out of place on a day that was over a hundred in the shade, and they did not look exactly the thing at a dainty tea-table in a swell cafe, but we clung to those greatcoats as our only salvation, for they *did* hide the blue horror beneath. I should have explained that our civilian clothes had been taken from us, and we were forbidden, under severe penalty, to wear any but regulation dress. Nevertheless, the lucky dogs who had relatives nearby would take the risk and borrow a cousin's rig-out, but we hated them as mean dogs, feeling they were taking an unfair advantage; and, if we got a chance, we would, by innuendo, hint to the lady in the case that these fellows did so much *dixie*-cleaning that their dungarees were too stiff to wear!

Nearing the close of a long, sunny Australian day—the air soft, warm, and sweet, and the sky suffused with a lovely pink. It was visiting-day—Friday. In the camp, rows of figures in blue dungarees and white hats were marching round and round the drill-ground, turning from left to right, forming fours, then back to two deep, and, so on and so on. Out across the flat ground between the camp and the railway-station, coming steadily toward the camp, was a very straggly line of white figures. As they came closer, one saw they were women and girls, fresh and dainty in summer frocks and hats, all carrying big baskets, suitcases, and all manner of strange and weirdly shaped parcels. A few odd males among them, mostly nearing sixty, or under ten. Some were portly, puffing a little, some old, their heavy parcels making their lips quiver and their step slow—and girls, just multitudes of them, all sizes, ages, and shapes—blondes, brunettes, in-betweens, and from every rank in the social scale—mostly in groups of any number from two to twenty—some chaperoned, some not. Here and there one saw one alone carrying an extra heavy suitcase, which somehow you knew contained extra-specially good things to eat, and when you looked at her face under her big hat a certain something there told you that on the third finger of the left hand under her glove you would surely find a diamond half-loop, and even, perhaps, a *very* plain new gold band!

From the drill-ground the soldiers could see this crowd of womenfolk steadily coming toward them, and grew acutely aware of their shapeless, grubby dungarees, dusty boots, and perspiring faces under tired-looking white hats. Agonized glances were turned on the sergeant-major as, with his face utterly expressionless, ignoring the oncoming feminine figures, he still right-about-turned and quick-marched them. The fluttering white frocks came closer and closer, and as they began to get near the gate imploring glances were turned in the direction of the guard, praying they would not let anyone in. Then suddenly, to their immense relief, they were dismissed; then it was just one mad rush for tents. Swearing breathlessly as they bumped into each other or tripped over tent-pegs and ropes, they ran, putting on an extra spurt every time they glanced over their shoulders and saw the women advancing upon them in mass formation. Changing was soon accomplished, not without a good deal of confusion, mixing up of garments, and splashing water around, but when they were finally all dressed and again in khaki uniforms smiles of satisfaction spread over clean and shiny faces as they glanced down at neat uniforms and well-polished boots—Smoke-o that day had seen much activity in the business of brushing and polishing.

Down at the gate the picket was having a busy time answering questions:

"Could you tell me where I will find Private McIntosh?"

"What tent is my brother in, d'you know?"

But as many of the eager questioners were, well, very delightful, none of the boys on picket duty kicked at their job. Some of the boys who were quicker dressers than the others now began to come down to the gate, bustling into the crowd of womenfolk, looking eagerly for their own particular visitors, and, seeing them, dashing up, hugging mothers and sisters, shaking bashfully the hand of sister's friend, gathering up all their parcels, and, with them all following close behind, leading the way to a dandy spot for supper. In course of time the sorting-out process was complete, and the camp was dotted with hundreds of groups, large and small, all laughing and talking, and busy unpacking those very weighty parcels. Boys who had changed into uniform with the others and gone down to the gate, though not really expecting any one as they were from

"On Show" before leaving home

out back and had no city friends, but still feeling lonesome, and, perhaps, having a forlorn hope that there might be someone, had helped rather bewildered girls, carrying their baskets and finding the man they wanted—these boys now looked longingly around at these groups, hoping someone would invite them to join in; and how their faces brightened when one of their tent-mates, looking up from a hunk of frosted cake, would see them and shout, "Hey, Bill! Here!" and, after the agony of being presented to "My mater, my sister, and Miss Stephenson," things were just O. K.

Yet there were a good many lonely ones, boys who hadn't even bothered to change, still in their ill-shaped blue dungarees, dusty boots, and cloth hats, some of them walking round, their heads down, and kicking at every clump of grass or stone that came within reach of their boots—some of them, too lonely even to look at the fun, hanging over the fences, occasionally exchanging a few peevish words with each other, while others gathered round the old man who kept a stall just inside the gate and bought lemonade, ginger ale, and arrowroot biscuits, consuming them with much assumed gusto, while others still sat inside their tents or the Y. M. C. A. hut.

Looking at these boys gave one a deep heartache, but the sob in one's throat changed suddenly to a laugh as one looked at their hats. Americans in Australia have always held the prize for originality in headgear, but that same prize must now be handed over to our soldiers in camp. What they can do with one simple, unoffending, white-cloth cricket-hat passes all belief. Seldom, as is the case with their dungarees, did these boys have a hat that really fitted them, those with big heads had the smallest hats, and those with extra small heads got the largest size. They were all shades, from their original pure white down, or up, to an exact match with Mother Earth. And the shapes! Some wore them turned down all round, some turned up all round, some turned up in front and down at the back, some vice versa, some turned up on the left side and down at the right, and some down at the left and up at the right; some had tucked the front part in, leaving a large expanse of bare brow, while the back part, turned down, shaded the nape of their neck. Some applied this idea reversed, turning in the back; some turned the brim right in except for a small peak *à la* Jockey; some had a peak back and front, made by rolling in both sides, and some settled the question by turning the whole brim in, the resultant skull-cap effect being such as to bring tears to the eyes of all beholders.

These disconsolate, lonely faces, with, in the cases of the younger boys, tear-filled eyes, surmounted by these absurd, preposterous hats—it was truly a case of not knowing whether to laugh or to cry; so by laughing hard, the women who saw them hid their tears.

It soon began to get dark—in Australia our twilight is short—so suitcases and baskets were repacked, but only this time with plates, cups, spoons, etc.—and one by one the parties rose and went over to the Y. M. C. A. tent for the concert. In the tent tables had all been moved out and rows of chairs and forms filled it. In a short time they were all occupied, the officers sitting in front, some with visitors, others alone and casting very longing eyes at the lovely girls coming in with the men.

The concert was given, as they mostly were, by an amateur club, and had its ups and downs. But everyone enjoyed it—the items that took the popular fancy were loudly applauded, and the others that weren't so good—well, no one minded, as everyone was happy, and the lights were very dim!

By the end of the concert it was nine o'clock, the time for all visitors to be shooed off home. The bugles blew the First Post, and everyone, very unwilling, made their way slowly down to the gate. Here good-byes were said, meetings arranged for the boys' next leave, promises made to come out next week, with much chattering and laughing, though here and there, back in the shadows, would be couples, very quiet, maybe engaged, perhaps just married, hating to separate.

At last the remaining white frocks flutter through the big gate and join in the stream already straggling across country toward the railway-station, everyone quiet and very tired.

In camp the boys stroll over to their tents, exchanging an occasional word with pals, but for the most part silent, and turn in, tired also, and a little thoughtful. In an hour all the stars shine brightly from the velvety, blue-black sky, the soft-scented air wafts in through open tent-flaps, lights are out, and all is quiet in the camp, except for the periodical changing of pickets and the occasional roar of a passing train in the distance.

CHAPTER 6

Many Weeks at Sea

A troop-ship has no longer a name, but although the ship we boarded at Port Melbourne docks was designated by the number *A 14*, it was not hard to discover that we were on a well-known ocean-liner, for on life-buoys and wheelhouse the paint was not so thick that inquisitiveness could not see the name that in pre-war days the Aberdeen line proudly advertised as one of their most comfortable passenger-carrying ships. That meant little to us, for her trimmings of comfort had been stripped off but for a few cabins left for the officers, and when we were mustered in our quarters, we wondered where we would sleep, for no bunks met our eye.

Embarkation is for everyone concerned the most tedious, red-tapeist incident in a soldier's career. For fear of spies the exact day had been kept secret, and although we had expected to leave weeks previously, and had, at least, twenty times said our tearful farewells, when the actual day arrived there was no expectation of it and no farewells. The night previously men had said to their wives, "See you tomorrow, dear!"—meetings were arranged with best girls, for the movies—in fact, not the faintest rumour had spread through the camp that there was any likelihood of our sailing for weeks, and here in the early dawn we were lined up on the wharf, being counted off like sheep, and allotted our quarter cubic foot of ship's space; preparing for our adventure overseas without the slightest chance of letting anyone I know what had happened to us. We could sympathize with the feelings of our folks as they would journey out to camp with the usual good things to eat only to find we had gone. By this time we would be well out at sea, en route for the Great Adventure, but it was hard luck for mothers and wives suddenly to find us gone without warning, and having to wait many weeks for the first letter.

It was wet, it was cold, it was dark on that wharf. If we were counted once, we were counted fifty times, and for hours we stood in the rain because there were two men too many. No, not men, for they were found to be boys of fifteen who had stolen uniforms and had hidden near the wharf for days to get away with the troops, but they were discovered, as every man had his name called and was identified by his officer as he passed up the gangway. One of them was not to be kept off, however: he slipped round the stern and climbed up the mooring cables like a monkey, and as no one gave him away he was undiscovered until rations were issued, so, perforce, he was a member of the ship's company and went with us to Egypt.

It's marvellous what quantities of men a troop-ship can swallow. There were a thousand men on our ship and we wondered how we would possibly move about, for we were marched 'tween decks, and seated on benches ranged alongside deal tables, and when all were aboard there was not room for a man more. It was explained to us that these were our quarters. We could understand them as eating quarters, but where were we to sleep? It was soon evident; above our heads were rows of black iron hooks; these were for our hammocks, which, with a blanket apiece, were in bins at the end of each deck. Hammock sleeping was not new to me, so I got a good deal of fun seeing the early-to-bedders climb in one side of their hammock, only to fall out the other, and very few could manipulate their blankets. One could see that nearly everyone was nervous for fear of turning over in his sleep, but there was really no danger of falling out, for when all the hammocks were up they were packed so closely that if you did roll over, you would only roll into the next hammock on top of some fellow who would, no doubt, think the mast had fallen. There were a good number of men to whom life would have been much pleasanter the next few days if they could have stayed in their hammocks all day, as, no matter how the ship rolls, a hammock, being swung, always keeps level. Unfortunately, all hammocks had to be taken down at 6 a.m. so we could sit at the tables for breakfast, and to most of the boys that first morning getting out of their hammocks was like stepping onto a razzle-dazzle. We were now well at sea and the general cry was in the words of the song: *Sea, Sea, Why Are You Angry With Me?* Discipline had to be relaxed those first days, for a seasick man is quite willing to be shot and has no interest in the war, and doesn't care which horse wins the boat-race. Seasickness never gets any sympathy from those who are immune, but sometimes just retribution comes on the scoffer, and it is some satisfaction to see a man's face turn green who but a few hours ago had been whistling with a selfish cheerfulness while you were revealing your own sticky past to the mermaids.

After about a week parades were announced, and in the early morning we were lined up for *physical jerks*, by which is meant calisthenics, or setting-up exercises. We now realized the appropriateness of the nickname, for the first stretching would cause a number to rush to the side, where they would attempt to jerk their hearts out, and also, standing on tiptoe on a rolling ship, one can only bend in jerks. To our joy these parades were short affairs, for there was only the limited space of the boat and saloon decks and each platoon had to take its turn in occupying this very limited parade-ground—so the greater part of the time was spent in passing remarks about the slovenly work of every other squad but one's own. Of course there were always fatigue and guard duties. I'll never forget my first butcher's fatigue, for when I stooped to pick up a carcass of mutton, I thought the best way to carry it would be to hang it round my neck like a feather boa, but no log of wood was stiffer or more unbending than that frozen woolly, and I asked if we were expected to eat that. No wonder so much coal is used on a ship when the food has to be thawed out! But this job was very comforting, for I saw the inside of the ship's storehouse, and never feared, though we were wrecked on a desert island, there would be any danger of our starving.

We turned out some pretty ragtime guards—sentries were posted at different parts of the ship, the most important being the guard over the liquor, and another sentry at the saloon gangway, whose duty it was to prevent any private or other common person trespassing on the hallowed ground sacred to the cigarette-ash and footprints of officers. This last sentry was expected to salute the O. C. troops and commander of the ship, all other salutes being dispensed with, as on board ship we saw our officers some five hundred and ninety times a day, and their arms would have been whirling like windmills had they been compelled to return our salutes. I remember one sentry failing to recognize the Commander-in-chief, and presently the colonel spoke to him thus: "What are you doing here, my man?"

"I'm supposed to be a —— sentry."

"Well, do you know that I am supposed to be the —— colonel?"

"Oh! Well, I'm supposed to give you a —— salute!"

And the sentry forthwith performed his belated duty.

On this ship the officers were all pretty popular, especially one who was never known by any title or other designation than Jerry. Jerry had more self-confidence than any man I have ever met. He could not correctly put a platoon through its formations, but would not hesitate to take charge of a battalion. When he had given some orders and had hopelessly mixed up a company, he would look at the mess with an air of superiority that proclaimed to all and sundry that he was commanding a lot of imbeciles, and then he would calmly throw the responsibility of disentangling themselves upon the men by the order: "As you were!"

It was a puzzle to all as to how he got his commission. He was tall and spruce, most scrupulous in the fit of his uniform, but absolutely too lazy to learn his job. He was something of a joke as an officer, yet his men got to like him for his good humour and absolute indifference to the censure of his superiors. In instructing a squad he would quite calmly read aloud out of a drill-book right under the eyes of the colonel, and his air of calm assurance under rebuke would so annoy his superiors that he frequently escaped much censure, for few senior officers are willing to display a loss of temper in front of the men, as it makes for a loss of dignity. One day Jerry found a sentry asleep at his post while he was on visiting rounds as officer of the guard. All Jerry did was to drawl out: "Next time you go to sleep, my lad, you'll wake up in hell!" As a matter of fact, he was too good-natured to have a man punished, and as the boys realized this, they would not let anyone take advantage of him. We did not think there was anything that Jerry could do properly until the first concert.

These concerts were weekly affairs, and we had three artists who were equal to the best. Tom Dawson, the Tivoli comedian, who was afterward killed in France, was one of us and always willing to provide half a dozen songs, with his India-rubber face stretched to suit each part. He was a prime favourite. Then we had an operatic tenor who could sing a solo from almost any Italian opera, but his talent was not appreciated—someone would be bound to call "Pretty Joey!" in the middle of his most impassioned passages. He got plenty of applause when he sang about "the end of a perfect day," even though the day had been as beastly as a severe storm could make it for a thousand-odd men cooped up so closely that only a third of them could see the sky at one time. His efforts to educate our musical taste completely failed, for the announcement that he was going to sing in Italian always raised cries of *"Steaka-de-oyst!"* "Fiji banana!" etc.

Another real artist played the mandolin, and when he appeared with it first of all he was greeted with cries of "Gertie!" As he played, however, he held the boys spellbound and never after failed to get an encore, though many still held that a mandolin was only a "sissy" instrument. But the star performer, to everyone's surprise, was Jerry. Here was one thing he could do, at any rate! His recitation of *Gunga Dhin* brought tears to our eyes, and thereafter no programme was complete without this item.

Toward the end of the voyage the concerts lost popularity, as there were only three or four artists; and there was no stock of music on board, so their two or three songs became as wearisome as a much-played gramophone record. The boxing and wrestling matches always held the crowd, and there was no lack of competition, for the runner-up was always *sure* that he would have won but for bad luck and was ever ready for another try. These were no "pussy" shows, for we had some professionals among us: Sailor Duffy, one of our second lieutenants, was middleweight champion of Victoria, and one of the ship's crew was champion wrestler of London. There were others who required convincing, at any rate, that they were not as good as the champions, and anyway there were always plenty of disputes during the day that by general consent were settled in the ring at night. This was how we passed the long weeks to Colombo, our first port of call.

To the white man having to make his home at Colombo it may

not be paradise, but to the sea-weary landlubber who has been weeks without a sight of land, there never was place more delightful. The first day we weren't allowed ashore, but there were other troop-ships lying in the harbour, and soon pretty well every man who could find a footing on the rigging was semaphoring like mad: "Who are you? Where'd you come from? Where are you going?"

We discovered one boat was full of New Zealanders and we *coo-eed* and waved wildly to them, feeling that New Zealand ought to be part of Australia, anyhow, and they were almost homelanders. There were also some Indian troops bound for the Persian Gulf, and immediately the rumour started that that was where we were bound, and everybody looked pretty blue. Pretty soon some coal-lighters came alongside—that is, we discovered there was coal in them after they had discharged their living freight, for they were simply black with niggers. There did not seem to be an inch of boat space that was not covered up by nigger. About half of them started to work, for the method of coaling in these parts is for the niggers to carry aboard about a teaspoonful in a wicker basket. By working in shifts and maintaining a constant stream of men hurrying from lighters to ship each with his spoonful of coal, sufficient is taken inboard in a very long time. Those who were not coaling, loudly proclaimed that they would dive for money and thereafter, by day and night, our ears were assailed by their cries:

"Me di'."

"Gib it money."

"You throw."

It was very amusing for the first hour or two, but we soon got heartily sick of their importunity and their incessant chatter.

The second day we were allowed a couple of hours ashore, and as many had a three-weeks' thirst, they saw no more of Colombo than the inside of a hotel bar. Others of us were amused at being escorted through the streets by the nigger policemen with whips, who did not hesitate to belabour very energetically any niggers who approached us too closely; but while the policeman was chasing one nigger another would seize his chance and offer for sale native jewellery of exquisite workmanship, at what would seem to us a ridiculously low price, but we were assured by everyone that whatever price they asked was ten times its value. Some of the boys were after souvenirs, and as soon as it was realized that we had money to spend we were followed about, during our whole stay, by scores of merchants, some simply loaded down with the entire stock of their shops. Our time ashore was too short for us to see what Colombo really was like, but it was delightful to be able to stretch our legs ashore again, and the novelty and charm of the streets and the luxuriant tropical vegetation made us feel that we would be willing to remain a lifetime amid scenes of such fascination and colour.

After Colombo the days were more wearisome than before. The weather was scorching and only a few of us could get on deck at a time for a breath of fresh air. Long before nightfall the decks would be covered with men lying on their blankets, for permission was given to as many as there was room for to sleep on the boat and saloon decks, and as there was only room for a twentieth of the complement, one had to grab one's position early. Some preferred a comfortable night's rest to their tea, and so would occupy their man's length of deck space while the others were eating.

Going through the Red Sea was a feast of beauty, for the evening colours of the sand-hills were gorgeous, and inconceivable to any but an eye-witness. We were now on biblical ground, and great were the religious arguments that waged. One boy wrote home that one of the ship's anchors had brought up a wheel from the chariot of Pharaoh, and his mother had replied that she was glad he was visiting such historic country, but when he later on told her that *Big Lizzie* was firing shells twenty-seven miles at the Dardanelles, she wrote him that she was afraid life in the army was making him exaggerate things and that he should keep strictly to the truth!

There was fighting going on at Aden when we passed—some Bedouins were attacking the town from the desert side, but evidently it was not serious, for, to our disappointment, we were not asked to join in. We were merely examined by a British war-ship and told to pass on.

At Suez we disembarked and we were none of us sorry to say good-bye to the old ship, and there were no fond farewells taken of the crew, for they were as unpatriotic a set of scoundrels as ever sailed under the British flag. They robbed us right and left. They stole our ration jam, selling it to us in the form of a drink. A penny a glass would buy "pineapple cordial," which was merely a tin of pineapple jam mixed up in a ship's bucket of iced water. "Orangeade" was marmalade jam and water. Strange to say, there were always enough "boobs" among us soldiers to fall for it. On board ship we were not allowed to wear boots, as the hobnails in our military footwear could cut up the deck, so those that hadn't shoes went barefoot, but at the end of the voyage when we began to search for our boots there was the deuce to pay. Only half the men could find them at all, and it was only through a search of the whole ship that many of us did not have to walk in the sands of Egypt barefooted. The missing pairs were found among the sailors, of course, one of them even having six. It is a wonder those sailors didn't cut our hair when we were asleep to stuff their pillows—they certainly skinned us as close as they could.

Part 2
Egypt

CHAPTER 7

The Land of Sand and Sweat

How we hated Egypt before we left it! It may be a land of fascination to the tourist who drives about in *gharris* to view its wonders and stays at a European hotel, but to be there as a soldier, to lie in its vile sand, to swallow its conglomerated stinks, to rub the filth off the seats in the third-class train-carriages, to have under your eyes continually the animated lump of muck that the *Gyppo* is, to have your ears filled continually with the vile expressions that the Egyptian conceives as wit, is an experience that makes one so disgusted that few Australians that were there will ever want to see the rotten country again. At first, however, all was novelty, and we were like children on a picnic as we marched from the wharf into the third-class carriages of the Egyptian state railways waiting for us just outside the gates. It was some job getting into those carriages. Ordinarily white people travelled first-class, but we were troops, and it was like pushing against a wall to pass the smell that came from the doors of these carriages that had been the preserves of the unwashed nigger of varied age and sex for the Lord knows how many years.

We left the ship with twenty-four hours' provisions, which were all consumed on that train. Some of us managed to get a little sleep by packing all the equipment in the end of the carriage and sitting on the floor back to back. Now and again the train would stop at nowhere in particular, when we would be assailed by anything-but-clean niggers, who would draw oranges and other fruit from inside their shirts. We had been warned against eating anything in Egypt that could not be skinned, and when we saw the niggers and where they kept their stock in trade we knew the reason.

So far we had nothing but English money, and, though we had been given lectures before disembarking on the values of Egyptian money, we had to pay liberal exchange to these train-side merchants. Oranges cost us about two cents apiece, though later on with Egyptian money we bought them three for a half *piastre* (three cents). The only station I remember on this trip was because of its curious-sounding name, Zagizig, where we had a stroll along the platform and met some of our lordly Sikhs from India, who were all smiles when they discovered we were Australians. In the early dawn we disentrained at Koubbeh and after straightening ourselves out from having been cramped up in those horse-boxes, we started our march of about ten miles, carrying full pack, to the camp at Zeitoun. But here there was no arrangement for our breakfast. The New Zealanders and Australians already camped there had only their own day's rations, and we had consumed ours on the train. How we cursed the powers that be! We had humped our eighty-pound packs those weary miles and when we thought we had arrived—no tucker! There might have been some trouble; grumbling might have led to action in a raid on somebody's stores, but for the Y. M. C. A. hut. They served out hot tea and in a few moments grumbling gave place to *chiaching*; criticism that a few moments ago had been edged was now good-humoured. Give an Australian soldier hot tea and it will pick him up quicker than any other drink on earth.

CHAPTER 8

Heliopolis

Our camp was just outside the new city of Heliopolis, which was built at the cost of about $40,000,000 by a Belgian syndicate to rival Monte Carlo, but it was a fiasco as a money-making concern. Nevertheless, there were some gorgeous buildings, and it was a source of constant interest to us. The Palace Hotel was the most magnificent building I have ever seen; used by us as a hospital. There was no lack of marble, and the mosaics were marvellous. The lamp-stands were of a unique and exquisite design. The contract provided that the pattern should be destroyed after they were made, so they would not be copied. It was rather incongruous to see nothing but rows and rows of army cots, and the white-robed nurses flitting about in rooms that were manifestly intended for luxurious divans and the evening dress of fashion. Lying in those cots, one had but to gaze ceiling-ward, and forget that one was in a hospital. It required little imagination to people the rooms with the same splendour and fashion that fills Monte Carlo, and maybe, had the war not come and the gambling license been granted, all this barbaric splendour would have been perfumed with the scents of attar of roses and lily-of-the-valley instead of *iodoform* and carbolic.

Another hospital was in Luna Park, which had been built to cater to the amusement of thousands of joy-seekers, but the only joy there now was in relief from pain. It was fun to make the round of the wards, for many beds were on the scenic railway, and you would visit one poor chap in a high fever, lying amid painted ice and snow, while another nursed his broken leg alongside a precipice that might well have caused it. I walked in to see the sights one day, and passing through a cave almost fell over a bed whereon was my own brother, whose whereabouts I had been trying to discover for days. Such are the coincidences of life.

The streets of this town were spacious and very clean and were bordered by fine buildings with granite and marble pillars and some fine masonry lacework. Unfortunately, poor taste was often shown, with plaster alongside the marble, and the stone used was too soft and already in places was crumbling. In Egypt, where it rarely rains, the climate is kind to the jerry-builder, and it's only when Jupiter Pluvius wants a laugh and sends a regular tropical downpour that the buildings that were a thing of beauty and a joy forever come to earth and are no more. We ourselves were on one occasion victims of this god's fun. We were told that it never rained, and our huts were built just to shelter us from the sun, but at 2 a.m. the grim old weather-god turned on the shower, and no doubt it amused him a good deal to hear our curses as we tried to shelter ourselves and tucker beneath greatcoats and water-proof sheeting. There was no chance of "getting in out of the rain," for there was not a water-proof shelter for miles. Egypt is not the only place, though, where the residents know least about their own climate!

Heliopolis, anyway, is a skeleton of a town, for most of these buildings were merely occupied in the front, by Greek and Indian merchants who had anticipated our coming. In these shops anything could be bought, from a microbe (which was sometimes given away) to an elephant (nearly always a white one)! However, there were silks galore and filigree-work of beauty, but the biggest trade was done in coloured handkerchiefs, crudely worked on a sewing-machine with a design of the pyramids and "Advance Australia." The cuteness of these merchants was also evidenced in the signs on their stores. The first Australian to stroll down those streets was amazed to see, in huge lettering, The Melbourne Store, next door to The Sydney Shop. They even knew our slang, for here was The 'Fair *Dinkum*' Store, and across the way Ribuck Goods. Prices were pretty much what you liked to pay. At any rate I never failed to get an article by paying only a quarter of the first-named price.

The most persistent of professionals were the bootblacks. You *had* to have your boots cleaned whether you liked it or not! Stop for a moment to talk to a friend and there was a nigger on each foot, industriously brushing away as if his life depended on it. They would follow you on to a tram-car, and whether you got a seat or not there would be somebody working on your boots two seconds after boarding it. Another nuisance were the sellers of swagger-sticks, and I have frequently bought one just for the pleasure of laying it across the back of its previous owner. They soon picked up our language and its choicest words, but one word they never understood was *No!* The first Egyptian word we learned was *imshi*! literally, "Get!"—but it generally required the backing of a military boot to make it effective. The Australianese that the *Gyppos* picked up is not commonly used in polite society; maybe *they* thought it correct English, but it was sometimes very embarrassing when walking down the street with a nurse. And some polite merchants were sorely puzzled when the effect of their well-chosen words and bow was an unintentional biting of the dust.

We must pass a vote of thanks, however, to the syndicate for providing us with some ideal club-rooms. I guess the Y. M. C. A. never had such quarters before or since, and must have had to do some squaring of conscience in calling these Army *huts*. It was a hut, though, all right, out at the camp, made of grass mats, held together with string, but it was the usual boon and blessing to men, and I guess there were few letters left camp that weren't on Red Triangle paper. I may as well mention here, too, that the best meals I had since leaving home were in the Y. M. C. A. building in the Esbekiah Gardens in Cairo, so here's a thank-you to those ladies and the management.

CHAPTER 9

The Desert

I know more about the desert in Egypt than any other part of it, for it was on the desert we trained. There were sham fights galore, but it was mostly squad and company drill, until if some devil had scooped out our brain-boxes and filled them with sawdust we could have carried out the orders just as well. In fact, one fellow must have gone mad with the monotony of it and perpetrated the rhyme, to the tune of *The Red, White, and Blue*:

> At the halt, on the left, form platoons,
> At the halt, on the left, form platoons,
> If the odd numbers don't mark time two paces,
> How the hell can the boys form platoons?

I don't know whether the author was ever found, but I know plenty that were laid out for singing it. We began to have a sinking feeling that we would not be in the real scrap at all, for a good part of our time was taken up in forming *hollow square*, a formation that is famous in the British army as having been only once broken, but is only of value against savages, and *furphies* (unfounded rumours) spread that we were going into Darkest Africa or the Soudan. However, we also practised echelon for artillery formation, that is, breaking a company into chunks and throwing it about at unequal distances, so that a shell falling on one chunk would not wipe any of the others off the map. Then there was more gloom, for that looked as if the war was real, and there must be something in what the papers were saying after all. About this time some of the boys' letters began to contain more war news even than the papers, for the padre, who was regimental censor, informed us that if he let our mail go home unpencilled there would be many mothers weeping at the danger their boys were in, as they described fierce battles in the desert. Even as it was, letters were published in home papers that showed our regiment to have been four times annihilated while we were in training! The only shots these fellows heard all day were the popping of the corks in the wet canteen! (No charge to the *drys* for this story!)

And then, of course, we route-marched—in the desert, please remember; a very different thing, Mr. Rookie, to the same thing on made roads! For one thing, we were not supposed to do more than fifteen miles a day, but on the desert there were no milestones, and the distance was "estimated" by the officer in command. Some of these officers must have been city treasurers in private life, for their estimate of distance was like estimated annual expenditure, generally much under the mark. Mostly they would know when we had gone far enough, which for us was too far, and then we would get lost coming back. Fortunately, there was a lot of men camped in that desert, and as it is customary for a man lost to travel in a circle, we would generally run into some camp or other, otherwise I'm afraid we would now be a petrified army, *somewhere in Sahara*. Ten miles with an eighty-pound pack on your back, through heavy sand, is as much as a man can endure; after that he doesn't endure, he just carries on, and on, and on, and on. At that time your company are all feet and are walking on your brain. Anyway, the man behind you does actually walk on your —— heels every second step.

In the desert, also, did we dig trenches. No, not the same thing as digging trenches anywhere! For it is really nearly as easy to dig trenches in the ocean. For every spadeful you throw out two fall in, and if, by the use of much cunning, you *do* manage to get a hole dug, then you must not leave it for a single instant, for it is only waiting until your back is turned to disappear. There is one thing—those trenches were good cover, for we would no sooner occupy them than we would be covered up entirely. I would defy an aeroplane with the best *made in Germany* spectacles to discover whether we were men or mummies.

But we had one very exciting trench-digging expedition. We dug, if you please, into an old city, and broke into tombs umpteen thousand years old. There were scarabs and ancient jewels there that the Field Museum would give their eye-teeth for. We were ordered to deliver our finds to the authorities, but I am afraid many of the boys had *sticky* fingers. It was all jolly interesting, but there is a fly in every box of ointment, and the supposed age of these relics brought home to us the fact that this soil had been lived on for thousands of years by people much like our present neighbours, without any sanitary ideas; and one of our fellows with a scientific mind pictured to us every grain of sand as being a globe inhabited by germs. This was comforting, for we each of us swallowed a few billion of these *universes* every day! They got in our eyes, in our ears, in our nose and mouth, but if they got into a cut by any chance, then we were subjects for the doctor.

"Oh Egypt, thou land of teeming life, how healthy wouldst thou be if you weren't so overcrowded!"

Yet there was beauty in the desert. We would frequently pick up agates, sapphires, and turquoise matrix. But its beauty was chiefly suggestive. There were gorgeous sunsets—poetry there, but more poetry still in the wonderful mirages. Why, here, hung above the earth, were scenes from every age: Cleopatra's galleys, Alexander's legions, the pomp of the Mamelukes, Ptolemy and Pompey, Napoleon and Gordon—their times and deeds were all pictured here. Perhaps the spirit world has its *movies*, and only here in the desert mirage is the *screen* of stuff that can be seen with mortal eyes.

But beauty is not for soldiers—the desert was our *schoolmaster*. It was the right-hand man of Kitchener, and well did it perform its task of putting iron into our spirits and turning our muscles into steel, and making us fit for whatever job the Maker of Armies had for us. He knew the place to train us—where the weaklings would fall and only the very fit survive. Any soldier who passed through his grades in the *academy of the desert* might not shine in a *guard of honour to a princess*; his skin would be blistered, his clothes would be stained, but he'd be the equal in strength of any man on earth, and would have fought the attacks of every known disease. It was Egypt and the desert that made Gallipoli possible, and the Australian army owes much to the astuteness of Kitchener, who knew the ideal training-ground for the daredevil freeman from down under.

Chapter 10

Picketing in Cairo

No man in the British Empire knew Egypt better than Lord Kitchener, and he had very good reasons, apart from training, in sending us there. There can be no doubt whatever that the majority of the Egyptians were pro-Turkish if not pro-German. The educated Egyptian, like the Babu in Bengal, is specially fitted by nature for intrigue, and if he sees a chance to oppose whatever government is in power and keep his own skin, it is his idea of living well. Egypt was immediately put under martial law, but there was plenty of scope for a while for the midnight assassin and the poisoner. Here and there soldiers would disappear and street riots would be started by the wind. Who would not turn round on seeing an R. S. V. P. eye in a face whose veil enhanced the beauty it did not hide? But there would always be some sedition-monger to immediately fill the street with a thousand yelling maniacs who would scream that their religion had been insulted by the accursed infidels. *Religion* they knew nothing about, but to make trouble was their meat and drink. There was a good deal of Irish blood among us, and many men who would rather fight than go to the opera, so there were some good old ding-dong scraps. Of course the *Gyppo* is no fighter, but he can stand behind and throw stones and can't resist plunging the knife into an inviting back, so sometimes our boys would get laid out. A street row is always a dangerous thing, for those in front cry "Back!" and those behind cry "Forward!" and there is likely to be a jam in which the innocent, if there are any, get hurt. I saw a pretty ugly-looking crowd dispersed with a characteristic Australian weapon. Firing over their heads had no effect, nor threats of a bayonet charge, but when two Australian bushmen began plying stockwhips, those niggers made themselves scarcer than mice on the smell of a cat. As a good manipulator of the stockwhip can pull the cork from a bottle, maybe these plotters were afraid of having their guilty secrets picked from them. At any rate, there were some who lost flesh in a part that would insure them having a smaller following thereafter.

There was a battle fought in Cairo for which there will be no medals distributed and to which stay-at-home Australians think there is no honour attached, but I doubt if any one who took part in the battle of the Wasir, except maybe the military police, are ashamed of what they did. Anyone who knows Cairo knows that there is a part of it that is not mentionable at dinner-table. It is the sink of the world. Every large city has its sore, but Cairo has an ulcer. This vile spot made the clean lads from the wind-swept plains and scented bush of Australia absolutely sick. The Australian is a practical idealist, and for him to see dirt is to want to remove it. Besides which, this place was a nest of spies and enemies. There were several of our boys who disappeared, and, though it may be said they had no right there, the sign "No Admittance" is one that the average Australian has never been able to read. It was one of those scraps that no one starts but that breaks out of itself, because it has been brewing so long. There were a few thousand of the boys in Cairo that night, and when the news spread it did not take long for more to come in from Mena and other camps. They did not wait for the motorman to start his car, but in many cases commandeered it for the time being. Things moved quite warmly for an hour or two: ladies of low degree scuttled like rats and panders dashed for safety, while *owners* in princely motorcars turned almost as white as their livers as they saw their *warehouses of virtue* going up in flame. Two incidents are very vivid—the sight of a grand piano tumbling out of a five-story window and one of the aforesaid *owners* trying to remonstrate with the avengers, and having his car run into the fire. The military police tried to interfere early in the game, but only made matters worse, as they were pretty well hated by the boys as being mostly slackers. The attitude of many of the officers may be judged from Jerry. He was looking on smoking a pipe when an English major dashed up to him, very apoplectic.

"Are you an Australian officer?"

"Ye—es!" drawled Jerry.

"Well, why don't you take your men in hand?"

"Can't see they are doing any harm!" said Jerry. In the end strong-armed guards were brought in from the camps, and as the boys were just about tired anyway of their self-appointed policemanship, things soon quieted down. There were rumours that it cost the Australian Government a tidy sum of money, but the burning of those pest-houses must have risen like incense to heaven, and one very good effect it had, about which there will be no dispute—it put the fear of God into the *Gyppo*, and Australian soldiers after that even singly and in small groups received nothing worse than black looks.

After this Cairo was very thoroughly picketed—the streets were patrolled all night by parties of ten or a dozen under an N. C. O. I was in charge of one of these parties for a couple of months and had a good deal of fun playing *policeman* among the cosmopolitan crowds that infest Cairo. We were only armed with the handles of our entrenching tools, which were sticks of hardwood about twelve inches long with an iron band at the upper end, but they made very effective batons. I remember once we had to settle a dispute at a wedding-feast. I suppose there must have been a lack of room in the house, for the meal was spread in the street—long tables with a couple of hundred guests seated at them right in the way of the traffic. We strolled past a couple of times, but as we had no instructions to prevent folk using the public street for their domestic affairs, we saw no call to interfere, but our mouths watered at the sight of the good things to eat, and we thought it rather a tempting of Providence to spread this abundance of food in the open street of a city where there are always about a million of people who had not enough to eat at any time. We had only gone a couple of blocks away when some wildly excited niggers rushed after us and informed us: "Plenty men kill 'um back there!"

We went back at the double and there was as ugly a riot as ever Irishman longed for. There seemed to be a couple of thousand yelling maniacs packing both sides of the street. Our instructions were to prevent the gathering of crowds. There were only ten of us and we had but our improvised batons, but I told the boys to get into the crowd and tell them once to *imshi* (get) and then hit. "Be sure and never speak twice." We soon dispersed the crowd. There was something about our *Nulla-nullas*[1] that looked very businesslike, and none stopped to argue the point.

Sometimes the boys were pretty thirsty in those long tramps through the streets, and the open cafes were very inviting. But we had an experience that warned me against allowing any of them to go in and get a drink. One of them had certainly not been gone more than a couple of minutes, and he swears he only had one drink; nevertheless, he had to be put in a cab and sent back to the barracks. We had pretty dull times in those barracks—the Kasr-el-nile just alongside the bridge of the same name. The chief amusement was to feed the hawks that all day hovered in the courtyard. We would drop pieces of meat and bread from the balcony, but so quick were the birds that I never knew a piece to reach the ground.

Jerry was one of the officers of the picket, and we had to report to him at midnight at a shelter in a part of the city with an evil reputation. From here we would issue in force to close for the night the various dens of iniquity. Jerry would generally stroll ahead with his cane and walk into the resort of the worst ruffians on earth with all the assurance of a general at the head of a brigade. He would announce to these, the most lawless men and women in the world, that it was time to close up, and there was something in his bearing that commanded prompt obedience.

In fact, nothing ever ruffled Jerry. One night a senior officer attached to the commandant came down in a tearing rage, and began to dress Jerry down for having presumed to close up a certain gambling resort without consulting the authorities. After about twenty minutes' harangue in which he threatened Jerry with all manner of punishment, he collapsed at the drawled retort: "And then you'll wake up!"

Jerry was still on the picket when I left to go down to the Suez Canal defences, and I did not hear any more about him until I met him in Melbourne a few weeks ago, when I asked him if he had been over to France, and his reply was: "No. I—I came back."

No explanation as to whether he was invalided or wounded.

---

1. Australian native weapon.

Jerry was quite equal to telling a field-marshal to go to a place even warmer than Egypt. Maybe his extraordinary self-assurance got on the nerves of some general so much that to protect himself from those critical eyes he had to send Jerry home.

The two principal hotels in Cairo, Shepheard's and the Continental, were out of bounds to all but officers. Some of our boys resented this discrimination while not on parade, for many of the privates were, in social life, in higher standing than the majority of the officers. There was one of our colonels who took his brother in to dine with him at Shepheard's. A snobbish English officer came up to this man who happened to be only a private, and said: "What are you doing in here, my man?"

But he got rather a setback when the Australian colonel said to him: "Captain, let me introduce my brother."

There was another Australian private whom an English officer objected to have sitting at the same table with him at the Trocadero in London. Next day this private reserved every seat in this swell restaurant and provided dinner for several hundred of his chums, putting a notice on the door: No Officers Admitted. Another illustration of snobbishness, this time in Australia, was when some officers at a race-meeting instructed the committee to refuse admittance to the saddling paddock and grand stand to all privates and N. C. Os, but they looked pretty small when informed that the owner of the race-course was a private and could hardly be debarred from his own property. Few Australian officers are of this type, however, and in the trenches our officers and men are a happy family. When the men realize that an officer knows his job and has plenty of pluck, they will follow him through hell.

A favourite rendezvous in Cairo was the Ezbekiah Gardens of a Sunday afternoon. There were beauties there from many nations, dressed in the *dernier cri* of fashion, who were tickled to death to be escorted by the bronzed giants from down-under, and though one failed sometimes to find words that were understood, yet sufficient was said in glance and shrug to make a very interesting conversation. And the Sultan's band was always there to fill in pauses and, in fact, played so well as to be an encouragement to flirtations that were delightful in spite of differences of nationality.

There was always plenty to see around Cairo, and the education of the Australian bushman has been widened considerably through those months in Egypt, though I am afraid some of us swallowed the yarns of the guides and garnered a vast store of misinformation. These guides were a set of blackmailers, but once you had engaged one he looked on you as his personal property, and would let no one rob you but himself. I would like, even now, to have within reach of my boot the old scoundrel who took me inside the Great Pyramid. After following him in and by the light of a candle climbing very carefully in stockinged feet the granite passage (polished by millions of toes until it was as slippery as glass), the old ruffian led me into the Queen's chamber, and then announced that he had lost his candle but would show me the height of the chamber by burning magnesium wire for the price of one *piastre* (five cents) per second. After I had a good flashlight view of the inside of this room, and marvelled sufficiently at the enormous size of the blocks of marble in the walls and out of which the *sarcophagus* was made, the old son of a thief told me it would be at the same rate that he would light my way to the outside air again. I only had stockinged feet, and made the foolish mistake of striking out in the dark. The old boy howled, but I verily believe that I very nearly displaced one of the eighty-ton blocks of marble. We arrived at the opening at the same moment and I got a "full-Nelson" on the greasy blackguard. He handed over the magnesium wire, also the candle, and was quite willing to give me as many of his wives as I required before I released him. I have never been in any place as hot as the inside of the Great Pyramid, and no longer wonder that a mummy is so dried up. For in five minutes pretty nearly every drop of moisture in my own body came out through the pores of my skin.

I also was barmy enough to climb to the top of the Great Pyramid; each separate block of stone to be surmounted was like the wall of a house, but the view from the top was worthwhile, and might have been enjoyed but for the thought of getting down again; especially as old Job (my new guide) persisted in telling me about several people who had been killed, bouncing all the way to the bottom. I did pretty well all the tourist stunts in Egypt. I rode a donkey when my feet touched the ground on either side, also mounted a camel that lifted me to a dizzy height. I gazed into the imperturbable face of the Sphinx and wandered among the numerous pyramids of Sakkara. I visited the tombs of the Mamelukes and feasted on the beauty of the mosques (having my feet shod with the provided sandals so that my infidel dust might not defame the hallowed floor). I also viewed the citadel; but the place of most charm was the streets of old Cairo. I was never tired of elbowing my way through the bazaars and it was worth it to buy something you didn't want for the sake of being waited on by *Abraham in the flesh*. Here was the Arabian Nights in very reality, and all the romance and lure of a thousand dreams. The smell was a bit overpowering, but bearable if you surrounded yourself with the smell of your favourite tobacco.

CHAPTER 11

Nipper

On the sheep and cattle station of Wyaga in south-western Queensland there is a shepherd's hut about fifty miles from the homestead.

One night my father was camping in this hut, and before lying down had piled a lot of dry dung on the fire outside so that the smoke would drive away the mosquitoes. Somewhere about midnight he woke with the sense of some human being near him. Then he was startled to see the fire scattered before his eyes, but never found sight nor sound of anything living.

Many months later he again visited the hut. This time it was occupied by old Mullins, the shepherd. Again about midnight he was roused, this time by the whining of the sheep-dog Nipper. Every hair on the dog was bristling, but he made no attempt to attack whatever it was he saw. Suddenly the fire was again scattered. The old shepherd said that this happened about once a month, and that on one occasion he had seen a woman kick the fire apart and then disappear.

To the railway-station at Goondiwindi came Mullins one day in December, 1914, and bought tickets to Brisbane for himself and Nipper. The regulations of the Queensland government railways will not allow dogs to travel in passengers' carriages. As Nipper had to travel in a dog-box at the end of the guard's van, old Mullins insisted on occupying a seat in the van, and at every station would get his friend a drink.

When the train stopped for meals at midday and evening Mullins would seize the plate served to him and make for the door. The manager of the refreshment-room made him pay for the plate before taking it outside, not trusting his looks, but the old shepherd only wanted to have Nipper's hunger satisfied before his own. At the end of the journey there were several china plates in the box that were of no further use to either of them.

The recruiting-officer in Brisbane was not surprised to see a weather-beaten old *bushie* walk into the depot, for there were many such seeking to join the young lads in this *ding-dong scrap*. It was only too evident that he was well over the age limit, but when they told him he was too old, he offered to fight them singly or collectively, or take on the best fighter their blank-blank army could produce. They managed to get him outside the door, but not before both he and Nipper had left behind them proof of their quality in lost skin and torn clothes.

Some days later old Mullins appeared again, leading Nipper on a chain. Almost everyone entrenched himself behind a table, but the old man had no fight in him, declaring in a choking voice that Nipper had come to enlist alone. "He is not too old, anyway, and will deal with more of the blank-blank swine than a hundred of your sissy, white-faced, unweaned kids!"

One of the doctors had a heart in the right place and wrote a letter to the commandant of a regiment soon going overseas, asking him if he could not take the dog as a regimental pet. He gave the old man the letter and told him to take his dog out to the camp.

The colonel was not without understanding, and that is how Nipper joined up to fight for democracy.

There were some who started out to teach Nipper tricks, but it was soon discovered that he knew a good deal more than most of us. He had a keen sense of humour, and after someone would spend hours trying to teach him to sit up, all of which time he would pretend he could not understand what he was wanted to do, with a sly look he would suddenly go through a whole repertoire of tricks, not merely sitting up, but tumbling over backward, generally ending the performance by *heeling-up* (nipping in the heel) all and sundry. He never really bit any one, but a lot of the new boys were nervous during this heeling-up process.

Nipper was certainly the most intelligent of the whole canine race. He was continually trying out new tricks for our amusement and was in ecstasy if they brought applause. On a shot being fired he would stretch out and pretend he was killed, but if you said, "White Flag! Treachery!" he would come to life again as savage as a wolf. If anyone scolded him he would lie down and wipe his eyes with his paw, which was irresistible and turned the scolding voice into laughter.

There was one senior officer that Nipper suspected was a German, and every chance he got he would sneak up and, without preliminary warning, take a good hold of the seat of his trousers. This major returned Nipper's dislike with interest, and had it not been for the protection of the colonel Nipper's career might have been cut short before we left Australia.

Nipper never seemed to entertain much respect for the Army Service Corps, and sometimes he would attack one of their wagons with such fury as to clear the men off it and start the horses bolting.

These were his dislikes, but his one and only hate was a military policeman. Perhaps he had a guilty conscience; but the very sight of a red-cap would make him foam at the mouth, and they sent in several requests that they might be allowed to shoot him for their own protection. The boys in camp had no special love for the M. Ps either, and there was very nearly a pitched battle when Nipper appeared one day with two raw welts across his back, suspicion being immediately laid at their door.

Nipper always appeared on parade, and considered his position to be the right flank when in line and right ahead of everybody when in column of route. If motor-car or horse vehicle was slow in giving way to us, Nipper informed them who we were, which was one of the few occasions on which he was heard to bark. At first he had some narrow escapes, but soon discovered that "heeling-up" a horse or the rear wheel of a moving automobile was more risky than nipping at the heels of sheep or cow.

Once our adjutant had an argument with the owner of an automobile for breaking through our column. Nipper objected to a certain remark of the slacker in the car, and without joining in the conversation leaped into the car and dragged out his overcoat into the mud, not relinquishing it until it was well soaked.

On board the troop-ship Nipper pined for the smell of the gum leaves, and it was the only time when we lost patience with him, for every night he would stand in the bow and howl.

The smells of Egypt disgusted Nipper, remembering the scents of the Australian bush. Only once did he make the mistake of heeling-up a *Gyppo*, after which he made a great pretence of being very sick. On other occasions when he wanted them to keep their distance, he found mere growling to have the desired effect.

The atmosphere of Egypt had a bad effect on Nipper's morals, and he would sometimes disappear for days. After a while the old reprobate acquired the disgusting habit of eating sand, which not only showed how far he had fallen from grace, but also had a serious effect on his health. On several occasions he had to be taken to the army medical tent, and only the most drastic remedies saved his life.

One day the colonel read a letter he had received from old Mullins inquiring if Nipper was still alive and reminding us that his meat had always been cooked for him. It almost made one believe in reincarnation, for it was really uncanny, as no human being could more contritely express remorse than did Nipper as he listened with tail between his legs, whining most piteously.

He accompanied me on some scouting expeditions in the desert, but his powers were failing, and I never trusted him after one occasion on which he made a fool of me. He showed all the symptoms of danger being near; and sure enough on looking through my glasses I saw what appeared to be a man with a rifle crouched behind a bush. I took three men with me and we made a long detour to approach from behind, but after all our precautions and alarm we found nothing but a long stick leaning against the bush and the shadow of a rock that looked something like a man.

In the end Nipper committed suicide, and this was the manner of his going. He was in the habit of swimming across the canal every morning while we were at Ferry Post. This morning, however, one of the boys noticed him go under, and diving in after him was able, after some difficulty, to get his body ashore. He was quite stiff and we all of us believed that he swam out a certain distance and gave up.

His bearing for days indicated that something was preying on his mind, and as we did not know what cloud overshadowed his canine soul we forbore to judge him.

His memory will remain for long in the hearts of those who knew him, and we buried him in the burning sand of Arabia with the simple inscription on a pine board:

Here lies Nipper
Died on active service, a true comrade,—— sacrificed to On,[1]
No. 0000——regimental pet—— ——th brigade——heathen.

and his identification disk was sent home to old Mullins and maybe hangs in the old hut where, perhaps, the ghost walks no more and the ashes of the fire smoulder undisturbed.

---

1. The Egyptian sun-god.

Part 3
Gallipoli

Chapter 12

The Adventure of Youth

Fate has decided that Gallipoli shall always be associated with the story of the Anzacs. This name (which is formed from the initial letters of the Australian New Zealand Army Corps) does not describe more than half the troops that were engaged in that fated campaign, but it has so caught the popular fancy, that in spite of all historians may do, injustice will be done in the thought of the public to the English, Scotch, and Irish regiments and the gallant French Colonial troops who played an equally heroic part. There were certainly no finer troops on the Peninsula—probably in the whole war no unit has shown greater courage than did the glorious Twenty-ninth British Division in the landing at Cape Helles.

No writer who accurately pictured these memorable months of our "treading on the corns of the Turkish Empire" could leave out even the loyal dark-skinned Britishers from the Hindustani hills and from the Ganges. There both Gourkas and Sikhs added to their reputation as fighters.

Australia and New Zealand's part does not, in actual accomplishment or in personal daring and endurance, outclass the doings of these others, the larger half of the army. But there is a romance and a glow about the Anzac exploits that (rail at the injustice of it as you may) makes a human-interest story that will elbow out of the mind of the *man in the street* what other troops did. In fact, every second man one meets has the idea that the Australians and New Zealanders were the only men there.

I don't intend to try and write the story of Gallipoli—I haven't the equipment or the experience—John Masefield has written the only book that need be read, and only a man who was in that outstanding achievement of the landing on the 25th of April has a right to the honour of associating his name in a chronicle of *What I did!* What I am going to attempt to do is just to picture it as a *winning of the spurs* by the youngest democracy on earth.

There was something peculiarly fitting in the fate that ordained that this adolescent nation of the South Seas should prove its fitness for manhood in an adventure upon which were focussed the eyes of all nations. The gods love romance, else why was the youngest nation of earth tried out on the oldest battlefield of history? How those young men from the continent whose soil had never been stained with blood thrilled to hear their padres tell them as they gathered on the decks of the troop-ships in the harbour of Lemnos, that tomorrow they would set foot almost on the site of the ancient battlefield of Troy, where the early Greeks shed their blood, as sung in the oldest battle-song in the world.

These young Australians were eager to prove their country's worth as a breeder of men. Australians have been very sensitive to the criticism of Old World visitors—that we were a pleasure-loving people, who only thought of sport—that in our country no one took life seriously, and even the making of money was secondary to football, and that we would all rather win a hundred pounds on a horse-race than make a thousand by personal exertion. Practically every book written on Australia by an Englishman or an American has said the same thing, that we were a lovable, easy-going race, but did not work very hard, and in a serious crisis would be found wanting.

The whole nation brooded over these young men, guardians of Australia's honour, and waited anxiously for them to wipe out this slur. That explains Australia's pride in Anzac. It meant for us not merely our baptism in blood—it was more even than a victory—for there, with the fierce search-light of every nation turned upon it, our representative manhood showed no faltering—but proved it was of the true British breed, having nevertheless a bearing in battle that was uniquely its own. In this age of bravest men the Australian has an abandon in fight which on every battlefield marks him as different from any other soldier.

There is an insidious German propaganda suggesting that the Australians are very sore at the failure on Gallipoli and that we blame the British Government and staff for having sent us to perish in an impossible task. I want to say, that while in the Australian army, as private, N. C. O. and officer, I never heard a single criticism of the government for the Gallipoli business. There is no man who was on the Peninsula who does not admire General Sir Ian Hamilton, and most of the officers believe that Britain has never produced a more brilliant general. That the expedition failed was not the fault of the commander-in-chief nor of the troops. And, anyway, we Australians are good enough sports to realize that there must be blunders here and there, and we're quite ready to bear our share of the occasional inevitable disaster.

But Gallipoli was not the failure many people think. Some people seem to have the idea that a hundred thousand troops were intended to beat a couple of million, and take one of the strongest cities in the world. There never was a time when the Turks did not outnumber us five to one, when they did not have an enormous reserve, in men, equipment, and munitions, immediately at their back, while our base was five hundred miles away in Egypt. The Turks had a Krupp factory at Constantinople within a few hours of them, turning out more ammunition per day than they were using, while ours had to come thousands of miles from England. Of course, we were never intended to take Constantinople. The expedition was a purely naval one, and we were a small military force, auxiliary to the navy, that was to seize the Narrows and enable the ships to get within range of Constantinople, and so compel its surrender. We failed, in this final objective, but we accomplished a great deal, nevertheless. We held back probably a million Turks from the Russians, and we left, in actual counted dead Turkish bodies, more than double our own casualties (killed, wounded, and missing). But, above all, we definitely impressed the German mind with the fact that Great Britain did not only mean the British Isles but the equally loyal and brave fighters from Britain overseas.

Here is no history of Gallipoli, but let me try to sketch four pictures that will show you the type of men that there joked with death and made curses sound to angel ears sweeter than the hymns of the soft-souled churchgoer.

CHAPTER 13

The Landing That Could Not Succeed—But Did

Picture yourself on a ship that was more crowded with men than ever ship had been before, in a harbour more crowded with ships than ever harbour had been crowded before, with more fears in your mind than had ever crowded into it before, knowing that in a few hours you would see battle for the first time. Having comrades crowding round, bidding you good-bye and informing you that as *your* regimental number added up to thirteen, you would be the first to die, remembering that you hadn't said your prayers for years, and then comforting yourself with the realization that what is going to happen will happen, and that an appeal to the general will not stop the battle, anyway, and you may as well die like a man, and you will feel as did many of those young lads, on the eve of the 25th of April, 1915. There was some premonition of death in those congregations of khaki-clad men who gathered round the padres on each ship and sang *God be With You Till We Meet Again*. You could see in men's faces that they knew they were *going west* on the morrow—but it was a swan-song that could not paralyze the arm or daunt the heart of these young Greathearts, who intended that on this morrow they would do deeds that would make their mothers proud of them.

For if you 'as to die,
As it sometimes 'appens, why,
Far better die a 'ero than a skunk;
A' doin' of yer bit.[1]

---

1. Robert W. Service.

As soon as church-parade was dismissed, another song was on the boards, no hymn, maybe not fine poetry, but the song that will be always associated with the story of Australia's doings in the great war, Australia's battle-song—*Australia Will be There*—immortalized on the *Southland* and *Ballarat*, as it was sung by the soldiers thereon, when they stood in the sea-water that was covering the decks of those torpedoed troop-ships. It was now sung by every Australian voice, and as those crowded troop-ships moved out from Lemnos they truly carried *Australia*, eager, untried Australia—where?

The next day showed to the world that Australia would always be *there!* where the fight raged thickest. Her sons might sometimes penetrate the enemy's territory too far, but hereafter, and till the war's end, they would always be in the front line, storming with the foremost for freedom and democracy.

The landing could not possibly be a surprise to the Turks; the British and French warships had advertised our coming by a preliminary bombardment weeks previously—the Greeks knew all about our concentration in their waters—and wasn't the Queen of Greece sister to the Kaiser?

There were only about two places where we could possibly land, and the Turks were not merely warned of our intentions, but they were warned in plenty of time for them to prepare for us a warm reception. The schooling and method of the Germans had united with the ingenuity of the Turks to make those beaches the unhealthiest spots on the globe. The Germans plainly believed that a landing was impossible.

Think of those beaches, with land and sea mines, densely strewn with barbed wire (even into deep water), with machine-guns arranged so that every yard of sand and water would be swept, by direct, indirect, and cross fire, with a hose-like stream of bullets; think of thousands of field-pieces and howitzers ready, ranged, and set, so that they would spray the sand and whip the sea, merely by the pulling of triggers. Think of a force larger than the intended landing-party entrenched, with their rifles loaded and their range known, behind all manner of overhead cover and wire entanglements, and then remember that you are one of a party that has to step ashore there from an open boat, and kill, or drive far enough inland, these enemy soldiers to enable your stores to be landed so

Anzac Cove, Gallipoli

that when you have defeated him, you may not perish of starvation. Far more than at Balaclava did these young men from down under walk *right into the jaws of death, into the mouth of hell!* And the Turks waited till they were *well* within the jaws before they opened fire. No one in the landing force knew where the Turks were, and the Turks did not fire on us until we got to the zone which they had so prepared that all might perish that entered there. They could see us clearly, the crowded open boats were targets of naked flesh that could not be missed. Was there ever a more favourable setting for a massacre? The Turks in burning Armenian villages with their women and children had not easier tasks than that entrenched army. Our men in the boats were too crowded to use their rifles, and the boats were too close in for the supporting war-ships to keep down the fire from those trenches. How was any one left alive? By calculation of the odds not one man should have set foot on that shore. Make a successful landing, enabling us to occupy a portion of that soil! What an impossible task!

To the men in those boats and the men watching from the ships, it appeared as if not merely the expedition had failed, but that not a man of the landing force would survive. Boats were riddled with bullets and sunk—other boats drifted helplessly as there were not enough alive to row them—men jumped into the bullet-formed spray to swim ashore but were caught in the barbed wire and drowned. Who could expect success, but it nevertheless happened! The Turks were sure that we could not land, yet *we did*. Not only did those boys set foot on those beaches, but the remnant of that landing-party drove the Turks out of their entrenchments up cliffs five hundred feet high, and entrenched themselves on the summit. How did they do it? No one knows; the men who were there don't know themselves. Did heaven intervene? Perhaps spiritual forces may sometimes paralyze material. It must be that right has *physical* might, else why didn't the Kaiser get to Paris? Mathematics and preparedness were on his side; by all reasoning Germany ought to have overwhelmed the world in a few months, with the superiority of her armament, but she didn't. The Turks ought to have kept us off the Peninsula, by all laws of logic and arithmetic, *and they didn't*. I really think the landing succeeded because those boys thought they had failed.

They must have believed themselves doomed—they could see that there were too few to accomplish what was even doubtful when the force was intact. When they were on the shore they must have felt that it was impossible that they could be taken off again. All the time more were falling, and soon it seemed that every last man must be massacred. They made up their minds that, at any rate, they would get a few of the swine before they went. Every man believed that in the end he must be killed, but determined to sell his life as dearly as possible, and that made them the supermen that could not be held back. A whole platoon would be cut down, but somehow one or two would manage to get into the trench, where, of necessity, it was hand-to-hand work, and with laughing disregard of the odds would lay out a score of the enemy and send the others fleeing before them, who would yell out that they were fighting demons from hell. After the confusion in the boats, and from the fact that in most cases companies were entirely without officers, there was no forming up for charges—indeed, there were no orders at all, but every man knew that he could not but be doing the right thing every time he killed a Turk, so they just took their rifle and bayonet in their naked hands and went to it. There was no line of battle, it was just here, there, and everywhere, khaki-clad, laughing demons, seeking Turks to kill.

Never was there fighting like this. All that day it went on. On the beach, up the cliff, in the gullies, miles inland were men fighting. It was not a battle; it would have made a master of tactics weep and tear his hair, but these man-to-man fights kept on. Many were shot from behind, many were wounded and fell in places where no one would find them—some, fighting on, went in a circle and found themselves back on the beach again. However, at nightfall some had begun to dig a shallow line of trenches, well inland across the cliff. Single men and small groups of them, not finding any more Turks where they were, fell back into this ditch and helped deepen it.

Fresh Turks were massing for counter-attack, and soon came on with fury, but we were something like an army now, and although the line had to be shortened it never broke. The landing had been made good, the impossible had been achieved. But there were many who died strange deaths, many left way in, helpless, who could not be succoured—many whom the fighting lust led so far that when they thought of seeking their comrades they found the barrier of a Turkish army now intervening. Strange, unknown duels and combats were fought that day. Unknown are the Bill-Jims who killed scores with naked hand—there were many such. Though we beat the Turk with the odds in his favour, yet this day and afterward he earned our respect as a fighting man.

> *East is East and West is West, and never the twain shall meet*
> *Till Earth and Sky stand presently at God's great Judgment Seat.*
> *But there is neither East nor West, Border, nor Breed, nor Birth,*
> *When two strong men stand face to face, tho' they come from*
>   *the ends of the Earth.*

The Australian had proved himself the fiercest fighter of the world...As one naval officer remarked, they fought not as men but devils. Many have said that much of the loss of life was needless, that had the Australians kept together and waited for orders not so many would have been cut off in the bush. It was true that the impetuosity of many took them too far to return, but it was that very quality that won the day. They did not return, but they drove the Turk before them and enabled others to dig in before he could re-form. You would have to go back to mediaeval times to parallel this fighting. There were impetuosity, dash, initiative, berserker rage, fierce hand-to-hand fighting, every man his own general.

These were not the only qualities of the Australian fighting men, but these alone could have succeeded on that day. When the time came for evacuation of those hardly won and held trenches, these same troops gave evidence of the possession of the opposite attributes of coolness, silence, patience, co-ordination; every man acting as part of a single unit, under control of a single will—which is discipline!

CHAPTER 14

Holding On and Nibbling

There are people who think that the Australian dash petered out with that one supreme effort of landing. We had achieved the impossible in landing—why did we not in the many months we were there, do the comparatively easy thing and advance? Surely, now that we had stores and equipment and artillery, we could more easily drive the Turks out of their trenches. So many seem to think that so much was done on that first day, and so little thereafter.

But the Peninsula is not a story of mere impetuosity and dash, it is a story of endurance as well. As a matter of fact, those eight months of holding on were as great a miracle as the landing. There is a limit to the physical powers even of supermen. These men were not content with the small strip of ground that they held, and they did attack and defeat the Turks opposing them again and again, but as soon as a Turkish army was beaten there was ever another fresh one to take its place. The Turks could not attack us at one time with an army outnumbering us by ten to one, not because they had not the troops, but because there was not room enough. As a matter of fact, that little army (only reinforced enough to fill up the gaps) defeated five Turkish armies, each one larger than its own. Remember, too, that the Turks were always better equipped and supplied—it was so easy with their chief city of Constantinople just within *coo-ee*. Our little army had to be supplied with every single thing over thousands of miles of water. General Hamilton said the navy was father and mother to us, and when it is remembered that every cartridge, every ounce of food, every drop of water, every splinter of firewood had to be brought by the ships, it will be seen that we could not have existed a single day without their aid. The Turks said often enough that they would push us into the sea—they continually called on Allah to aid them—we were only a handful after all; we only held a few hundred acres of their filthy soil, but onto that we clung, sometimes by the skin of our teeth. And it was the weather, not the Turks, that made us leave in the end.

Ever and anon we alarmed the Turk by nibbling a piece nearer to his sacred city. Never did men live under worse conditions than in those eight months of hell, yet never was an army so cheerful. Bill-Jim, which is Australia's name for her soldier-boy, always makes the best of things, and soon made himself at home on that inhospitable shore.

The first thing he decided needed alteration was his uniform. Breeches and puttees were not only too hot but they closed in the leg and afforded cover to the lively little fellow who lives indiscriminately on the soldiers of both sides. As each soldier began to trim his uniform to his own idea of comfort, it was soon, in very reality, a *ragtime* army. Some felt that puttees were a nuisance—everybody realized that the breeches were too long, but differed on the point as to how much too long. Some would clip off six inches from the end, others a foot, and others would have been as well covered without the article at all. Almost everybody decided that a tunic was useless, but some extremists threw away shirt and singlet as well. A Turkish army order was captured which stated that the Australians were running short of supplies, as they made one pair of trousers do for three men. Evidently Johnny Turk could not understand the Australian disregard for conventionality and his taking to nakedness when it meant comfort and there were no women within hundreds of miles to make him conscious of indecency. Clothes that couldn't be washed wouldn't keep one's body clean and became the home of an army that had no interest in the fight for democracy. The Australian showed his practical common sense in discarding as much as possible—but, say, those boys would have caused some amusement if drawn up for review!

Water was certainly the most precious thing. There never was enough to drink, but even then there are always men who would rather wash than drink, and to see these men having their bath in a jam-tin just showed how habit is, in many of us, stronger than common sense, for there was never water enough to more than spread out the dirt or liquefy it so that it would fill up the pores. Others who must bathe adopted a more effective but more dangerous proceeding. Of course, the sea was there—surely plenty of water for washing! Just so, but this bath was pretty unhealthy, for it was practically always whipped by shrapnel and you went in at the risk of your life. Some of the best swimmers used to say it was all right so long as you dived whenever you heard the screech of a shell—that the shrapnel pellets did not penetrate the water more than a few inches. Most men did without either of this choice of baths, and used a scraper. It was evidenced on the Peninsula that one of the greatest of civilizers is a razor. By necessity few could shave, and you soon could not recognize the face of your best chum as it hid itself beneath a growth of some reddish fungus. Really handsome features were quite blotted out, and it is now evident to me why, in civilized life, we all so gladly go through the conventional daily torture of face-scraping.

Thirst is not a thing to joke about, however, and there were times when the allowance of water was not enough to wash down a half-dozen bites, and the food would stick in one's throat.

There was generally enough food but mighty little variety except just before the evacuation when stores had to be eaten to save them being taken away or destroyed. It is all very well to say a man will eat anything when he is hungry, but you can get so tired of bully-beef and biscuits and marmalade-jam that your stomach simply will not digest it. Machonochie's, which was a sort of canned Irish stew, wasn't bad, but there wasn't always more than enough of that to supply the quartermasters. Still there were some great chefs on the Peninsula, men who had got their training as cooks in shearers' camps, where anything badly cooked would be thrown at their heads. It was marvellous how some of them could disguise a bully-beef stew, and I have been told of men coming to blows over the merits of their respective company cooks.

There were more flies on the Peninsula than there was sand on the shore, and they fought us persistently for every atom of food. Getting a meal was a hard day's work, for all the time you had to fight away the swarms, and no matter how quick you were with your fork, you rarely got a mouthful that hadn't been well walked over, and it didn't do to think where those flies might have been walking just previously. No army ever had a better directed sanitary department, but, no matter how clean we kept our trenches, the Turks just *loved* dirt and *worshipped* flies, and their trenches were only ten yards away in one place, and in no place were they far enough to make it a record-breaking aerial flight for a fly. Perhaps it was because they were all Turkish-bred that the flies did us so much harm, for they certainly accounted for more deaths than the shells or bullets. Dysentery was rife all the time and there were times when not one man was well. If the doctors had known enough they would have put a barrage of disinfectant in front of our trenches. We put up sandbags to stop the bullets, but no one had devised a method to stop those winged emissaries of death. Those who died from lead-poisoning were but a score to the hundreds who died of fly-poisoning.

This is but a little of what holding on meant to that little force. The Turk was not only a brave, but a "wily" fighter—snipers were always giving trouble, and one never knew from which direction the next shot was coming. Men with "nerves" declared that our line must be full of spies—sometimes a shot would come through the door of a dugout facing out to sea. These snipers were certainly brave fellows—some were found covered with leaves—one was found in a cleft in the rock where he must have been lowered by his comrades and he could not get out without their help. In the early days some of the Turkish officers who could talk English even took the extreme risk of mixing among the troops and passing false orders. One of these spies was only discovered through misuse of a well-known Australian slang-word. No one in the Australian army but knows the meaning of *dinkum*. Its meaning is something the same as the American *on the level* and is probably the commonest word in the Australian soldier's vocabulary. He will ask: "Is that *dinkum* news?" State that, "He's a *dinkum* fellow!" and so on. Well, one day a man in an Australian officer's uniform spoke to some officers in a certain sector of trench, and said he brought a message from headquarters. He was getting a lot of information and seemed to know several officers' names, but he bungled over one of them, and on the officer he was speaking to inquiring, "Is that *dinkum*?" he answered: "Yes, *that's* his name!" There was no further investigation, he was shot dead on the spot. The officer who did it may have been hasty, but there can be no doubt that justice was done, for he must have been either a Turk or a German and had already found out too much.

CHAPTER 15

The Evacuation

Without warning, winter came down upon us. No one guessed he was so near. We were still in our summer lack of clothing, and were not prepared for cold weather, when like a wolf on the fold the blizzard came down upon us. This was the worst enemy those battered troops had yet encountered. Hardly any of those boys had ever seen snow and now they were naked in the bitterest cold. There were more cases of frost-bite than there were of wounds in the whole campaign. More had their toes and fingers eaten off by Jack Frost than shells had amputated. In those open, unprotected trenches, in misery such as they had never dreamed could be, the lads from sunny Australia stood to their posts. When the snow melted the trenches fell in and Turk and Anzac stood exposed to each other's fire, but both were fighting a common enemy and so hard went this battle with them as to compel a truce in the fight of man against man.

Soon it was evident that our final objective of capturing the Narrows could not be accomplished with the forces we had. Directly the winter gales would arrive and on those exposed beaches no stores could be landed. We had to leave and leave quickly, or starve to death. So the evacuation was planned.

No achievement in military history was better conceived or more faithfully carried out. Here was scope for inventive genius and many were the devices used to bluff the Turk. We schooled him in getting used to long periods of silence. At first he was pretty jumpy and could not understand the change, when the men who had always given him two for one now received his fire without retaliating. After a while he decided that as we were quite mad there was no accounting for our behaviour. Then we scared him some more by appearing to land fresh troops. As a matter of fact, a thousand or so would leave the beach at night and a few hundred return in the daylight under the eyes of the Turkish aeroplanes, causing them to report concentration of more troops. Stores were taken out to the ships by night, and the empty boxes brought back and stacked on the beaches during the day. It must have appeared as if we were laying in for the winter.

There were many inventive brains of high quality working at great pressure during all the days of holding on, but one of the cleverest ideas put into operation was the arrangement devised by an engineer whereby rifles were firing automatically in the front-line trenches after every man had left. There is no doubt the Turks were completely bluffed. When the remaining stores were fired after being well soaked with gasoline, the Turkish artillery evidently thought they had made a lucky hit and they poured shells into the flames and completed for us the work of destruction. I doubt if they even found the name of a Chicago packing-house on a bully-beef case, when next day they wandered curiously through the abandoned settlement that for many months had been peopled by the bronzed giants from farthest south.

The last men to leave the actual trenches were the remnant of the heroic band that were the first to land. They requested the honour of this post of danger *and it could not be refused them*. They must have expected that their small company would be still further thinned; but this place of miracles still had another in store, as the evacuation was accomplished from Anzac itself without a casualty.

The last party to leave the beach was a hospital unit—chaplain, doctors, and orderlies. It was intended that they should remain to care for the wounded, though they would necessarily fall into the hands of the Turks. It was not feared that they would be ill-treated, for all the reports we had of prisoners in the hands of the Turks went to show that they were well cared for. In this as in other respects the Turk showed himself to be much more civilized than the German. It was a pleasant surprise to be able to greet again these comrades, who but a few minutes before we had commiserated on their hard luck; for they came off in the last boats, there being no wounded to require their services. The padre, who was a Roman Catholic priest, said that he missed the chance of a lifetime and would now probably never know what the inside of a harem was like!

They were sad hearts that looked back to those fading shores. It almost seemed as if we were giving up a bit of Australia to the enemy. Those acres had been taken possession of by Australian courage, baptized with the best of the country's blood, and now held the sacred dust of the greatest of our citizens, whose title to suffrage had been purchased by the last supreme sacrifice. Never were men asked to do a harder thing than this—to leave the bones of their comrades to fall into alien hands. These were men white of face and with clenched fists that filed past those wooden crosses and few who did not feel shame at the desertion. Some there were who whispered to the spirits hovering near an appeal for understanding and forgiveness. They wondered how the worshippers of the Crescent would treat the dead resting beneath the symbols that to them represented an accursed infidel faith. There are cravens in Australia who suggest that she has done more than her share in this struggle, but while one foot of soil that has been hallowed by Australian blood remains in the hands of the enemy the man who would withhold one man or one shilling is not only no true Australian but no true man—a dastard and a traitor.

When peace shall dawn and the Turk shall heed the voice of United Democracy as it proclaims with force, "Thou shall not oppress, nor shalt thou close the gates of these straits again!" then shall visitors from many lands wander through these trenches and marvel what kind of men were they that held them for so long against such odds, and gaze at the honeycombed cliff where twentieth-century men lived like cave-dwellers, and sang and joked more than the abiders in halls of luxury.

Today the name Anzac is the envy of all other soldiers, and while none would want to live that life again, every man who was there rejoices in the memory of the association and comradeship of those days. Read the *Anzac Book* and you will see that there was much talent and many a spark of genius in that army. But only those who were there know of the many busy brains that worked overtime devising improvements in the weapons that were available, and ever seeking to invent contrivances that added to comfort. Many of the inventions are forgotten, but some are in use in France today, notably the periscope rifle or *sniperscope* and the thumb periscope which is no thicker than a man's finger. It was found that our box-periscopes were always being smashed by the Turkish snipers; so one ingenious brain collared an officer's cane and scooped, out the centre. With tiny mirrors top and bottom, it was a very effective periscope, and soon most officers were minus their canes. Some very good bombs were made from jam-tins with a wad of guncotton, and filled up with all manner of missiles. These improvised bombs were risky to handle, and some men lost their lives through carelessness, though probably there were nearly as many accidents through over caution. They would generally be provided with a five-second fuse, and you were supposed to swing three times before throwing. Some men who had not much faith in the time-fuse threw the bombs as soon as the spark struck, which gave the Turks time to return them. Both sides played this game of catch, but I think we were the better at it. The way of lighting the fuse was to hold the head of a match on the powder stream, drawing the friction-paper across it. This generally caught immediately, but after a while someone introduced the idea of having burning sticks in the trench, and a *torchman* would pass down the trench lighting each fuse. One man was not sure that the spark had caught and began blowing on it and was surprised when it blew his hand off. We would drop on top of the Turks' bombs a coat or sand-bag, and it was surprising how little damage was done. If you put a sheet of iron on top of one, or a sand-bag full of earth, it would make the explosion very much worse, but loose cloth would spread out and make a spring-cushion by compression of the air above.

There was another use made of empty jam-tins: they were tied to our barbed wire so that if any Turk tried to get through he would make a noise like the cowbells at milking-time. Talking about barbed wire, Johnny Turk played a huge joke on us on one occasion. As the staking down of wire was too risky, we prepared some *knife-rests* (hedges of wire shaped like a knife rest) and rolled them over our parapet, but opened our eyes in amazement to find in the morning that they had only stopped a few feet from the Turkish trenches. The Turks had sneaked out and tied ropes to them and hauled them over to protect themselves. Thereafter we took care to let Abdul do his own wiring.

CHAPTER 16

Ships That Pass . . .

Although we did not capture the Narrows (that narrow stream of water through which a current runs so swiftly that floating mines are carried down into it faster than the mine-sweepers could gather them up), this did not prevent at least one representative of the navy from passing that barrier. This was the Australian submarine, *A2*.

It may not be generally known that Australia had two submarines at the outbreak of war. These would appear antediluvian alongside the latest underwater monster, but, nevertheless, one of these accomplished a feat such as no German submarine has ever approached. The first of our submarines met an unknown fate as it disappeared somewhere near New Guinea. There has been much speculation as to what happened to it, but its size can be guessed at when I mention that a naval officer told me he thought it probable that a shark had eaten it. As was the same type, but it achieved lasting fame in that it passed under the minefield, through the Narrows, across the Sea of Marmora, and into the port of Constantinople. Right between the teeth of the Turkish forts and fleet it sank seven Turkish troop-ships and returned safely. A certain town in Australia that was called Germanton has been rechristened Holbrook in honour of the commander of this gallant little craft.

****

Everyone has heard the story of the destruction of the *Emden* by the Australian cruiser *Sydney*, but it is worth bringing to notice that the captain of the *Emden* was of a different type from the pirates who have made the German sailor the most loathed creature that breathes. It is hard to believe that he was a German, for it seems incredible that a German sailor would refrain from sinking a ship because there was a woman on board. One can imagine that he would be ostracized by his brother officers of the wardroom, for he actually had accompanying him a spare ship on which to put the crews of the ships he sank. One can hardly imagine him sitting at mess with the much-decorated murderer of the women and children on the *Lusitania*, and it is the latter who is the popular hero in Germany. There are none more ready than the Australian soldiers to show chivalry to an honourable foe, and when the *Sydney* brought Captain Mueller and the crew of the *Emden* among the troop-ships these prisoners were cheered again and again. They could not understand their reception, but the lads from Australia admired these brave men for their plucky fight and clever exploits. Would they, had they not been captured early in the war, have changed and become like the vile, cowardly sharks that infest the seas in U-boats?

****

The Great War is writing history on such a large scale that the old classic stories of heroism and devotion to duty will be forgotten by the next generation. The story of the *Birkenhead* has always been considered the highest illustration of discipline and steadiness in the face of death evinced by any troops, but the citizen-soldiers from the young Australian democracy have in this war given on two occasions proof that they possessed the same qualities. The *Southland* has been written in letters of gold on the pages of Australia's history.

When the sneaking U-boat delivered its deadly blow in the entrails of this crowded troop-ship, there was no more excitement than if the alarm-bugles had summoned them to an ordinary parade. Some of the boys fell in on deck without their life-belts, but were sent below to get them. They had to go, many of them, to the fourth deck, but they scorned to show anxiety by proceeding at any other pace than a walk. It was soon evident that there were not enough boats left to take all off and so none would enter them and leave their comrades to go down with the ship. They began to sing *Australia Will Be There*—

> *Rally round the banner of your country,*
> *Take the field with brothers o'er the foam,*
> *On land or sea, wherever you be,*
> *Keep your eye on Germany.*
> *For England home and beauty*
> *Have no cause to fear—*
> *Should old acquaintance be forgot—*
> *No—no—no, no, no—*
> *Australia will be the-re-re-re!*
> *Australia will be there!*

Someone called out, "Where?" and the answer came from many throats—"In hell, in five minutes!" and it looked like it. But nothing in a future life could hold any terrors for the man who had campaigned during a summer in Egypt. In the end volunteers were taken into the stokehole and the *Southland* was beached. The colonel was drowned and there were a few other casualties, but most escaped without a wetting, so what looked like an adventure turned out to be a pretty tame affair after all. But Australia will ever remember how those boys stood fast with the dark waters of death washing their feet and, like Stoics, waited calmly for whatever Fate would send them. This epic of Australian fortitude was written in September, 1915, and is part of the Dardanelles story.

But the latest troops from Australia are of the same heroic stuff as those who wrote the name "Anzac" with their blood on the Gallipoli beach. For the *Southland* incident was duplicated in almost every particular on the *Ballarat* in April, 1917. This story was enacted in the waters of the English Channel, and there were no casualties, for the work of rescue by torpedo-boats was made easy as each man calmly waited his turn and enlivened the monotony meanwhile with ragtime, and again and again did the strains of *Australia Will Be There* ring out over the waters. As they sang *So Long, Letty,* many substituted other Christian names, and it looked as if it might be *so long* in reality. But they knew that to an Australian girl there would be no "sadness of farewell" when she realized that her lover had been carried heavenward by the guardian angel that waits to bear upward the soul of a hero.

****

Big Lizzie (the *Queen Elizabeth*) was for many months queen of the waters round Gallipoli. Her tongue boomed louder than any other, and it was always known when she spoke. She was the latest thing in dreadnoughts then, just commissioned, and the largest ship afloat. Though since that time the British navy has added several giants that dwarf even her immense proportions. The boys in the trenches and on the beach at Anzac never failed to thrill with pride as they heard her baying forth her iron hate against the oppressor. We knew that wherever her ton-weight shells fell there would be much weeping and gnashing of teeth among the enemy. We readily believed all the stories told of her prowess, no matter how impossible they seemed. No one doubted even when we heard that she had sunk a boat in the Sea of Marmora twenty-seven miles away, firing right over a mountain. She was there before our eyes an epitome of the might and power of the British navy that had policed the seas of the world, sweeping them clear of the surface pirate and also confining the depredations of the underwater assassin, so that all nations except the robber ones, might trade in safety. How true it is that the British navy has been the guarantor of the freedom of the seas, so that even in British ports over the whole wide world all nations should have equality of trade! Never has this power been used selfishly: take for instance, the British dominions of the South Seas, where American goods can be sold cheaper than those of Britain, for the shorter distance more than compensates for the small preference in tariff. The almost unprotected coast of the American continent has been kept free of invaders; its large helpless cities are unshelled, because *out there* in the North Sea the British navy maintains an eternal vigilance.

After some valuable battleships were sent to the bottom by the German submarines it was realized that *Big Lizzie* was too vulnerable and valuable to be kept in these waters; so in the later months her place was taken by some weird craft that excited great curiosity among the sailormen. These were the *monitors* which were just floating platforms for big guns. They were built originally for the rivers of South America, but it was discovered that their shallow draft made them impervious to torpedo attack; and as they were able to get close in shore, their big guns made havoc of the Turkish defences. They do not travel at high speed and appear to waddle a good deal, but they have been most invaluable right along, and were of great assistance lately to the Italians in holding up the German drive. They have been used also around Ostend and are of prime importance wherever the flank of an army rests on the sea. I have picked up portions of their shells and seen the shrapnel lying like hail on sand-hills in Arabia (more than twenty miles from the Suez Canal, which was the nearest waterway).

We also passed some other amazing-looking craft which were being towed down the Red Sea. They looked like armoured house-boats, and were for use up the Tigris. I should not like to have been boxed up in one, for it looked as if they would have to use a can-opener to get you out, and it did not appear to me as though the sides were bullet-proof. But trust the Admiralty to know what they are doing! Pages could be filled with the mere cataloguing of the various kinds of ships used by the navy in this war, and I am told that these *river tanks* were the prime factor in the advance in Mesopotamia.

A marine court would decide that the *River Clyde* was not a ship at all but a fortress. There was a naval engagement in this war when two ships were refused their share of the prize money for the capture of German ships because they were anchored, the sea lawyers decreeing that they were forts.

But the old, sea-beaten collier *River Clyde* deserves to be remembered as a ship that has passed, for before she grounded on the beach she carried in her womb as brave a company of heroes as have ever emblazoned their deeds on a nation's roll of honour. The wooden horse that carried Ulysses and the heroic Greeks into the heart of ancient Troy did not enclose a braver band than were these modern youths shut within the ironsides of the old tramp steamer which bore them into the camp of their enemies somewhere near the supposed site of the Homeric city.

Doors had been cut in the sides of the old steamer, and lighters were moored alongside with launches. When she ran aground these lighters were towed round so as to form a gangway to the shore, and the troops poured down onto them. The Turks were as prepared in this case to repel an attack as at Anzac, and held their fire until the ship was hard and fast. They then had a huge target at point-blank range on which to concentrate leaden hail from machine-guns and rifles aided by the shells from the Asiatic forts. Few lived in that eager first rush—some jumped into the sea to wade or swim, but were shot in the water or drowned under weight of their equipment. Again and again the lighters broke from their moorings, and many brave swimmers defied death to secure them. One boy won the Victoria Cross for repeatedly attempting to carry a rope in his teeth to the shore. But the crosses earned that day if they were awarded would give to the glorious Twenty-Ninth Division a distinction that none would begrudge them. The regiments of the Hampshires, Dublin, and Munster Fusiliers added in a few hours more glory to their colours than past achievements had given even such proud historic names as theirs.

The landing at Cape Helles and the wooden horse are beacons of the Gallipoli campaign that shine undimmed alongside the Australian-New Zealand landing at Anzac which, as a rising sun, proclaimed the dawn of the day of their nationhood.

Another *ship that passed* and in its passing wrought havoc on the enemy was one too small to support a man. It was a tiny raft, and it was propelled by one-man power, who swam ashore from a destroyer, towing this craft which was to bluff the Turks into believing that a whole army was descending upon them. The man was Lieutenant Freyberg, and on the raft he carried the armament that was to keep a large Turkish force standing to arms at Bulair (the northern-most neck of the Peninsula) when they might have been preventing the landing on the other beaches. The weapons this gallant young officer used were merely some flares which he lit at intervals along the beach, and then went naked inland to overlook the army he was attacking. Leaving them to endure for the rest of that night the continual strain of a momentarily expected attack, he then swam out to sea, for five miles, searching anxiously for the destroyer that was to pick him up. After several more hours of floating he was sighted by the rescuing ship and taken on board, exhausted and half dead. The Turkish papers stated that "the strong attack at Bulair was repulsed with heavy losses by our brave defenders."

This hero, who is a New Zealander, and now Brigadier-General Freyberg, V.C., is well-known in California and was at Leland-Stanford University.

PART 4

The Western Front

Chapter 17
Ferry Post and the Suez Canal Defences

The first attack on the Suez Canal caused the authorities to realize the need of protecting the canal by having a line of defence in Arabia far enough east to prevent the enemy reaching the waterway itself. For if the Turks should again appear on the banks of the canal, they might easily put enough explosives in it to blow it up. So vital is this artery of the British Empire that a German general stated that if they struck a blow there they would sever the empire's neck. The Turkish attempt to cross the canal was easily frustrated, and of the Anzacs only a few New Zealanders had a part in the scrap; but the iron boats that they carried across the desert are in the museum in Cairo and will be for generations *souvenirs* of this enterprise.

After the evacuation of Gallipoli there were constant rumours of another attack being contemplated, and for several months the Australians and New Zealanders were kept in Egypt for the defence of the canal. Before we dug the trenches in Arabia (which were about ten miles east of the canal) passengers on steamers passing through it had some lively experiences, as the Bedouins of the desert would sometimes amuse themselves by sniping at those on board, and the wheel-house and bridge had to be protected by sand-bags.

We were camped first at Tel-el-Kebir and then at Ferry Post, near Ismailia (where the canal enters the Bitter Lake). Those who took part in the march from Tel-el-Kebir will not forget it in a hurry. The camels bolted with our water and we only had our water-bottles in a hundred miles across the desert. By the time we reached the Sweet Water Canal we were panting like dogs, our tongues swollen and hanging out, our lips cracked and bleeding. There were many poor fellows just crazed for need of a drink, under that awful sun that was like the open furnace-door of hell, with the sand filling every orifice in our faces and parching our throats till they were inflamed. We were warned that the Sweet (or fresh) Water Canal was full of germs and that to drink it might possibly mean death, but most of us were too far gone in the agony of thirst to care whether the drink were our last, and we threw ourselves down at the water's edge and lapped it up like dogs. Fortunately, there were few ill effects, and the medical staff was not overworked because of it. There might have been many casualties, though, if it had not been for the New Zealanders, who, hearing of our plight, came out with water-carts and ambulances and picked up those who had fallen by the way.

At Ferry Post there was a reorganization of the Australian battalions and we lost many of our old pals—alas! never to meet again this side of eternity.

This was the concentration camp whence brigades were despatched for a spell of trench-digging and guard duty at the outpost line. There was a good deal of rivalry between us and another brigade known as the Chocolate Soldiers. They received this nickname because they were the most completely equipped unit that ever left Australia. They were commanded by a well-known public man, and the womenfolk had seen that they lacked nothing in sweaters or bed-socks. They had a band for every battalion, while we had to tramp along without the aid of music to enliven our lagging steps. Maybe we were a bit jealous, because they on several occasions went by train when we had to hoof it. When we went to relieve them in the trenches we met on a narrow concrete roadway where there was only room for one set of fours. The proper way to pass would have been for each to form two deep, but our boys spontaneously called out, "Give the gentlemen the road!" and we stepped aside into the sand. It took us about half an hour to pass, and all the time there was a running fire of comment. To no one in particular our fellows would remark, "Why, look? Some of them even shave!"

"What a nice *figure* that captain has!"

"They let them have real guns, too!"

And as the transport passed piled high with officers' kits, there was a shout of "There go their feather beds!"

We had a sports meeting in the desert, and everybody in our brigade from the brigadier down to the cook's off-sider was delirious with joy when we carried off the *championship cup*, beating the Chocolates by two or three points. We might not have been so elated had not the Chocs been such *nuts* on themselves, for they had been offering ten to one on their chances.

The part of the trenches that we occupied was known as Hog's Back. On our left was Duntroon (named after the Australian West Point). In front of us was a peculiarly shaped hill called Whale Back. We did not live in the trenches themselves, as they were continually falling in and had to be cleaned out again practically every day. Our supplies were brought within about three miles on a light tramway. Sometimes we went short, as this train had a habit of turning over when rounding a corner and emptying our much-needed tucker in the bottom of the gully.

From the rail-head, which was also the end of the pipe-line, food and water were loaded onto camels; and as I had seen something of camel transport in western Queensland, I was for a few weeks put in charge of the camel-loading. Camels are curious beasts and know to an ounce the weight they carried yesterday, and if you attempt to put on them one jam-tin more they will curse you long and loud, end up with some very sarcastic and personal remarks, and then submit to the injustice under protest. They are very revengeful and will harbour a grudge for days, waiting their chance to bite your arm off when they can catch you unawares. A camel's load has to be equal weight on each side, and it was some problem making a ham and a side of beef balance a case of canned goods. These camels were a mongrel breed, anyway, and poor weight-carriers. We usually put an eight-hundred-pound load on a camel in Queensland—I have seen one carrying two pianos—but these beasts would not carry more than two hundred pounds. A camel has never really been tamed and they protest against everything they are asked to do. They growl and swear when made to kneel, and make as much fuss again when urged to get up. Their skin never heals from a cut or sore, but they can have no feeling in it, for the Arabs simply stitch a piece of leather over the place. An old camel is all shreds and patches. They have to be provided with separate drinking-places from the horses, for they put germs in the water that give the horses some kind of disease. They are unsociable brutes and ought to be segregated, anyway. No wonder every high-bred horse is terrified at the smell of a camel; the first time you meet one it is like a blow in the face and remains a weight on your mind until the camel is a long way to leeward. They had a special objection to carrying fresh water, and nearly always bolted when they discovered it was Adam's ale that was swishing about on the outside of their hump. Perhaps it reminded them of their last week's drink. The result for us was that when the transport arrived there would be no water, and Mr. Ishmail and his camel would have to beat a hasty retreat from the rage of the boys, for water was our chief need, and it seems to me that there never was a time in those trenches that I wasn't thirsty.

I had some fun scouting in the desert, but on several occasions was very nearly lost when there were no stars, and hills had been altered in shape by the wind since I last passed them. We were expecting an attack by the Turks, and some camel patrols we sent out reported signs of camps but no sight of the enemy. As a consequence of these rumours our sentries were very nervous, and we scouts ran considerable risk returning to our lines before daylight. I was very nearly shot on several occasions, and once was within an ace of firing on one of my best pals. I saw a figure in the dark and, sneaking up to it, called out: "Put up your hands!"

He did so, but then foolishly dropped them again. If he had not called out, "Who the hell are you?" at the same moment, he would have been a dead man.

A squadron of our Light Horse discovered a Turkish well-boring party in the desert. They were under command of an Austrian engineer, but soon surrendered when they saw that they were surrounded. This made us sure that the Turkish army could not be far away, but our aeroplanes reported no signs of it. A few weeks later an attack was made by about twenty thousand Turks on the Scottish regiment holding the line to the north of us and we had a bit of a skirmish with their flank guard. They surprised us completely; the fight was fought mostly in pyjamas on our part, but we had little difficulty in driving them off. This raid was

An Australian Camel Corps

some achievement and I take off my hat to the man who planned it. They came across those many miles of desert without being seen, bringing with them even six-inch guns. They bluffed our aeroplanes by only travelling at night and hiding under sand-coloured canvas in the daytime. Their heavy transport was moved by laying a track in front of it, taking it up behind as it passed on and putting it down in front again.

We captured a lone Turk soldier nursing his blistered feet in the desert and he was delighted to join us. We also brought in at the same time a Bedouin who evidently thought we were some species of game, for although he fired on us he had no love for his Turkish companion and could not be persuaded to keep him company. The only request I heard this Turk make was for one of our uniforms. He kept pointing out the filth of his own clothes, so I had some water given to him to wash them, but this did not satisfy him at all. It was not the cleanliness of our uniforms he admired, but the cut and material. Perhaps this was policy, for generally the Turkish prisoners would remark: "Englisher very good—German damn bad!"

After this we returned to Ferry Post again and it was almost like going home for we had daily swims in the canal and plenty of liquid refreshment, the wet canteen doing a roaring trade. We were also able to buy luxuries, such as biscuits and canned puddings; and even relieve the monotony of marmalade jam with *bullocky's joy*. This last is merely molasses or golden syrup called *bullocky's joy*, sometimes *cocky's delight* because it is the chief covering for slices of bread with the bullock-driver or cocky farmer in Australia.

When a steamer was passing through the canal during our bathing-parades we had to get in up to the neck as we were warmly clad with merely a tin identity-disk hung round our necks on a piece of dirty string. Some of the passengers would throw into the water tins of tobacco and cigarettes; and there were some sprints for these made in record time, I tell you. Sometimes we would receive messages from home and it was surprising how often the man whose name was called out would chance to be present. There were occasions, however, when someone would call out from the ships: "D'you know Private Brown of the Yorkshires?" and we would have to explain that we were Australians. I suppose we could not expect them to recognize us dressed as we were, though our language should have given them a hint. On our part we would inquire if the war was still on, and tell them to give our regards to King George.

One morning the camp was all agog and the air thick with *furphies*. We were ordered to get ready for embarkation, and speculation was rife as to our destination. Some said we were going to Mesopotamia. Others had it from a reliable source that we were bound for Salonika. *Someone said, that someone told them, that they had heard*, that a sentry outside the general's tent had overheard the general talking in his sleep and *we were to make another attack on the Dardanelles!* There were few who guessed we were going to France, such being too good to be true, and only the bold ones dared to whisper that it might be so, but they were immediately told to "Shut up! Don't be an ass! Hasn't our luck been out ever since we left Australia?" I really think we were afraid to voice our hopes aloud lest Fate should overhear us, and if the word France was mentioned by accident we all immediately touched wood, a handy pal's head serving the purpose.

When we took train for Alexandria our hearts beat almost to suffocation and it was only when the troop-ship cleared the harbour, and eager eyes watching the compass saw her course was set N.W., that we gave a cheer, feeling that at last we might have a chance to show our mettle with the Canadians and Tommies, where the biggest fight was raging.

Before we left the wharf our kits were inspected and cut down to absolutely the minimum weight. Transport space was limited, but it broke many of our hearts to part with the sweater "Phyllis" made. We could only keep two pairs of socks; some boys had at least fifty. In one boy's pack there was a red pair and he was thereafter always known as Coldfeet. No one wept at leaving Egypt, and France held all the fruit of our dreams.

Chapter 18

First Days In France . . .

We had some excitement crossing from Alexandria to Marseilles, and the troop-ship ahead of us was torpedoed, though no lives were lost. But it was great to see our watch-dog of a destroyer chase after the submarine. The transport I was on was going over twenty-two knots, but the destroyer passed us as though we were standing still. The captain of our ship said she was doing forty-seven knots. At any rate, she rammed the submarine and must have appeared, through their periscope, just as a huge wave.

How excited those French people were over us Australians! They pelted us with flowers and sweets, and, while no one objected to the embraces of the girls, we thought it a bit too much when the men as well threw their arms around us and kissed us on both cheeks. French customs were new to us, and some of the boys thought the men were crazy. We weren't allowed much time to enjoy the gayeties of this lovely French seaport, but were marched off to the train and sent north to the big show. We thought we had never seen such lovely scenery as the south of France. I am not going to say that we have not just as good in Australia, but the wonderful greenness and the trees were such a change to us after Egypt that the boys just hung from the carriage-windows, and as there was a good number that could not get these vantage-points, they scrambled onto the roofs of the carriages, so as not to miss any of that wonderful panorama of ever-changing beauty.

We did not leave that train until we were well within sound of the guns, and then disentrained at a small village named Morbecque. We went into tents in a farmyard, and the very first evening began to make acquaintances among the villagers.

The Huns had only been there a day or two in their march on Paris, and during that time the inhabitants had made themselves scarce. But enough damage had been done in the houses during those two days to make every man, woman, and child speak with disgust of the filthy *boche*.

Everybody was very willing to make friends with us Australians, but the difficulties of language prevented a very rapid growth in knowledge of each other. All were on the hunt for souvenirs, and on the second day hardly a man had a button left on his coat. Orders were issued that the buttons be replaced before the next parade, and it was amusing to hear the boys trying to explain to the village shop-mistress what they wanted. It ended in their ransacking the stock themselves, but I do not think anyone found many buttons of the same kind, and our uniforms did not look as smart as usual, as somehow blouse-buttons do not seem to go well with a uniform.

These people were simple and religious, as I found most of the French people to be, at least the country-folk. I received no less than six crucifixes that I was assured by the charming donors would protect me from all danger, as they had been blessed by certain archbishops, the favourite being the archbishop of Amiens. I was mean enough to remark to one of them that it was a wonder any of the Frenchmen ever were killed. After I had been in the trenches I met again the daughter of the mayor, who had given me one of these crucifixes to wear around my neck. I informed her how a bullet had passed between my eye and the telescope I was using, laying open my cheek. She was quite sure that the bullet was going through my temple but had been diverted by the power of the charm, and fourteen *aves* she said for me every day.

While at this village I saw both a wedding and a funeral, but the funeral was by far the most spectacular of the two. The whole of the outside of the house was covered with black cloth—it must have taken a hundred yards—and processions of boys and girls went back and forth from church to house for several days, singing the most doleful music. Everyone in the village attended the burial, and I really think enjoyed the show.

For six days we lay snug in this village, every day going for route-marches of fifteen to twenty miles to harden us up again after the soft days on the transport. We knew we were on the lip of the caldron of war, for day and night we heard the rumbling of the guns.

Then on the seventh day I was chosen as one of a party to go up to the trenches and find out the positions we were to take over. We went by train a few miles nearer the line, and the guns grew ever louder. Then, after a ten-mile walk, we came suddenly to a barrier across the road, and a notice telling us that from this point parties of not more than six must proceed in single file, walking at the side of the road. Our flesh began to creep a little as we thought on the sinister need for these precautions.

After about five miles of this, on stepping through a hedge we suddenly found ourselves in a communication-trench. This trench was not very deep, and a tall man's head would project over the top. It was surprising how many of us thought we were six-footers and acquired a stoop, lest the tops of our hats show.

You are always nervous the first time in a new trench, as you do not know the danger-spots and are not even quite sure in which direction the enemy lies, for the communication-trench zigzags so. However, you generally acquire a bravado which you do not feel, for you see the old residents walking unconcernedly about, and you dare not let them see your nervousness. I remember on this morning we stepped right into hell. The *boche* evidently caught sight of one of our parties, and may have thought that a changeover was taking place, for we had hardly got to the front line when he started to pour shells upon it. Gaps were torn in the communication-trench behind us, and shells were falling so thick when we turned into the trench that we soon saw we had not chosen a favourable time to *talk dispositions* with the battalion in the line. When they realized, however, that we would most likely relieve them in a day or two, they almost fell on our necks with joy, for they had been five weeks in these trenches, and thought that they were there for good. There was little rejoicing among us, however, for, of our party of sixteen, seven were killed and four wounded in that visit of a few hours. Two sergeants (who had just been chosen for commissions) were blown to pieces as I was talking to them. As I turned to reply to a question addressed to me by one of them the shell came, and in a second there was not enough left of either for identification. I picked myself up unhurt. Shells seem to have a way with them—one man being taken, and the other left. And it is not always the man nearest the shell that is taken.

They told me to go back to the support-trenches for tea; about three hundred yards, and the communication-trench that I had to travel down was as unhealthy as any place I have ever been in. I was told the reason the enemy had its range so accurately was that it was of their own building. The support-trenches seemed to be getting more shells, even than the front line, and it looked as if I was walking out of the frying-pan into the fire.

Tea was the last thing I was wanting, but, as others were eating, I had to put up a bluff, though I felt it would be a sinful waste if I were to be killed immediately afterward.

That first day, however, took away most of my fears, and thereafter I got to fancy I possessed a charmed life and the bullet or shell was not made that would harm me.

The most surprising thing of the life over there is the narrow escapes one has. There are scores of men who have been in almost every battle from the beginning, and are still there, and that day it seemed truly as if I walked in a zone of safety, as shells would fall in front of me and behind, and even pushed in the parapet against which I was leaning, and I did not even get shell-shock.

I sat with my *dixie* of stew and lid of tea in the open doorway of a dugout, and the whiz-bangs passed within twenty yards of me and pelted me with pieces of dirt, but nothing hard enough to break the skin struck me. We did not learn much about those trenches on this visit, and were a sad little party that went back to our companions with the news of what had befallen our comrades and the perils awaiting them. The two remaining days spent in that little village were full of foreboding. Those who had *gone west* were well loved, and but yesterday so full of the joy of life.

Nearly everyone wrote home those nights, as it might be for the last time.

Under fire men are affected in different ways, but as for myself, I must admit that after that first day I felt I was not to die on the battlefield, and this gave me a confidence that many of my comrades thought was due to lack of fear. Strange to say, this feeling of security left me only on the night I was wounded, many months later. But of that in its proper place.

When we left Morbecque, the whole of the inhabitants turned out to bid us farewell. Many of the women wept, and though we had only been there a week, we felt we were leaving old friends.

We knew something of what these French people had already paid in defending that in which we were as much concerned. There was not a young man in the whole neighbourhood, and it was the old grandfathers and grandmothers that worked the farms.

Our hearts had warmed to France, before we knew the lovable French people themselves, because she had borne the brunt in the first years of the war, and her soil had been ravaged, and her women so unspeakably maltreated. And it seemed that the French people took especial interest in us Australians who had come twelve thousand miles to join in this fight in defence of the world's liberty.

This war has done more to make known to each other the people of the world than any other event in history. Many of the French people had hardly heard of Australia, but hereafter they will never forget the name of the land whence came those stalwart boys who marched singing through their country; who went to war with laughter, and when out of the trenches were ever ready to give a hand with the crops.

To their poverty it seemed as if we Australians were all millionaires, and our ready cash was a godsend wherever we went. Although we did not receive on the field our full six shillings a day, we always had more money to spend than the Tommies. In fact, frequently within a few hours after our arrival in a village we would buy out all of its stores. The temptation must have been great, yet I never knew a French farmer or storekeeper attempt to overcharge us. All we had, we spent, and though we grumbled enough that we were not able to draw our full pay, the French people thought that we were simply rolling in money.

The brigade did not go by train any of the distance, but marched the whole way to the trenches, taking two days. This part of the country was just on the edge of the Hun advance and, being only visited by some scouting-parties of Uhlans, had escaped most of war's ravages. We marched through beautiful woods, passed peaceful villages, and over sleepy canals that we saw not again in France in many long months—most of us, alas, never.

I do not know whether they wanted to show what Australians could do, but we did a forced march that day of eighteen miles with full packs up—eight of them without a breather. This may not sound much, but our boys were as nearly physically perfect as it was possible for men to be, and yet when we arrived at camp we left a third of them on the road.

We went into billets at Sailly, within five miles of the firing-line, where we found the civilian population going about their avocations as though war were a thousand miles away. There were plenty of ruins and even great holes in the streets that showed the Hun had not only the power, but the will, to send these death-dealing missiles among the women and children still living there. I thought the boys were too tired from their march to want to look 'round the town, but after "hot tea" had been served out, they were like new men, and went out to explore the place, as though they merely had had a morning stroll. Hot tea is to the Australian what whiskey is to the Scotchman, his best pick me up.

CHAPTER 19

The Battle of Fleurbaix . . .

Next morning it was "going in" with a vengeance. We did not enter the same trenches where I had been a few days previously, but about a mile farther south. These trenches were our "home" for over three months, so let me try and describe how they were built and looked to us on that day of entry. In this part of the line, near the borders of Belgium, you cannot dig down, the soil is so marshy, so the trenches are what is known as *breastwork*. They are built *up* about six feet from the level of the ground, a solid wall of sand-bags, ten to twenty feet thick. This will stand the hit of all but the heaviest shells, but is an unmistakable target if the enemy artillery have observation at all. The support and front line trenches were divided every two hundred yards, by communication-trenches, built in the same way, except that the communication-trench had *two* sides. These communication-trenches were distinguished by such names as Pinney's Ave., V. C. Ave., which latter was supposed to be built on the spot where Michael O'Leary won the first Victoria Cross of the war. Others were called Bond Street, Brompton Ave., and Mine Ave.

Later on my brigade held the length of trench that included all these, from Mine Ave. to Bond Street, over one thousand yards; but for the battle and the first ten days we only held about three hundred yards, using the three communication-trenches—Pinney's, Brompton, and V. C.

I had a good deal of apprehension as the brigade marched in, remembering the reception our reconnoitring party had received. If Fritz had spotted a score of us he could not well avoid noticing a thousand, though we were broken into little parties of six, that

"Us—Going In"

moved along the gutter in single file. But he must have been asleep this day, for the changeover was completed with little attention from him in the way of shells.

Leading up to Pinney's Ave., there was a short length of communication-trench very appropriately called Impertinence Sap, for it was merely a ditch, three feet deep, floored with duck boards. I could never get the reason why this trench was built. It only afforded protection for one's legs, which is the part of the body one would rather be hit in if one must be hit at all. The goose-flesh always crept around my head when I walked along this sap, for, strange to say, my head seemed to be the most valuable part of me, and at night the machine-gun bullets used to whistle through the low hedge that ran alongside it and frequently struck sparks from the flints on the old road just a yard or two away. I suppose I used that sap two hundred times, always with misgivings, for I have seen more than a score of men punctured along its length.

All these parts were unhealthy. The Rue de Bois, the street that ran parallel to the firing-trench, about a thousand yards behind the front line, was always under indirect machine-gun fire, yet was, nevertheless, used regularly every night by our transports. It was surprising how few mules were killed. Many times have I skipped, as the bullets struck sparks around my feet.

After a while we got to know that Fritz had a regular cut-and-dried system in the shelling of these trenches. He always took Mine Ave., Brompton Ave., and Pinney's Ave. alternately, and we later on saved a number of lives by having a sentry at the entrance to these communication-trenches to give warning to use the other trench while this one was being shelled. Weeks later I worked out the enemy's bombardment system more thoroughly, and had such notices as this posted: *Pinney's Ave. dangerous on Mondays, 2 to 6 p.m., V. C. unhealthy Tuesday afternoons*, and so on. I know I saved my own life several times by watching Fritz's *times and seasons*. I am quite sure that each battery over yonder had a book that laid down a certain number of rounds to be fired at a certain range on Mondays, and so on for every day in the week. And every relieving battery would take over this book of instructions. Of course there were times when Fritz got the wind up (lost his nerve), and then he would shell anything indiscriminately. The god of the German is *Method*, and his goddess *System*, and it hurt his gunners sorely when we tried something new, and made him depart from some long-predevised plan.

However, these were discoveries of a later date than the battle which wiped out about 70 per cent of our strength.

We had not been two days in the trenches before we knew that we were destined for an attack on the trenches opposite, and we had not had time even to know the way about our own lines. Few of us had even had a glimpse of No Man's Land, or sight of the fellow across the street whom we were to fight.

Our guns immediately began to get busy. In fact, too busy for our liking, for they had not yet got the correct range. This was before the days of total aeroplane supremacy, and the battery commander in those days had not an observer flying above where his shells were falling, informing him of the slightest error.

At any rate, we soon began to discover that the shells that were bursting among us were many of them coming from behind. This made us very uncomfortable, for we were not protected against our own artillery-fire; and accidents will sometimes happen, do what you can to avoid them. Our first message over the 'phone was very polite. "We preferred to be killed by the Germans, thank you," was all we said to the battery commander. But as his remarks continued to come to us through the air, accompanied by a charge of explosive, and two of our officers being killed, our next message was worded very differently, and we told him that "if he fired again we would turn the machine-guns on to them." I was sent back to make sure that he got the message. I took the precaution to take back with me one of his duds (unexploded shells) as evidence. At first he told me I was crazy—that we were getting German cross-fire, and that his shells were falling two hundred yards in front of us. I brought out my souvenir, and asked him if he had ever seen that before. He said: "For God's sake, bury it," but I told him it was going to divisional headquarters, and that his little mistake had already cost several lives. This battery did not belong to our division.

Our company commanders gathered us in small groups and carefully explained the plan of attack. We were to take the three lines of German trenches that were clearly discernible on the aeroplane photograph which was shown us; the first wave was to take the first trench, the second jumping over their heads and attacking the second German line, the third wave going on to the third German line. When all the Germans had been killed in the first trench, those left of the first wave were to follow to the third line. Unfortunately this photograph misled us, as one of the supposed trenches proved to be a ditch, and a great number of men were lost by going too far into enemy territory, seeking the supposed third line.

I have seen an actual photograph taken by an aeroplane during this battle, that shows a fight going on five miles behind the German lines. Many of the boys had sworn not to be taken prisoners, and though they knew they were cut off, they fought on until every last one of them was killed.

The Germans were thoroughly aware of our intentions to attack. Bad weather made a postponement for a couple of days advisable, and there had been so much artillery preparation that the enemy had time to get ready for us.

Considering the short time that our own artillery had been in their positions, and that they did not know a few days previously the range of the enemy's positions, their work was very thoroughly done. In most cases the wire had been well cut, and the enemy's front-line trenches were badly smashed about.

The Germans must have had some spies behind our lines, for they knew the actual moment of attack, and our *feints* failed to deceive them. Before the real attack the bombardment would cease for a moment or two, whistles being blown, orders shouted, and bayonets shown above the top of the parapet. The *idea* was that the Germans would then man their parapet to meet our attack, the artillery again opening fire on the trench. They failed to appear, however, until we actually went over the top, then the machine-guns and rifles swept a hail of bullets in our faces, like a veritable blizzard.

Nothing could exceed the bravery of those boys. The first wave went down like wheat before the reaper. When the time came for the second wave to go over there was not a man standing of the first wave, yet not a lad faltered. Each gazed at his watch and on the arranged tick of the clock leaped over. In many cases they did not get any farther than the first wave. The last wave, though they knew each had to do the work of three, were in their places and started on their forlorn hope at the appointed moment.

This battle was a disaster. We failed to take the German trenches, but it was like two other failures, the defence of Belgium and the attack of the Dardanelles—a failure so glorious as to fill a man with pride that he was enabled to play a part in it. In this battle we so smashed five divisions of Bavarian guards that it was months before they got back into the trenches. Had they gone to Verdun at that time it might have meant its fall, as they were the flower of the German army.

In places both first and second German lines were taken, but in others we did not get across No Man's Land.

It was not that certain companies fought better than others, but here and there were unexpected obstacles. In one place No Man's Land was only fifty yards across, while elsewhere it was three hundred yards. There was a creek running diagonally across in one section, too wide to leap, too deep to ford, and the only place where it was bridged was so *marked* by the German machine-guns that the dead were piled in heaps about it.

Those who actually reached the German trenches were too few to consolidate, and the German artillery soon began to take a heavy toll of them, knowing the range of their own trenches to a yard. So these had to come back again, and when night fell we were back in our old trenches—rather a few of us were; most of our division lay out in No Man's Land.

All were not dead, but we had no men to help the wounded. We had no stretchers, and those that were alive, unwounded, were so fatigued as to be hardly able to stand upright. But we could not stand the thought of the fellows out there without help, and we crawled among them, taking the biscuits and water from the dead and giving them to the wounded. We could only reach a few of them, and we crawled back at daylight, cursing our impotence, and fearing what the day might bring to these our comrades, lying helpless in full view of the brutal enemy.

The sight of our trenches that next morning is burned into my brain. Here and there a man could stand upright, but in most places if you did not wish to be exposed to a sniper's bullet you had to progress on your hands and knees. In places the parapet was repaired with bodies—bodies that but yesterday had housed the personality of a friend by whom we had warmed ourselves. If you had gathered the stock of a thousand butcher-shops, cut it into small pieces and strewn it about, it would give you a faint conception of the shambles those trenches were.

One did not ask the whereabouts of brother or chum. If we did not see him, then it were best to hope that he were of the dead.

It were folly to look over the parapet, for nearly every shell-hole contained a wounded man, and, poor fellow, he would wave to show his whereabouts; and though we could not help him, it would attract the attention of the Huns, who still had shells to spare—so that the wounded might not fight again.

I have found the Bavarian even worse than the Prussian, and this day, and the next, and again, did they sweep No Man's Land with machine-guns and shrapnel, so as to kill the wounded.

When darkness came the second night, we had organized parties of rescue, but we still had practically no stretchers, and the most of the men had to be carried in on our backs.

I went out to the bridge, and in between machine-gun bursts began to pull down that heap of dead. Not all were dead, for in some of the bodies that formed that pyramid life was breathing. Some were conscious but too weak to struggle from out that weight of flesh. Machine-guns were still playing on this spot, and after we had lost half of our rescuing party, we were forbidden to go here again, as live men were too scarce.

But the work of rescue did not cease. Two hundred men were carried in from a space less in area than an acre.

One lad, who looked about fifteen, called to me: "Don't leave me, sir."

I said, "I will come back for you, sonny," as I had a man on my back at the time.

In that waste of dead one wounded man was like a gem in sawdust—just as hard to find. Four trips I made before I found him, then it was as if I had found my own young brother. Both his legs were broken, and he was only a schoolboy, one of those overgrown lads who had added a couple of years in declaring his age to get into the army. But the circumstances brought out his youth, and he clung to me as though I were his father. Nothing I have ever done has given me the joy that the rescuing of that lad did, and I do not even know his name. He was the only one who did not say: "Take the other fellow first."

There were men who were forty-eight hours without food or drink, without having their wounds dressed, knowing that the best they had to hope for was a bullet. That the chances were they would die of starvation or exposure, and yet again and again would they refuse to be taken until we should look to see if there was not someone alive in a neighbouring shell-hole. They would tell us to "look in the drain, or among those bushes over there." During the day they had heard a groan. A groan, mind you, and there were men there with legs off, and arms hanging by a skin, and men sightless, with half their face gone, with bowels exposed, and every kind of unmentionable wounds, yet someone had groaned. Why, some had gritted teeth on bayonets, others had stuffed their tunics in their mouths, lest they should groan. Someone had written of the Australian soldier in the early part of the war, that *they never groan*," and these men who had read that would rather die than not live up to the reputation that some newspaper correspondent had given them.

I lay for half an hour with my arms around the neck of a boy within a few yards of a German listening post, while the man who was with me went back to try and find a stretcher. He told me he had neither mother nor friend, was brought up in an orphanage, and that no one cared whether he lived or died. But our hearts *rubbed* as we lay there, and we vowed lifelong friendship. It does not take long to make a friend under those circumstances, but he died in my arms and I do not know *his* name.

There was another man who was anxious about his money-belt; perhaps it contained something more valuable than money. I went back for it, stuffing it in my pocket, and then forgot all about it. When I thought of it again the belt was gone, and the owner had gone off to hospital. I do not know who he was, and maybe he thinks I have his belt still.

One of the most self-forgetful actions ever performed was by Sergeant Ross. We found a man on the German barbed wire, who was so badly wounded that when we tried to pick him up, one by the shoulders and the other by the feet, it almost seemed that we would pull him apart. The blood was gushing from his mouth, where he had bitten through lips and tongue, so that he might not jeopardize, by groaning, the chances of some other man who was less badly wounded than he. He begged us to put him out of his misery, but we were determined we would get him his chance, though we did not expect him to live. But the sergeant threw himself down on the ground and made of his body a *human sledge*. Some others joined us, and we put the wounded man on his back and dragged them thus across two hundred yards of No Man's Land, through the broken barbed wire and shell-torn ground, where every few inches there was a piece of jagged shell, and in and out of the shell-holes. So anxious were we to get to safety that we did not notice the condition of the man underneath until we got into our trenches; then it was hard to see which was the worst wounded of the two. The sergeant had his hands, face, and body torn to ribbons, and we had never guessed it, for never once did he ask us to "go slow" or "wait a bit." Such is the stuff that men are made of.

It sounds incredible, but we got a wounded man, still alive, eight days after the attack. It was reported to me that someone was heard calling from No Man's Land for a stretcher-bearer, but I suspected a German trap, for I did not think it possible that any man could be out there alive when it was more than a week after the battle and there had been no men missing since. However, we had to make sure, and I took a man out with me named Private Mahoney; also a ball of string. We still heard the call, and as it came from nearer the German trenches than ours we knew they must hear as well. When we got near the shell-hole from which the sound came I told Mahoney to wait, while I crawled round to approach it from the German side. I took the end of the ball of string in my hand, so as to be able to signal back, and from a shell-hole just a few yards away I asked the man who he was and to tell me the names of some of his officers. As he seemed to know the names of all the officers I crawled into the hole alongside him, though I was still suspicious, and signalled back to my companion to go and get a stretcher.

As soon as I had a good look at the poor fellow I knew he was one of ours. His hands and face were as black as a negro's, and all of him from the waist down was beneath the mud. He had not strength to move his hands, but his voice was a good deal too strong, for he started to talk to me in a shout: "It's so good, matey, to see a real live man again. I've been talking to dead men for days. There was two men came up to speak to me who carried their heads under their arms!"

I whispered to him to *shut up*, but he would only be quiet for a second or two, and soon the Germans knew that we were trying to rescue him, for the machine-gun bullets chipped the edge of the hole and showered us with dirt. In about half an hour Mahoney returned with the stretcher, but we had to dig the poor fellow's limbs out, and only just managed to get into the next hole during a pause in the machine-gun bursts. To cap all, our passenger broke into song, and we just dropped in time as the bullets pinged over us. These did not worry our friend on the stretcher, nor did the bump hurt him, for he cheerfully shouted "Down go my horses!"

We *gagged* him after that and got him safely in, but the poor fellow only lived a couple of days, for blood-poisoning had got too strong a hold of his frail body for medical skill to avail. His name I have forgotten, and the hospital records would only state: "Private So-and-so received ——; died ——. Cause of death—tetanus."

Chapter 20

Days and Nights of Strafe

We had only been a few days in the trenches in France when I was sent for by the General. I went in fear and trembling, wondering what offense I had committed; but I soon did not know whether I was standing on my heels or my head, for he said to me:

"I have recommended you for a commission, and you are immediately to take over the duties of intelligence or scouting officer."

This was a big step up, as I was only a corporal, though I had been acting in charge of a position over the heads of many who were my seniors in rank.

Now began for me many adventurous and happy days, for my job afforded me a great deal of independence and scope for initiative, and I was able to plan and execute many little stunts that must have irritated Fritz a good deal. When I was returning at dawn from my night's peregrinations, I would generally meet the brigadier on his round of inspection, and no matter in what mood he was in I always had some story of strafe to tell him that would crease his face in smiles, and I saved many another officer from the bullying that was coming his way.

Our brigadier was very popular because of his personal bravery. One morning I was showing him the remains of some Germans I had blown up, and in his eagerness he stuck his head and shoulders, red tabs and all, over the trenches, when—*ping!*—a sniper's bullet struck the bag within an inch of his head and covered him with dirt. Pompey roared with laughter and was in good humour for the rest of the day. On one occasion in Egypt this same General issued orders that no men were to wear caps. He said he didn't care where we got hats from, but that we were all old enough soldiers to obtain one somehow. He would punish any soldier who appeared on parade next day without a hat, and the only one whose head was minus a hat next morning was the brigadier himself! He laughed and said that the man who pinched his hat had better not get caught, that's all!

My chief business as intelligence officer was to keep an eye on Fritz and find out what he was up to. I had a squad of trained observers who were posted in certain vantage-points called O. Pips (O. P.—Observation Post). These O. Pips were mostly on top of tall trees or the top of some old ruined farmhouse. From these pozzies (positions) a good deal of the country behind the enemy lines could be seen, and the observers, who were given frequent reliefs so that they would not become stale, had their eyes glued to it through a telescope. Every single thing that happened was written down, including the velocity and direction of the wind; the information from all these and other sources being summarized by myself into a daily report for G. H. Q.

There was one O. Pip on top of a crazy ruin that was used for many months without the Germans suspecting. It really hardly looked as if it would support the weight of a sparrow. I used to wonder oftentimes how I was going to get up there, and then by force of habit would find myself lying alongside the observer sheltering behind two or three bricks. From this *pozzie* one of my boys saw a German Staff car pass Crucifix Corner. This was a stretch of a hundred yards of road which we could plainly see where a crucifix was standing, though the church that once covered it had been entirely destroyed. The car was judged to contain some officers of very high rank, both from the style of the car and the colours of the uniforms. When I got this information I prepared to make that road unhealthy in case they should return. I called up our sniping battery, and got them to range a shell to be sure they would not miss. At five o'clock in the afternoon my waiting was rewarded, and just by the pressing of a button eight shells landed on that car, and sent its occupants *down to the fatherland*. We received news about that time that one of the Kaiser's sons was killed, and though it was denied later, in my dreams I often fancy that he might have been in that car.

There was a landmark behind the German lines in this sector

known as the *hole in the wall*. It was marked on all our maps used by the artillery for ranging, and was the object on which we set our zero lines to get bearings of other objects. One day the hole in the wall disappeared, and there was much wailing and gnashing of teeth. Did the Germans destroy it or was it the rats that undermined its foundations? I fancy it was like the celebrated One Horse Shay—every brick in the wall that surrounded the hole had been wearing away for years, and at the stroke of Fate all crumbled into dust. We were able to do without our old friend, as Fritz very kindly built up in the churchyard at Fromelles a large red earthwork that could be seen for miles, and which our big guns sought unsuccessfully to destroy but made the entrance to it very unhealthy.

We had some crack sharpshooters or snipers in trees and also on top of ruins, but took care never to have them near our observation posts lest they should draw fire. I had one man who was a King's prize-winner, and he must have accounted for well over a hundred of the enemy, some of whom may have thought themselves quite secure when they exposed but a portion of their body eight hundred or a thousand yards from our trenches. Through the wasting of skilled men in unsuitable work which is prevalent in all our armies, this man was sent forward in a bayonet charge and killed. In his own job he was worth a battalion but in a charge of no more value than any other man. The snipers and observers make effective use of camouflage, and have uniforms and rifle-covers to blend with their background—spotted for work among trees with foliage, *à la* Mr. Leopard—striped when in long grass or crops like Stripes of the jungle. We have suits resembling the bark of a tree, and some earth-coloured for ploughed ground, also one made from sand-bags for the top of the parapet.

I could fill a volume with the happenings during our many months in these trenches.

We had great sport through the use of a dummy trench. This was a ditch which we dug about seventy-five yards behind our front line running parallel to it. We would light fires in this about meal-times, and now and again during the day send a file of men along it who would occasionally expose their bayonets to view above the top. This ditch would appear to the German aeroplanes exactly like a trench, and as they used their second line for a supervision and living trench they probably thought we did the same. Our boys laughed to see most of the German shells exploding on the dummy trench.

There were one or two occasions in which Fritz broke the unwritten law that there should be an armistice during meal-times. We soon cured him of this, however, as we systematically for a week put out his cook's fires with rifle-grenades. Thereafter both sides were able to have their meals in peace though we took care to change our hour from one to two instead of twelve to one.

Fritz's system now and again got on our nerves. It was deadly monotonous, always knowing when his severest shelling would start and I have known the boys run races with the shells, driven to take foolish risks by sheer ennui. We always expected some shells on V. C. House at 4 p.m., and were rarely disappointed. The men off duty would assemble in front of the old house and at the sound of the first shell race for the shelter of a dugout about a hundred yards away. Generally they would all tumble in together and in their excitement could not decide who won the race, and so would have it all over again. The officers were ordered to stop these "races with death" for there were some killed, but they would break out now and again when the last man who was killed had been forgotten.

The bombing officer had a good deal of sport with his rifle-grenades, and as I was hand in glove with him I enjoyed some of his fun. A favourite place for the firing of our rifle-grenades was at Devon Avenue, for most of Fritz's retaliation came to the Tommies whose flank joined ours at this point. One day their major came along to us in a great rage, and wanted to know why we were always stirring up trouble—couldn't we let well enough alone? He complained in the end to our brigadier, but the answer he got was: "What are you there for? What's your business?"

After this, whenever we had our strafe on this flank, they would squeeze up to their centre leaving fifty yards unmanned between us. These men were brave enough, and in a raid the same major held the trench with great bravery under a severe bombardment and attack by a strong force.

We also had an armoured train that we were very proud of. At least, that is what we called it, but it was only a little truck with six rifles fastened on it for firing grenades. We ran this along rails down the trench, and would fire a salvo from one place and then move to another by the time Fritz had waked up and was replying with pineapples and flying-fish, as his rifle-grenades were dubbed.

One day I was ordered to locate the enemy's *minenwerfer* positions, as his *minnies* were getting on our nerves. These huge shells, although they very seldom caused casualties, for they are very inaccurate, would nevertheless make the ground tremble for miles as they buried themselves sometimes fifty feet deep in the soft ground before they exploded. When these were about our boys would watch for them as they could plainly be seen in the air. We would watch their ascent, sometimes partly through a cloud, and, as the shell wobbled a good deal, we could not be exactly sure where it was going to land until it was on the downward curve, then we would scatter like sheep, and as it would generally be two or three seconds before it went off, we had time to reach a safe distance. The real trouble was that no one could sleep when they were coming over, as each of them had all the force of an earthquake. I have picked up pieces of the shell two feet long by a foot wide, jagged like a piece of galvanized iron that had been cut off with an axe.

Well, I had to locate the position of these mine-throwers, and the easiest way to do it was to make them fire and have observers at different points to get bearings on the exact position from which the shells were thrown. They were easy to see, as they were accompanied for the first fifty yards with showers of sparks like sky-rockets. But Fritz can be very obstinate on occasions, and all our teasing with rifle-grenades failed to make him retaliate with anything larger than pineapples (light trench-mortars). In desperation, I sent to the brigade bombing officer for some smoke and gas-bombs. Even these failed to rouse his anger sufficiently when—*Eureka!*—we discovered some *lachrymose* or tear bombs. These did the trick and overcame a rum-jar as the *minnie* shells are generally called. I had eight batteries on the wire, and we gave that *minnie* position a pretty warm time. By the same methods I located nine of these German trench-mortars on that front. Later on we captured one of them and I was surprised to see what a primitive affair it was. It consisted of a huge pipe made of wooden staves bound round and round with wire. The charge is in a can like an oil-drum and dropped in the pipe, and then the shell dropped in on top of it. A fuse is attached, burning several seconds so as to allow the crew to get well out of the way, as their risk is as great as those they fire it at. When I had seen the gun, I was not surprised that rarely did they know within a hundred yards of where the shell was going to land, only expecting to get it somewhere behind our lines.

While I am talking of trench-mortars, I must tell you about the *blind pig*. This was a huge shell with which we frequently got on Fritz's nerves. When it was first used there was some doubt about its accuracy and the infantry were cleared out of the trenches in its immediate front before it was fired. The first shot landed on our support trenches, the next in No Man's Land, and the third on Fritz's front line. Each time it seemed as if a double-powered Vesuvius were in eruption, and when the artillery got to know its pranks there was no need for us to get out from under. The aeroplanes reported that when the blind pigs went over, some Fritzes could be seen running half an hour afterward. Fritz does not like anything new; for example, they appealed to the world against our brutality in using tanks. Christmas Day, 1916, one of our aviators, with total disregard of the rules of war, dropped a football on which was painted "A Merry Xmas" into a French town infested by Germans. As it struck the street and bounced up higher than the roofs they could be seen scuttling like rats, and maybe, today, *that* airman is haunted by the ghosts of those who died of heart-failure as a result of his fiendishness.

This airman is a well-known character among the troops in Flanders, known to all as *the mad major*. His evening recreation consists in flying but a few hundred feet above the enemy's trenches, and raking them with his machine-gun to show his absolute contempt for their marksmanship. I have seen them in impotent fury fire at him every missile they had, including pineapples and *minnies*; but he bears a charmed life, for, though he returned and repeated his performance four times for our benefit, he did not receive a scratch. I went over the German lines with him for instruction in aerial observation. He said to me: "Do you see that battery down there?"

I replied "No!"

His next remark was, "I'll take you down," and he shot down about five hundred feet nearer. We were getting pasted by *archies* much more than was pleasant, so when he next shut off his engine, to speak to me, I did not wait for his question but assured him that I could see the German battery quite plainly. I hope the recording angel will take into account the extenuating circumstances of that lie.

We had a *spring gun* or catapult that came very near preventing this book ever being written. On one occasion we placed a bomb in the cup, but instead of taking the spring and lever out, which was the correct way, we tried a new experiment of holding the lever down with two nails which would release the spring as soon as it was let off. Unfortunately, the bomb rolled off at our feet, and we had four seconds to get to a safe distance. Some of us got bad bruises on our foreheads as we dived for an open dugout as though we ourselves had been thrown from a catapult. On another occasion we used Mills grenades with a grooved base plug. To our alarm, the first one exploded with a beautiful shrapnel effect just above our heads. I am sure a piece passed through my hair but I could not wear a gold braid for a wound because, not even with a candle, could the doctor find a mark.

Our tunnellers were always mining and we would see them by day and night disappearing into mysterious holes in the ground, and it was only when Messines Ridge disappeared in fine dust that we understood that their groping in underground passages was not in vain. They would sometimes tell us exciting tales of fights in the dark with picks against enemy miners; and now and again we would be roused by explosions when one side blew in on the other and formed a new crater in No Man's Land. With their instruments our miners discovered that the head of one of the enemy galleries was under the headquarters dugout of the English regiment on our right. I went along to inform them. With excitement in my voice I said to the officer in charge:

"Do you know that there is a mine under here?"

"Bai Jove, how jolly interesting! Come and have a drink."

I said: "Not in here, thank you."

"Why? It won't go off today," he said. "Anyway, we are being relieved tomorrow, so it won't worry us, but we'll be sure and leave word for the other blighters."

There was a dugout in our own sector in which were heard mysterious tappings, but though we had an experienced miner sleep in it he reported that the sounds were not those of mining operations. Maybe it was the rats, but we gave that dugout a wide berth, as someone suggested that it was haunted, and even in the trenches, better the devil you know than the devil you don't know!

We managed to have a good deal of comfort in these trenches, all things considered. We even rigged up hot baths in our second line. The men were able every second day to have a hot bath, get clean underclothing, and have a red-hot iron passed over their uniforms, which was the only effective method I have known of keeping us reasonably free from body-vermin. These baths turned us out like new men, as the Australian craves his daily shower. I doubt if there are any troops in the world who take such pains for cleanliness. Wherever we camp we rig up our shower-baths as a first essential, and in some of the French villages the natives would gather round these Hessian enclosed booths staring at the bare legs showing beneath and jabbering excitedly about the madness of these people who were so dirty that they needed a bath every day.

Although this sector of trench was during eight months known as "a quiet front," as no actual offensive took place, yet there was never a day or night free from peril, and all the time our strength in numbers was being sapped—men left us *going west* or said goodbye as they went to hospital, and sometimes would disappear in No Man's Land—gone, none knew where. We received reinforcements that did not keep pace with our losses and during all the time were never once up to half strength. Always we were on the watch to worst our enemy, and he was by no means napping. Gas was often used and sentries were posted with gas alarm-signals not only in the trenches but in the streets of the villages behind the lines. If by night or day the whitish vapour was seen ascending from the trenches opposite, then such a hullabaloo of noises would pass along the trenches and through the streets of the towns as to make the spirits of the bravest quail, and woe betide even the little child who at that signal did not instantly cover his face with the hideous gas-mask. These noises were made chiefly with klaxon horns, though an empty shell-case struck by iron was found to give out a ringing sound that could plainly be heard above even the screech and crump of the shells.

Our gas-masks are quite efficient protection, and I have been a whole day under gas without injury, by keeping the cloth in my mask damp all the time. Men sometimes lose their lives through lack of confidence in their masks. The chemical causes an irritation of the mucous membrane, and they fancy they are being gassed, and in desperation tear them off. It is the duty of an officer to decide when the danger has passed and test the air. I remember on one occasion I warned some men who were opening their coats that the danger had not passed, but when I returned I found they had removed their masks and three of them were very severely gassed. We are always on the lookout for gas, and when the wind is dangerous a gas-alert signal is given, when every man wears his mask in a ready position so that it can be donned without a second's delay.

I was really sorry to leave those trenches. So many months was I there that they were something like a home to me, and who knew what was awaiting one in another and an unknown section? I knew every shell-hole in No Man's Land, and constant observation of the enemy methods enabled me to anticipate his moves. I felt that nowhere else would I be so successful. I even parted with a rat that I had tamed in my dugout with a feeling of regret, though on all his kin I waged a bitter war, spending many hours when I ought to have been sleeping in shooting them with my automatic as they came into the light of the dugout doorway. It was there, too, that I experimented with the enemy grenades, and I remember once nearly scaring an Australian nigger white. He was the only coloured man in our brigade, and was just passing in front of the dugout as I threw a detonator on to the hard metal of an old road a few yards away. Evidently he was surprised at being bombed when he thought he was among friends! He, however, received nothing worse than the fright.

Chapter 21

The Village of Sleep

There was little element of surprise about the Somme offensive. Although there must have been some uncertainty in the mind of the German Staff as to just where the blow would be struck, for our papers were filled with rumours of a drive in the north, and troops and big guns were moved north every day and withdrawn at night, yet the intensity of the artillery bombardment around Albert, which day by day waxed ever greater, proclaimed in a shout that here was the point on which our punch would strike.

The selection of this place for an offensive was an indication that it was not the policy of the Allies to attempt to drive the German army out of France, but that their evident intention was to defeat the enemy practically in the present trenches. The German line in France and Belgium is shaped like the letter L, and the Somme battle was waged at the angle of the letter just where the line was farthest from Germany. Of course it would be madness to attempt to finish the war on German soil, if to do it we should have to devastate one-eighth of France and its fairest and richest province.

These smashes are rapidly destroying the morale of the enemy, as well as killing many of them, and will lead to the collapse of the army pretty much where they are now. If they attempt an offensive on the western front, where our armament is now so strong, it will hasten the end. The British artillery had at the end of 1917 a reserve of fifty million of shells, and pity help the German army if they bump into them. The British offensive of 1916 was hastened somewhat by the need of relieving the pressure on Verdun, and though the first blow was not as powerful as it would have been if delayed a few months, it accomplished much more than was expected.

Up the British line there crept news of big doings down south. There was a new sound in the air—a distant continued thunder that was different from any previous sound—the big drums of the devil's orchestra were booming an accompaniment that was the motif of hell's cantata. Up the line ran the rumour of a battle intenser than any yet fought—more guns being massed in a few miles than the world had ever seen before. Into every heart crept the dread of what might await us down there, and to every mind came the question: "When are we going?"

Close behind rumour came marching orders, and as we left our old trenches south of Armentières we said good-bye to scenes that had become homelike, and turned our faces south to make that "rendezvous with death" in the dread unknown to which duty called us.

But there were weeks of peaceful scenes that seemed to us like a forgotten melody of love and home and peace, and the train that bore us out of the war zone seemed to carry us into another world, but though the feast to our eyes was pleasant and like *far-off forgotten things and pleasures long ago*, we were not borne thither on downy couches. Never were there seats more uncomfortable than the floors of those French trucks, and we occupied them for days. When now and again the train stopped and we could unbend ourselves for a short stroll, it was like the interval in a dull play. We had taken our cookers with us on the train, but the French railway authorities would not allow us to have a fire burning while the train was moving, so we would have to draw onto a siding that our meals might be cooked. Now and again at these stops there would be canteens run by English and American women, and the home-cooking and delicacies they smilingly gave us were a reminder of the barracking of the womenfolk that makes courage and endurance of men possible. These are the untiring heroines that uphold our hands till victory shall come, and so the women fight on. There were French women, too, who brought us fruit and gingerbread, and with eyes and strange tongue unburdened hearts full of gratitude and prayer.

How glad we were to gaze on the earth, smiling through fields of waving corn and laughing with peaceful homes, with the church-spires still pointing heavenward, after so many months of associating with the scars of blackened fields and the running sores festering on earth's bosom, once so fair, where churches had swooned and in lost hope laid their finger in the dust.

But all journeys end in time, and one night instead of eating we loaded ourselves like the donkeys in Egypt and tramped off to the village of our sojourning. The billeting officer and guide were several days ahead of us and they met us at the train and told us it was only three miles to the village, but after we had tramped five we lost all faith in their knowledge of distance. It was *tramp, tramp, tramp, the boys are marching*, for three miles more, and when we had given up all hope of eating or resting again we saw, at the bottom of a hill, silhouetted against the violet sky the spire of a church, but we did not breathe our hopes lest it might vanish like a dream. Soon we came to a house, and instinctively the column halted, but it was *on, on, ye brave!* yet a little longer, then suddenly a company was snatched up by the darkness. Lucky dogs! They had found some corner in which to curl up and sleep, which was all we longed for, as we were now too tired to even care about eating. Chunk after chunk was broken off the column and almost all were swallowed by stables and barns, or houses that were not much superior, when there loomed ahead some iron gates, and like the promise of a legacy came the news that this was the headquarters billet; and never did the sight of four walls offer to weary man such a fortune of rest and shelter.

In the morning we discovered we were in the village of Ailly-sous-Ailly, the sleepiest place on earth. It nestled at the bottom of a cup and was hidden by trees; no passer in the skies would glimpse roof or street. No vehicle entered it from outside and the war was only hearsay. I think the hum of its labour can only be heard by the bees, and its drowsy evening prayers are barely audible to the angels. Its atmosphere crept over our spirits like ether and we did little else but sleep for the week that we were there. Parades would be ordered, but after a short time of drilling in the only field of the village, we would realize the sacrilege of our exertion, and the parade would be dismissed. Thereafter the only preparation for the day ahead that was persisted in consisted of lectures, when the droning voice of the officer would frequently be accompanied by snores from his men. My duties were to give instruction in scouting, but I seemed to be sounding a motor-horn in slumberland when I counselled my boys to always keep their eyes skinned as the genie of the village was weighting their eyelids with lead. I spoke in the language of different worlds when I said: "A scout's body should never be seen to move" (and the village hummed its applause), "but his eyes should be never still—" (and there was almost a hiss that came through the trees).

For the first day or two we did not see the inhabitants of the village at all. Much puzzled at this we questioned the *maire*, and he told us that they were very much afraid because we were Australians—that there had been much alarm when they heard we were coming. Perhaps they thought we were black, and into their dulled ears had crept a whisper of the fierceness in battle of these giants called Anzac. It was not long, however, before curiosity drew them from their hiding-places and our laughing good nature won their confidence. It was not surprising that our lavish spending of money should have roused their cupidity, for never had they seen so much wealth before, and never had we seen such poverty. Any of our privates was able to buy out the stock of a whole store, which was not worth more than a pound or two. One of them, to satisfy his hunger, on the first night walked into one of these stores, but when he saw the stock his face was a picture of blank disappointment.

"I want something to eat," he said, "and I think I'll take all you've got. It may make a fruit salad or something."

There were only one or two that could converse with us in anything but a language of signs, but the old *maire* spoke English of the kind that Queen Elizabeth used, and he acted as interpreter for the whole village.

When they understood that we were willing to pay for any damage done, the bills came in in sheaves. Some boys, in ignorance, cut up for firewood an old cedar log that was an heirloom. You would have thought it was made of gold from the value put upon it by its owner. Fifteen francs was asked for a bundle of straw that some boys made a bed of, and some of our Australian horses did not know any better than to eat the thatch off one old lady's bedroom, which not only cost us the price of the thatch when it was new but also damages for fright. There was a gap in the hedge that I had noticed when we entered the town, but it cost us ten francs all the same. These people were not unpatriotic, but to them it looked like the chance of a lifetime to acquire wealth, and I have no doubt we pensioned several of them for life.

The war was to them like a catastrophe in another world, and Australians did not travel farther to fight than in their imagination did the sons of this village when they went to the trenches less than a hundred miles away. I discovered one day how deep the knife of war had cut when I spoke to a grandmother and daughter working a large farm, as with dumb, uncomprehending pain in their eyes they showed me the picture of son-in-law and husband who would never return. Rights of peoples and the things for which nations strive had no meaning to these two, but from out the dark had come a hand and dragged from them the fullness of life, leaving only its empty shell.

Our headquarters billet was in the vacated house of the village squire. He was a major in the French army, and had taken with him the young men of the village committed to his charge. His wife had gone to nurse in a hospital and they had put their children in a convent. He then left the key in his door, saying that his house and its contents were at the service of the officers of any British regiment that should come that way. This house was a baronial castle, but in its furnishing knew as little of modern conveniences as Hampden Court of William IV. We did not smile, however, at the antimacassars, wax flowers, and samplers, nor the scattered toys of the nursery, for we were guests of a kindly host who, though absent himself, had entrusted to our care his household gods and was a comrade in arms.

Houses, especially old houses, absorbed the personality of the dwellers therein, and I fancy that our host is not unknown to me. Were I to meet him I would recognize him at once, for his spirit dwelt with us in his home, and my prayer is that when he returns he will not find that temple tainted by the spirit of any alien who occupied it in his absence.

The village church slumbered in the centre of the village, and was its sluggish heart. No discord or schism of sect or creed ever disturbed its atmosphere. Unquestioned was its hold on the faith of men, women, and children. Not more quietly did the dead rest beneath the stones of the churchyard than did the worshippers who knelt before the carved wooden images of the saints, trusting in their protection and receiving from their placid immobility a benediction of peace. The cure from a neighbouring town only visited the village once a quarter, and the old lady who kept the key was very reluctant to let us in; but when the *maire* knew of our desire, he brought us the key that we might view it at our leisure. Its pews were thick with dust, the images were chipped and broken, some saints were minus nose or arm, the vestments in the open cupboard were moth-eaten and tawdry, dried flowers lay on tombs of the village great; but its atmosphere was one of peace, and it was not difficult to realize that many had carried therein their burden of grief and unrest and left it behind them, soothed on the bosom of Mother Church, like a fretting child.

But it is not the business of soldiers to sleep, and suddenly came the awakening with the sound of the hundreds of motor-buses that were to carry us into the noise and devastation of hell! We marched up to the rim of the village, and amid the smell of gasoline, the tooting of the horns, and the roar of the engines we boarded these, thirty to a bus, and rumbled on toward the greatest noise and flame and fire that has ever torn the atmosphere asunder, outdoing any earthquake, thunderstorm, or tornado that nature has ever visited upon humanity.

On this journey we saw more of the tremendous organization needed to equip and feed an army than we had been able to visualize before. For thirty miles we were a part of a stream of motor vehicles flowing in one direction passing a never-ending stream going the other way. Through the city of Amiens we went without stopping. With longing eyes we gazed from the buses which hours of bumping and rolling on poor roads had made to us torture-chambers. How gladly would we have strolled through its streets gazing on the pretty girls and gaping at the novelty of its quaint buildings and the unusual ware in its shop-windows.

Later on I was a week in the hospital here with a sprained ankle, and I had a chance to explore this lovely city of Picardy. Its cathedral was a never-ending source of interest, and not a day passed during my stay that I did not hobble on crutches through its dim aisles and worship the beauty of its statues. There is one statue called The Weeping Angel which is world-famous, and I have gazed at it

MY OWN COMRADES WAITING FOR BUSES

for hours, feeling its beauty steal over me like a psalm. There was always music stealing gently through the air, but like a blow in the face were the walls of sandbags protecting the carving on the choir-stalls and the thousands of statues on the huge doors. The grotesque hideousness of the gargoyles gave a touch of humour that was not incongruous to religion, but these sand-bags were such an eye-sore against the beauty of the carved poems that suggested what an intrusion into God's fair world is the horror of war.

Several times while I was in Amiens the German aeroplanes came over and bombed the city. Opposite the hospital a three-story house collapsed like a pack of cards, burying seventeen people in its ruins. I saw a French airman bring down one *boche* by a clever feat. He evidently could not aim upward to his satisfaction, so he turned upside down, and while flying thus, brought down his opponent.

Through Amiens the buses carried us within a few miles of Albert, which was within range of the German artillery. It is in Albert that the remarkable hanging Virgin is to be seen. The cathedral and tower have been almost practically destroyed, but still on top of the tower remains uninjured the figure of the Virgin and Child. A shell has struck its base, and over the town at right angles to the tower leans the Virgin imploringly holding the babe outstretched as though she were supplicating its protection. The French people say that the statue will fall when the war ends, but some materialistic British engineers, fearing the danger to life in its fall, have shored and braced it up.

This is similar to the miracles of the crucifixes that are found standing unharmed amid scenes of desolation. I have seen several of them without a bullet mark upon them when every building in the vicinity has been laid in ruins. I know two cases in which there is not one stone remaining of the church, yet the crucifix that was inside stands in untouched security. There are always those who see in these things a supernatural agency as some saw "angels at Mons," and as for me I do not seek to explain them, knowing that there are more things in heaven and earth than are dreamed of in our philosophy.

I am reluctant to leave this chapter with its peaceful memories, for it is the antechamber of hell. There is little here that hints of the brimstone and fire just through the door. But our path lies that way and we must pass on.

CHAPTER 22

The Somme

The battle of the Somme lasted eight months, and never since the days of chaos and darkness has a portion of the earth been under the sway of such forces of destruction. Not even the Flood itself so completely destroyed the habitations of man. Flourishing towns were powdered into brick-dust, thousands of acres of forest were reduced to a few blackened stumps, and every foot of ground was blasted and churned and battered again, while every yard was sown thick with bullets more malignant than the seeds planted by Jason. Today nature is busy trying to hide the evidence of the hate of man, and long grass and poppies cover the blackened soil and grow in the shell-holes, until only in the memory of the men who strove nakedly in its desolation and death will the knowledge of that area as it was for those eight long months remain. If he visits it again the poppies and the grass will fade, and it will appear to him once more as the ploughed land of demons, and grinning at him in every yard will be the skulls of the countless unburied that there lie. The other birds will shun it, for there are no trees, but the lark will still sing on, as this brave-hearted bird continues to do even when the guns are booming.

Australian blood has sanctified much of that soil, and Australian bravery has monopolized some of its names. As surely as Gallipoli will Pozières and Thiepval and Bapaume be associated with the name and achievement of Australians in the minds of readers of the history of the great war. These are places that will ever be names of honour and glory in the thought of the Australian people as will be Flers to New Zealand and Delville Wood to South Africa.

At Pozières the First and Second Divisions demonstrated that the abandon and tenacity against odds that secured a footing on the Gallipoli Peninsula was still the special prerogative of the care-free lads from these South Sea nations. Our own artillery was unable effectively to silence the fire of the German batteries, and wave after wave melted like snow in the sun, yet the unconquerable spirit drove the remainder on until the positions were taken and held. There were wounded men who dragged themselves, not back to their own lines for attention, but forward toward the enemy so that they might be able to strike at least one blow ere they died. There were others that had their wounds dressed and then returned to the fighting. No one left the line that day who could help it, or his name would have been remembered as an outstanding exception among the many who, wounded again and again, and faint from loss of blood, still fought on. This engagement carved a line in my own heart, for therein died three comrades who enlisted with me, and our souls were grappled together by many common dangers shared and mutual sacrifices cheerfully made. There is no life in the world that tries out friendship like a soldier's in active service, and when it has endured that, it is stronger than the love of twin for twin, like the love of David and Jonathan, of Damon and Pythias, a love that passeth knowledge.

The Germans had one ally on the Somme that wrought us more havoc than all his armament. How we cursed that mud! We cursed it sleeping, we cursed it waking, we cursed it riding, we cursed it walking. We ate it and cursed; we drank it and cursed; we swallowed it and spat it; we snuffed it and wept it; it filled our nails and our ears; it caked and lined our clothing; we wallowed in it, we waded through it, we swam in it, and splashed it about—it stuck our helmets to our hair, it plastered our wounds, and there were men drowned in it. Oh, mud, thou daughter of the devil, thou offspring of evil, back to your infernal regions, and invade the lowest circle of the inferno that you may make a fit abiding-place for the slacker and pacifist! I take back all I said about the sand of Egypt. It was a mere irritant compared with this mud. I am sorry for the times I have been out of temper with the mud back in Australia, when it clung to my boots in tons, when I have been bogged in a sulky in the *black soil* country. Australia, you have no mud, just a little surface stickiness that I will never growl at again as long as I live:

It isn't the foe that we fear;
It isn't the bullets that whine;
It isn't the business career
Of a shell, or the bust of a mine;
It isn't the snipers who seek
To nip our young hopes in the bud;
No, it isn't the guns,
And it isn't the Huns—
It's the <u>mud</u>, <u>mud</u>, <u>mud</u>.[1]

Official reports of the later battles in 1918 tell us that the shell-fire on the Somme was a mere popgun show to these battles, but it is difficult for the imagination to grasp this fact, as it did not seem then that the air had any room for more shells. In fact, I have seen shells meet in the air, both exploding together. It seemed to us at times as if there was not a foot of air that did not have a shell in it. In one battle there were four thousand guns firing over a five hundred yards front, the heavies being seventeen and a half miles behind the lines, and the field-guns massed wheel to wheel a hundred and fifty to the five hundred yards, and row after row like infantry drawn up for review. Shells not merely whistled and screamed overhead, they leaped from the ground beneath one's feet with a flame that burned, a roar that deafened, and a displacement of air that swept one away. At artillery practice in peace times there is great excitement if one lone man happens to be in front of the gun, but on the Somme we walked about among them, over them, and round them, and we were never warned even when they fired but a couple of yards away. One day a red-hot shell from a gun about fifty yards away landed at my feet, but, fortunately, did not explode. For four months our artillery expended an average of half a million shells a day. The increase in artillery last year may be judged from the fact that in the last six months of 1917 one million tons of shells were used by the British on the western front. By day the drum-fire of the guns beat on one's ears like a devil's tattoo until one felt that in another week reason would be unseated. But at night was added the horror of flame that drove away the darkness with a ruddy glare. It seemed as if thousands of Bessemer furnaces were refining metal for the paving of hell. Into

---

1. Robert W. Service.

this caldron of man's making that outdid the fury of the elements young lads from farms and shops walked uprightly. Like ants impotent in their strife they swarmed, and to a watcher from another world they must have appeared like insects in the crater of Vesuvius in eruption. Yet the mind of man, so much greater than his body, had organized and planned this monstrous scene, and from his method it deviated not a hair's breadth.

We were encouraged and supported by the knowledge that the German was having a far worse time than we were, that the hell of flame and fire and smoke was for our protection and his annihilation. His shells came over blindly in most cases, and though we were so thick that they could not but get some of us, yet we knew that our shells were being directed by thousands of aeroplanes on top of the earth beneath which he huddled, with the sweat of fear pouring from him. There were many indications of the terror our shell-fire wrought and days when the prisoners could be counted in thousands, on one occasion sixteen men bringing back as many as four hundred. These men were imbeciles, crazed by the sound of the shells, and obsessed by one idea, the necessity of getting away. When we took their trenches we found that in most cases they were completely obliterated, and in some cases the entrances to the deep dugouts were blown in, smothering the men sheltering in them.

The wastage of man-power on the Somme was not a little due to the nervous strain. I think everybody's nerves were more or less on edge, and now and again a hurricane of fire would sweep the trenches because some man's nerve got past breaking-point. He would see an imaginary enemy bearing down upon his sentry-post and fire wildly, giving alarm to the whole line. A German sentry would reply to him, more of our men would fire back, more Germans join in, star-shells make the night as bright as day; then Fritz would get the wind up thoroughly and call for artillery support—our guns would blaze into reply and there would be many casualties just because one man lost his nerve and *saw things*.

Nerves are queer things, for frequently the man of a nervous, highly strung temperament is the coolest in action. Some men, too, get shell-shock a hundred yards from a bursting shell, while others are knocked down and buried and never even tremble. Men have

Ammunition going through a Somme city

the power of speech taken from them for months and as suddenly have it restored. I know of one case in which a boy did not speak a word for twelve months, and when viewing the play *Under Fire* in Sydney suddenly found his speech return at the sound of a shot. Another man had just been pronounced by the medical officer as cured when the back-fire of a motor-car heard in the streets of Melbourne brought back all the symptoms of shell-shock again. Once a man has had shell-shock he is never of any use under shell-fire again, although he might be quite brave under any other fire and suffer no ill effects in civil life. Where there is so much shell-fire the observation of the German sentries is very poor and surprise raids are easily carried out. Fritz is very reluctant to put his head up and periscopes are always being smashed.

There was only one place in the Somme where drinking-water could be obtained, and this was in the ruins of the town of Piers. The Germans had been driven out of this place too quickly to give them time to poison the water, but they made it very difficult for us to get at it by shelling continually. They had the exact range, and it was only in the hour before dawn that one could get near the wells without meeting with certain death. It was amusing to see the scamper of the water-carriers out of the ruins as the first shell announced that the relief of Fritz's batteries had been completed and the *hate* had recommenced. They were severely handicapped running with a fifty-six pound can of water, but it was a point of honour not to leave this behind. Of course, there was plenty of other water filling every hole around, but this was not only thick with mud but had the germs of gas-gangrene, and one knows not how many other diseases besides.

When the line had advanced a few miles "going in" was as tiring a day's journey as though one had walked twenty miles. I will never forget having to chase after my brigade to Bécordel-Bécourt. I left Albert just at dark and had to trust to my instinct for direction in finding the place, for no one could tell me the way, and the old road on the map was non-existent. It was only about three miles, but seemed like thirty as I wound in and out of the traffic that jammed the new road, defying the passage of even a dog. When I arrived at the place where the town of Bécordel had once been I found there were about five hundred thousand troops camped about the area, and in the dark to find the whereabouts of my own unit of five thousand was about as hopeless a task as I have ever attempted. I inquired of more than a score, but no one had seen anything of the Australians. I wandered about for hours and was hungry and thirsty and half dead when I stumbled on a Y. M. C. A. hut. They could not guide me in the right way, but they gave me a cup of hot tea, and no nectar of the gods could be as welcome. The Y. M. C. A. is welcome to all the boosting I can give, for they were my salvation that night, and at other times were a comfort and resting-place. When I found our camp at two o'clock in the morning I found the men in a worse plight than I was, for their transport had not arrived, and none had had anything to eat or drink.

In this huge camp which was within range of the German guns there were tens of thousands of camp-fires blazing in the open in utter contempt of Fritz and his works. We took the road again that same morning for our position in reserve at Montauban. I said we took the road—well, we were on it sometimes, whenever we could shove the horses toward the centre to enable us to squeeze past—otherwise we had to plough along above our knees in the soft mud. Even on the road the slush was up to our ankles, but it was metalled underneath. We discovered our transport in the jam of the traffic—they had taken twenty-four hours to go the four miles but our tongues blistered with the names we called them, and we threatened them with eternal damnation if they were not at the next camp with a hot meal when we arrived.

Where Montauban had once been we went into camp. We had no tents, but made ourselves comfortable in shell-holes, with a bitter-cold rain falling, by stretching tarpaulins over them. The engineers were putting up Nissen huts at the rate of twenty a day, but as soon as the last bolt was screwed home, forty shelterless men crowded each one to capacity. It was some days before our turn came and we waited lying half-covered with mud and slush. When we did get a hut allotted to us it was as if we had been transferred to a palace. These huts look like half of a round galvanized-iron tank, and were floored and lined. They were carried in numbered sections and could be put together in a few minutes. They were very comfortable. You could stand up in the centre, and there was plenty of room to sleep along the sides. I believe the inventor, Mr. Nissen, is an American and here's my hand to him as an ally who maybe saved me from rheumatism, and I am sure thousands of boys from the other side of the world bless his name continually.

The whole brigade was practically bogged when we came to move forward. The weight of our equipment sank us into the soft mud and the only way we got onto the road again was by hanging to the stirrups of the horses as they ploughed a way through. We also passed ropes back for the men to grasp and harnessed them to mules, and thus dragged them to firm ground. The road did not carry us far, and we soon had to struggle across the open toward the support trenches. This was not as bad as round the camp, not being churned up by the tramping about of men and horses. We could not use the communication-trenches as they were rivers of liquid mud, but had to wait till dark and go over the top in relieving the front line. On this occasion we took over from the Grenadier Guards, which numbers among its officers many of the English nobility. We *bushies* and *outbackers* from the land of the Kangaroo stepped down into the mud-holes just vacated by an earl, several lords, and as noble and proud a regiment as ever won glory on a battlefield. The Prince of Wales was a staff-captain in the army of the Somme doing his bit in the mud and misery like the rest of us. There is no "sacred privilege that doth hedge about a king" in the British Empire, and King George is respected among us for his manliness, and we cheered him sincerely when he twice visited us in the trenches, for we do not believe today in the divine right of kings, neither do we believe in the divine right of majorities.

In another chapter that tells of my wounding I have pictured our days and weeks as lived in these trenches, so I will bring this chapter to a close by summarizing some of the things that the great push on the Somme accomplished.

(1) It relieved the pressure on Verdun.

(2) It accounted for several hundred thousand German casualties.

(3) It demonstrated our ability to break through.

(4) It led to the perfecting of barrage-fire where-by casualties were reduced in our infantry to an astonishing degree.

(5) It gave confidence to our troops by enabling them to get to hand-grips with the German, and discover that he was individually no fighter.

(6) It weakened the morale of the German army enormously, and convinced the German soldier that his cause was lost.

(7) It gave to us possession of the high ground.

(8) It definitely established our supremacy of the air, and was the turning-point of the whole war.

CHAPTER 23

The Army's Pair of Eyes

The aeroplane has become so much a necessity to the army that it is difficult to imagine how wars were ever fought without them. I remember reading a statement by a military observer with the Japanese army that, if the Russians had had a single aeroplane, they could have annihilated the Japs more than once. Of the army's pair of eyes the airman is the sharper, but the old-time scout is not by any means superseded, though his methods have changed. Just as there is much behind the enemy lines that only the aeroplanes can see, there are some things that cannot be discovered except from the level of the ground along which the scout crawls. The airman makes the enemy's plans an open book, for he observes him as soon as he moves, but the airman travels on a different plane from the infantry soldier, and it is the infantry man who fights out the final phase of the battle. The ground has an altogether different aspect from the air, and aeroplane photographs sometimes mislead. The scout, however, goes ahead on the same ground that the infantry have to travel, and he can bring back news of exactly what is there. The airmen do not help us much in determining the condition of the enemy's barbed wire, and nothing is so fatal for an attack as being held up on the wire. Streamer wire cannot be seen a few yards away, and only by sending out advance scouting-parties can a commander know whether the wire has been sufficiently destroyed to allow an easy passage for his troops. As an attack is always planned to take two or three of the enemy's lines, these scouts have to find out the condition of the wire in front of the second or third line trenches as well.

Crawling in No Man's Land and behind the German lines is not as dangerous as it sounds. The greatest cause of casualties is shell-fire and the scout is safe from this, for, naturally, no enemy shells fall near him in enemy territory, and he has previously arranged with his own artillery to withhold fire from the sector in which he is working. He runs little risk even from machine-guns or rifles, for the ground is so honeycombed with shell-holes that he is nearly all the time in good cover. The only danger that he runs is that of discovery, and for a properly trained scout such is inexcusable.

The general idea the stay-at-home has of the trenches is that every yard contains a man who is watching out for signs of the enemy. But a trench is serrated with bays containing half a dozen men who are cut off from sight of their neighbours. Of these half-dozen men one or, at most, two are on the lookout while the others are sleeping, and a well-placed hand-grenade will put the whole six of them out of action. Experience has shown that where there has been much shell-fire the sentry's observation is very lax, as men will not stick their heads above the trenches any more than they can help and at night periscopes are not much use. I have repeatedly come back into our own trenches from a night's excursion without being seen by our own sentries, and on two occasions, in the daytime. There are some sectors that are only held by battle outposts with gaps of fifty and a hundred yards without them. Of course, it is an easy matter to get past in these places.

We have sometimes to get the artillery to make a way for us. We will have them bombard a hundred yards of German trench very heavily for about ten minutes while we lie within fifty yards waiting for the prearranged second when we will scuttle across; the enemy having been compelled to vacate that sector during the bombardment, it is some minutes before they realize that the shelling has ceased and return.

Once behind the German front trench, the work is easy, for they never look behind or imagine that any of their enemies could be in their rear, and there is no observation from the second or third line trenches. On other occasions we do without the help of the artillery, bombing a gap for ourselves. We arrange to have rifle-grenades fired along three hundred yards of trench except for fifty yards where is our gateway. Here we sneak up and carefully roll hand-grenades into two or three bays. The Germans on either side do not take any notice of these explosions as the same thing is happening all along the line, and the Germans *in the bays* are not in condition to take much notice either. We may have to administer the *coup-de-grace* with our hand-bayonets.

Getting back is fairly easy, for the sentry's back is toward us, and a scout should never have to strike twice. He may leave a Mills grenade with the pin out as a gift to the sleeping men in the bay. He only has a two or four-foot-wide trench to cross, and even if the alarm be given he is back among the million and two shell-holes of No Man's Land before any action can be taken: even though they bomb their front thoroughly the chances are in the scout's favour; though they make No Man's Land bright as day with star-shells and flares there are plenty of shell-holes deep enough to completely hide him from view.

There is other important information that only the scout can obtain as when we once found a dummy trench filled with barbed wire and controlled by machine-guns. Had our men gone forward in the attack without the knowledge of this they would have jumped down into it to be massacred like rats in a trap. Machine-gun positions are also generally indistinguishable to the airman's glass or camera. I used an instrument of my own construction which would give me the map reference of any object that I observed in relation to any other two objects the position of which I knew on the map. At night I would have the two known positions marked by distinguishing lights or have coloured flares sent up from them at regular intervals.

The training of our scouts is very severe. For in this work men have to have complete confidence in their own superiority to the German soldier, and must be able to depend entirely on their own resources as they generally have to work singly or in pairs. It is necessary that they be picked men with unusual keenness of observation. They are trained for work in the dark by being made to go through the ordinary soldier's exercises blindfolded. In this way they get the extra sense that a blind man has. A blind man will not put his weight onto his foot until he has felt if it is on firm ground; and by habit he does this without hesitating. Our scouts are able after a while to walk along using their eyes for observation all the time not needing to watch where they are stepping. We also train them to have complete control over their muscles and among the final tests for first-class scouts are to remain an hour without showing any movement whatsoever and to take half an hour in getting from the prone or lying position to standing upright on their feet. These two last ideas were borrowed from the Zulu who has no equal in the world in escaping observation. They are also taught many methods for finding directions as a compass is unreliable where there is so much unidentified iron lying about.

We have abundantly demonstrated in several sectors on the western front that it is always possible for properly trained men to surprise the enemy. As a matter of fact the Germans have carried out surprise raids on us, and I am quite satisfied that it is never possible completely to guard against surprise. In one sector I had trip wires in No Man's Land connected with buzzers in our own trench so arranged that I would know if there were any one out there and to within fifty yards of where they were. But this was only possible on a quiet front where there was no actual offensive taking place, and not many shells falling in No Man's Land. I even placed buttons in the German wire so as to be sure that our patrols did not just go outside our own trench and lie in a shell-hole until it was time to return, for they had to signal by pressing these buttons at intervals. They had to repair any of these wires they found severed, and this somewhat elaborate scheme was the means of our capturing some German patrols and gave us entire control of No Man's Land.

We also took advantage of every possible means to make Fritz's sentries jumpy. We would have our snipers on certain days smash all their periscopes. I myself have shot down sixty in an afternoon when the sun was shining on them. This made them afraid that they would not have any left for emergencies and gave them a wholesome respect for our shooting so that they were very shy of exposing themselves. We would also set a rifle to fire exactly into a loophole so that when it opened we had only to pull the trigger to send a bullet through the brain of the man using it. There were other dodges that it is not wise to speak of just yet.

This may be a good place to describe the two kinds of raids. In a raid with artillery support the artillery cut out a sector of the enemy trench with a *box barrage* which means that they fire on three lines of a square leaving the open side for our troops to enter. They also put a barrage on this side until the prearranged moment when the attackers go forward. This leaves the raiders to deal with the troops within that box preventing any others coming in to support them. The weakness of this method is that it lets the whole German line know what we are doing, and the raiding-party frequently gets cut up badly by the enemy's artillery when they are returning across No Man's Land.

The most successful raid is always the silent one if you have dependable troops. The chief obstacle is the enemy wire, but beforehand the artillery can cut this in many places, and machine-guns can be ranged on these gaps to prevent their being repaired. The enemy does not know, even if he suspects a raid, exactly where it will come. It is even a good idea if you only have a small party to enter one of these gaps, crawl down fifty yards inside the wire before attacking, and, when finished, come out through another gap lower down, but every man of the party needs to scout over the ground beforehand so there will be no confusion during the attack. We have carried out successful raids in this manner when none but the Germans who were attacked knew anything of what was going on until we were back in our own trenches, and rarely were there any of these who could give evidence except by means of their dead bodies. I remember that one of our men, who was champion wood-chopper of Australia before the war, drove his bayonet through a German and six inches into a hardwood beam, and as he could not withdraw it had to unship it, leaving the German stuck up there as a souvenir of his visit. Probably not another man in the army could have done it, but it no doubt added to the reputation of the Australians, as these Fritzes must have thought us a race of Samsons.

There is a strong bond between us and the airmen, and the army's pair of eyes are focussed together, for the information from both sources is co-ordinated. Our trench maps are constructed chiefly from aeroplane photographs, and it was only occasionally that some object would be seen in the photograph that could not be identified; when we scouts would have to crawl over to it and find out its family-tree.

All our intelligence officers are given schooling in aerial observation, and I have been several times over the German lines with a pilot, and have a very high admiration for these birdmen who are not merely the bravest of the brave but princes of good fellows. I had some wonderful aeroplane photographs of some of our attacks wherein I could recognize the stages of our progress, and so expert has this work become that a German soldier can hardly even brush away a fly without a permanent record of it being obtained. Probably the greater number of our aeroplanes on the battle-front are engaged in ranging for the artillery, and in actual offensive warfare, but their greatest value is in reconnaissance, and so it will always be.

Airman and scout—one flies, the other crawls, yet both seek information from the enemy, and are the twin eyes of the army. There is a romance about the work of both that attracts adventurous youth, and neither is as dangerous as it appears to a layman. In the element of the airman he is a difficult target to hit, and it is estimated that it takes thirty thousand anti-aircraft shells to bring him down. And his machine is now so perfect that peace flying will be much safer than motoring.

In No Man's Land, the hunting-ground of the scout, shells only fall by accident, and he is camouflaged to defy detection. A black crawling suit is used at night, with hood and mask, but the most important thing is to break the outline of the head, so the hood has several peaks and corners. A human head on the sky-line cannot be mistaken for anything else, except maybe a pumpkin or melon, but in these hoods it appears like a large lump of dirt, and should the scout chance to move suddenly while in such a position, the likelihood is he would be dirt in a second or so.

All day long when the shells sail over
I stand at the sand-bags and take my chance;
But at night, at night I'm a reckless rover,
And over the parapet gleams romance.[1]

---

1. Robert W. Service.

Chapter 24

Nights in No Man's Land

How little I thought that my time was coming
Sudden and splendid, supreme and soon;
And here I am with the bullets humming
As I crawl and I curse the light of the moon.

Out alone, for adventure thirsting,
Out in mysterious No Man's Land;
Prone with the dead when a star-shell, bursting,
Flares on the horrors on every hand.

Yet oh, it's great to be here with danger,
Here in the weird, death-pregnant dark,
In the devil's pasture a stealthy ranger,
When the moon is decently hiding.

Hark! What was that? Was it just the shiver
Of an eerie wind or a clammy hand?
The rustle of grass, or the passing quiver
Of one of the ghosts of No Man's Land?[1]

The first night *out there*. The memory of it still quickens the pulse and makes the cheek grow pale. How my teeth chattered, my heart beat almost to suffocation, every splash of a rat was an enemy scout, and every blade of grass magnified itself into a post for their barbed wire. I had but gone a few yards when I expected the next instant to bump into the enemy trenches. There are strange sounds in No Man's Land; not human sounds, for such carry far—the beat of a hammer on a post, the sharp twang of unrolling barbed wire

---

1. Robert W. Service.

as it catches, and then springs away—voices even come as through a megaphone in the eerie silence—but these are long-drawn sighs that penetrate the inner consciousness and hushed murmurs that fall on the ear of the soul. I have felt a touch on the shoulder as though one would speak to me when there has been no one by.

It is the grave of ten thousand unburied dead, but the grinning skulls and quivering jelly or the few rags that flutter in the wind are not the comrades that we knew. I think their spirits hover near, for they cannot go to their abiding-place till victory has been won. They are ever seeking to pierce the veil of sense so that they may add their strength to our arms, and these make for us of No Man's Land *no strange place*, and give to our sentries encouragement until the land of No Man vanishes and our possession reaches to the barrier of the enemy barbed wire. My nights in No Man's Land if added together would total many months, and I grew to feel that it was one of the safest places on the whole front.

There was one night when I got a huge fright. I was crawling alongside a ridge—it had been an old irrigation farm, and this was a low levee running across—I heard on the other side a splash which I thought was made by one of the innumerable rats, but I put up my head and looked over—so did Fritz, not a yard away! We both stared blankly in each other's face for a long second and then both of us turned and bolted. This was excusable for a German, but I have no defence. When I went back to look for him, after a court martial by my own conscience, he was nowhere to be seen.

There was another night when Fritz got the better of me. In my explorations I came across a path through his barbed wire which was evidently the place where his patrols came out. I thought I would provide a surprise-party for him, so I planted some percussion bombs and put a small Union Jack in the centre. In the morning the Union Jack was gone and a German flag in its place. Everybody from the brigadier down rubbed it in that Fritz was too smart for me.

But after this the tide turned and came in in a flood of ill luck for Fritz. It was a pitch-black night and the occasional star-shells only served to make the black more intense when they faded. As we crawled out one behind the other each had to keep a hand on the foot ahead so as not to get separated. We made several ineffectual attempts to find the opening in our barbed wire and then cut a new one. Was this like the darkness after Calvary? The red signal-rockets ascending from the enemy's trenches gave no light, but only burnt for a second or two as a ruddy star. And the green lights turned the vaporous fog a sickly yellowish green as though it were some new poison-gas of the devils over there. I led the way straight across. It was too dark to pick a path and we committed no sacrilege as we trod on the bodies of forgotten comrades. It was impossible to repress a shudder as the hand met the clammy flesh, and the spilt light from a rocket exposed the marble eyeballs and whitened flesh of the cheek with the bared teeth gleaming yet more white. Our mission was to wait for a German patrol at the gap in their wire I had previously discovered. We were seeking identification of the regiments opposing us, and we desired to take at least one of them alive.

We waited drawn-out minutes while the dark smothered us and our thoughts haunted us. Minute piled on minute while we suffered the torture of the heretic who was fastened so that the falling drops of ice-water would follow each on the selfsame spot. Home and love of life sought to drag us back to the shelter of our trenches, but Duty like an iron stake pinned us there. But the stake was fast loosening in the soil of our resolution, when we heard the guttural gruntings that announced the approach of our quarry. We let them pass us and get well away from their trenches, then silently, like hunters stalking wild beasts, we followed them. When we were close enough to be almost overpowered by the smell of sauerkraut and sausage mingling with stale sweat, my voice rapped out, though muffled by the thick air: "Hands up!"

There was no hesitation in obeying, although there were eight of them and only six of us. We pointed out the direction for them to go, and reminded them with our boots that there was no time to waste. We had only crossed a couple of shell-holes, however, when we came to a full stop. Presently I understood that they had discovered we were Australians and were terrified. Probably they had been fed up with tales about our savagery, that we tortured our prisoners. Anyway, they would not budge, and we could not carry eight hulking Germans and had no means of tying them together. Presently, the disturbance attracted notice from both trenches and there was only one thing to do. My sergeant called out: "Look out, sir! We'll be seen in a minute. What will we do?"

The contest was short and sharp; they outnumbered us, but we went to it with a will. It was sheer butchery, but I had rather send a thousand of the swine down to the fatherland than lose one of my boys. And perhaps it was charity to some wife and daughter who would now be free from the brutality of her Teutonic lord and master.

There is nothing so easy as to be lost in No Man's Land. A compass is useless, for you may be lying on a fifteen-inch shell just covered with a few inches of earth, and the stars refuse to look down on its pain, and the sky is always thickly veiled. Turn round three times, and you don't know which trench to return to. It is an awkward predicament, and many a time I went blindly forward praying that it was in the right direction. The German's horn-rimmed glasses but bewilder him the more, and we have had several of them walk into our arms without intention, though they soon found that thereby they had bettered themselves. There was one young Bavarian officer who made this miscalculation. I saw him moving near our wire in the early dawn. I called to some men to draw a bead on him but he came toward us and at the last with a run jumped down into our trench.

"Good morning!" I said to him, looking down my automatic, and you never saw such a crestfallen countenance in your life. It must have been some shock, expecting to join his own people and suddenly finding himself in the camp of his enemies. I found out afterward that he was a young cadet qualifying for his commission, and this was his first night in the trenches. He evidently was seeking an iron cross very early in his career. I spat question after question at him: "What's your regiment? How long have you been in the trenches?" etc., but in English he replied:

"I won't tell you anything. You can't make me!"

"All right, old chap, don't get excited! Come along with me."

I took him to the dugout which I shared with the medical officer in the support-trenches and sent Pat, my batman, to get together the best meal he could. Pat was a genius as a provider. None of the other officers liked him, for they suspected he was the medium for the loss of some of their luxuries, and I always had a blind eye. On this occasion Pat got together a real slap-up feed—some tinned sausages, mashed potatoes, strawberry jam, preserved pears and cream, not forgetting a bottle of champagne. I sent for the doctor and we fell to with gusto, and never offered his nibs a bite, though the eyes were popping out of his head, and his mouth watering with hunger. Toward the end of the meal I said to him: "I can't compel you to tell me anything, but I am not compelled to feed you. But you know how to earn something to eat." He began to tell me something I knew was all rubbish and I swung at him with "You swine! If you tell me those lies I'll strip your badges off you and send you in as a private."

I was surprised at the effect this threat had on him, though I knew that was the one thing that never failed in bringing a German officer to book. He trembled and paled and gave me a lot of information that I afterward proved to be correct.

Here's a good story of Pat, my old batman, who had been a shearer's cook in Australia, and looked after me like a father. He was really too old for the trenches, but this job just suited him. I was very surprised one day to see him with a German prisoner. He was never in a charge, and had no business having this man. Probably he had borrowed him from some other chap. I said to him: "Pat, what on earth are you doing with Fritz?"

"To tell yer the truth, sorr-r, Oi haven't yet made up my moind!"

"Let us have no humbug, take him back to the cage!"

"Very well, sorr-r!" About ten minutes later I saw Pat without his prisoner.

"Here, Pat, what on earth did you do with Fritz?"

"Well, sorr-r, he kept beggin' and beggin' to be let go, so Oi just put a Mills in his pocket with the pin out, and tould him to run for his loife!"

He would not get fifty yards before it went off!

The trained scout moves very cautiously in No Man's Land, with all his senses at high tension. After moving from one shell-hole to the next he lies and listens for a full minute. If there are any human beings near they will likely betray themselves by loud breathing, a muffled sneeze, or some rattle of equipment. If satisfied that the way is clear, he moves forward into another hole. Should he suddenly come into sight of the enemy, he is taught to freeze instantly, and the chances are he will not be noticed.

There was one night when I was making a way through the German wire, and had my hand up cutting a strand, when a sentry poked his head over the top and looked straight at me not three yards away. I froze instantly in that attitude but he fired a shot at me which, of course, went wide, being aimed in the dark. He then sent up a flare, but the firing of this dazzles a man for several seconds, and then so many shadows are thrown that I was no more distinct than previously. He went away, returning a minute or two later to have another look. By this time I was feeling quite stiff, but he was quite satisfied that no live man could be there. Had I jumped into a shell-hole, as fear prompted me to do, he would have roused the whole line, and a bomb would likely have got me. However, I thought this would be a good opportunity to take a look into the trench, for I reasoned that this sentry must be alone or someone else would have put up the flare while he fired the shot. Probably the rest of his regiment were on a working fatigue not far away. It was a breastwork trench and I climbed up the sand-bags, but tripped over a wire at the top and came down with a clatter. A red flare went up and I heard the feet of many soldiers running along the duck-boards. I only had time to roll into the ditch at the foot of the back of the parapet, where I was quite safe from observation, when they manned their trench to repel the raid. After several minutes when about a hundred rifles, several machine-guns, and a trench-mortar were pouring their fire into No Man's Land, I began to recover my nerve and saw that it would be a good opportunity to mark the position of one of these machine-guns which was firing just above my head. In fact, I could, with ease, have had my hand drilled just by holding it up. I tore a page out of my note-book and placed it in a crevice between the sand-bags, just under the gun. Hours afterward when all was quiet I returned to our own trenches and fastened another piece of white paper to a bush half-way across No Man's Land that I noticed was in line with a dead tree close to our *sally-port*, and my first piece of paper. In the morning the artillery observation officer could see these two pieces of paper quite plainly with his glasses, and that trench was levelled for fifty yards.

    No Man's Land is a place of surprises where death plucks its victims without warning. There have been some strange deaths there when bodies lay with unbroken skin, having neither mark of bullet nor shell. Times when the spirit laid the body down, fair and unmarred human flesh, but other times when the flesh was rent to ribbons and the bones smashed to splinters by the force imprisoned in a shell.

Such was the death meted out by justice to six Germans in a listening post fifty yards in advance of their trench. This party was in the way of our raid. We could not enter their trench by surprise without first removing it, and the job fell on me. I prepared a mine of my own. I took two Stokes shells, changed the time-fuse for instantaneous, took out the safety-pins holding the lever down by means of an iron ring. I crept out with these shells just a little before dark so as to arrive at the position before the Germans. I then put the shells, one on either side, and connected them with a fine trip-wire tied to each ring. I hurried from the spot as though the pestilence were after me, and got back safely—to the surprise of my brother officers who very consolingly said that they all expected I would blow myself up. At half past eight, however, there was music in our ears of a loud explosion in the direction of my mine. Next morning, through the telescope, could be seen what remained of several Hun carcasses. Pat, my batman, who was always a Job's comforter, informed me that the Germans would lie in wait for me to revenge this outrage; but if I had taken any notice of him, I would never have been able to do my job. He would come to me some mornings and beg me not to go out in No Man's Land that night as he had dreamed that I was "kilt," when I generally consigned him to a place where the English cease from troubling, and the Irish are at rest.

The enemy did his share in surprises. There was one occasion when I received word from the Tommies on our right that a large German patrol had been out on their front all night. As they did not attack I was considerably worried as to what they were up to, knowing they would not be there for the benefit of their health. I was responsible that our portion of the line should be guarded from surprise, and fear of some unknown calamity that might spring upon us from the dark made me so concerned that I lay pretty nearly all day on top of the parapet covered with sand-bags searching every inch of No Man's Land for a sign of the cause of their nocturnal activity. The setting sun revealed something shining that looked like the barrel of a Lewis gun. I determined to go out and get it after dark. When I went out I found I could not get near the place, for a machine-gun was playing round it to discourage curiosity, which it very effectively did. I reported next morning that the only chance of seeing what it was was to go out in the daytime; and it was suspicious enough to justify the risk. I donned a green suit and with a snail's progress crawled through the long grass and discovered that the Germans had laid a five-inch pipe from their trenches to within fifty yards of an indentation in our own. They would be able to enfilade us with gas before we could don our masks. We looked on our dangerous wind being one that blew across No Man's Land, but with this pipe we would be gassed when the wind blew down the line from the Tommies to us. The engineer officer wanted to blow up the pipe, but I thought if we blocked it up the enemy might not discover it, and put through gas which would come back on himself. Some concrete dugouts were being constructed at this time, and I took out a bucket of concrete and dumped it over the end of the pipe in broad daylight without having a shot fired at me or being seen. Afterward I found crawling in the daylight in No Man's Land to be less dangerous than at night. On a quiet front there is very little rifle or machine-gun fire by day for fear of betraying machine-gun and sniper positions. Never once in two or three daylight excursions into No Man's Land was I seen by the enemy or our own sentries.

Darkness always holds fear for the human heart, and it is the unknown danger that makes the bravest quail, and not so many are cowards in the daylight. But who can tell which holds the more peril for the soldier? He faces the terror that cometh by night, the destruction that walketh by day, and the pestilence that wasteth at noonday. But night is often kindly—it brings the balm of sleep to our tired bodies and covers coarseness and filth with a softening veil. No Man's Land at night is more beautiful than by day, for we need not know of the horror we do not see, and it shuts us off from sight of our enemies, and lets us feel that the wall is thick and strong that stands between our homes and women kin, and the savagery and bestiality of the monster who ravaged the homes and raped the women of Belgium and France.

> But if there's horror, there's beauty, wonder;
> The trench lights gleam and the rockets play.
> That flood of magnificent orange yonder
> Is a battery blazing miles away.[2]

---

2. Robert W. Service.

CHAPTER 25

Spy-Hunting

Man is by instinct and tradition a hunter, and there is no sport so thrilling as man-hunting, especially if the hunted be a menace to society, and more especially if he be a spy that threatens the safety of yourself and comrades. There is also in this branch of intelligence service an appeal to the clash of wits that holds fascination for the keen mind. The German spy system is not more clever than our own, but has been more carefully organized and much longer in operation. He spies also on friend and neutral, while we only use this back-door method of gleaning information from an enemy. The word, too, has associations that are ugly, and I fancy that our spies do not boast of their service, but spy-hunting is a service that has no taint, and there is much satisfaction both to the conscience and intellect in routing out the underground worker who, for "filthy lucre," would sell the blood of his fellow man. The traitor and the spy have in all ages been rightly considered as foul beings who poison the air and whose touch contaminates. In Germany alone is the spy given honour which is fitting in a country which has substituted *Expediency* for *Honour* and *Plausibility* for *Truth*, on whose throne is a maniac, and where *Conscience* has been unseated by *Pride*, and *Reason* displaced by *Method*.

Germany's espionage of her neighbours has been in existence so long, and so much time and money have been expended on it that we must prepare for its reassertion after the war even in countries where it has been for a time suppressed. Its hands have been cut off, but the plotting brain and the murderous heart of the system still persist and will be used after the war to rehabilitate the trade of Germany under many disguises, and will also seek, through appeal to our pity for a fallen nation, to lull us into slumber, until the claws and fangs of militarism have grown again.

We are so new in the game that our methods in spy-hunting are clumsy, and we frequently give warning to the brains of the system to seek cover when we strike at its puppets. By arresting the agents of the German master spy we cut off his activity for a time but allow him to spread his ramifications in other directions, and the first knowledge we have that he has sprung to life again is by the destruction of property and loss of life that ensue. It would sometimes pay us to give these agents more and more rope, keeping them under observation until we can strike at the centre and heart of all this plotting. When we have enough evidence against one of these agents for a death penalty we should allow him to purchase his life by betraying his master, and as these agents only serve for hire and know not what loyalty is, they are always ready to turn king's evidence if the price offered be high enough. Of course, they should not be given their liberty again, but segregated like the carrier of a contagious disease.

It should always be remembered that a man who in war-time talks sedition and disloyalty in public is not a spy. He is too big a fool to be ever employed in a service that requires, above all things, secrecy and the ability to avert suspicion. The first thing a spy seeks to do is to find a suitable cloak to cover his designs, and also to place himself in a position where he will gain information. Among the first things he would do would be to seek to join the Red Cross, and he would be almost certain to enlist. In these days the man to be suspicious of is the one who is always protesting his loyalty and showing what *he* is doing *to help the cause.* The true patriot knows that he has no need to proclaim his loyalty, and is shy of boasting of service that is really a *privilege and a duty.*

Among the most useful equipments for a secret-service agent is lip-reading, and if he can signal with his eyelids in Morse so much the better. Dark goggles, one glass of which is a small mirror, are also very useful, as one can sit with one's back to a party in a cafe or train, and read what they are saying. Women are the most dangerous spies, and trade on the instinctive chivalry that men cannot help but extend to them. There are many officers whose deaths at the front have been suicides because they were betrayed by some woman who had sucked valuable information from them, and their chivalry would not let them deliver her over to justice. Men in high place in England and in France have betrayed the public trust through faith in a woman who was false and who sold their confidence to the enemy for a price that was so strong to their hearts as to be irresistible, more than love, honour, or country.

Even in the army there are mysterious happenings—shots from behind and strange disappearances. There was one Australian general whose death created many rumours, and other officers who were supposed to have been shot from within our lines.

Of course, in the war zone among a strange peasantry there are many spy scares, and maybe some of the things we were suspicious of were quite innocent; but it was strange that whenever a gray horse appeared near a battery that battery was shelled, and when they painted all the gray horses green their positions were not so frequently spotted. Sometimes the old Flemish farmers would certainly plough their fields in a strange fashion but, perhaps, zigzags and swastikas are common patterns in French fields. It may have been our alarmed ears that fancied the paper boy played a different tune on his horn every day, but pigeons did certainly rise from the middle of paddocks contrary to the habits of these birds.

One of the hardest things I ever did was to arrest a young Belgian girl nineteen years of age who undoubtedly was the means of the death of thousands of our boys. It was in this wise. One night I observed a light a good way behind our trenches go out then come again. I watched it very carefully, and found it was signalling by the Morse code with dashes ten seconds long and the dots five. If you were not watching it very carefully you would never have dreamt it was anything but a flicker of light. The letters I read were—*nrudtveauaoiln*, which, when decoded, gave important information regarding the movement of troops. I took a line through some trees of the direction from which the light came and walked toward it. Just off an old drain I found an overturned wagon with a loophole cut through the backboard. There were footprints in the drain, and the grass was pressed down where a body had been lying. For five nights I lay in wait, my hopes keyed up to the highest point of expectation. At last to me was to fall the good fortune of capturing a spy—perhaps to end the leakage of information of our plans that we knew the Germans were getting. But on these five nights nothing happened. The day afterward, some boys of a battery whom I asked to watch this drain caught an old farmer in it. This farmer, however, who lived next door to our brigade headquarters had been carefully watched, and the information had come from outside the zone which he never left. Someone must have brought the information to him. Everybody using those roads had to have a passport issued by the French intelligence service, and countersigned by the intelligence officer of the area. Elimination narrowed suspicion to a paper girl who, it was found, sold out her papers round the batteries and billets at ten o'clock, and did not return until after three. The excuse she gave was that she was visiting her brother's grave, but on looking up her records we found that she had never had a brother. One day I kept her in sight on the road while I rode across the fields. After she entered the house where she was living at Estaires I followed and opened the door. As soon as she saw me she fainted. I blew my whistle, and on arrival of the picket we searched the house and found the German code with some maps and other incriminating documents. I never did a harder task in my life than hand that girl over to the French authorities for possible execution. She was a very pretty, happy little girl, red-haired and blue-eyed, and, although one could show no pity because the safety and life of thousands were at stake, yet it wrung the heart to think of the wastage of the young, bright life, the victim of German gold, and the treachery that is the handmaiden of war, and preys on the weakness of the moral nature.

There was another occasion when I unearthed a spy's burrow. One night a man in D Company stopped me on the road, and pointing out a lonely farmhouse, told me he had seen some blue sparks flashing from the chimney. We walked across and, entering the flagged kitchen, asked for *cafe au lait*. Sitting at the white table worn with much scrubbing, and slowly sipping the coffee, we engaged the old man and woman in conversation. They were very bitter in their denunciation of *les boches*, and spoke of their sacrifices as nothing. "Why, *monsieur*, it is for France! It is not for us to complain if she ask much from us."

My companion spoke French very fluently (his name was Davies), and he acted as interpreter. I noticed that they seemed anxious to get rid of us, but we stayed for several hours getting the old lady to cook us eggs and chipped potatoes, and talking on almost every topic but the war. One suspicious circumstance that had caught my eye as soon as we entered the kitchen was the fact that the flue of the stove did not lead up the chimney, but out through a hole in the wall.

At last, when we rose to go the old man in an excess of hospitality accompanied us fifty yards on our way. We promised to bring some companions on another day. "But no, *monsieur*, that will not do—we cannot get more eggs, and my wife she is a little afraid of the *soldat* from *Australie*."

After he left us and returned to the farm we doubled back, and round to the other side. Soon we heard the crackle of wireless. Expecting that the door would be fast bolted, we smashed-in a window, almost knocking over the old woman as she barred our way. Looking up the chimney, I found there as neat a small set of wireless as was ever made in Germany. The motor was in the cellar and well-muffled. The old chap hesitated to come down, but a shot that brought down some plaster hurried his decision. In spite of the old woman's pretended fear of Australians, she evidently did not think we were adamant to pity. On her knees with much weeping she begged us to let them go away, and shifted rapidly from one ground of appeal to another. She said her husband was crazy and his wires and things did no harm; he was trying to talk to *le Président*, but no answer ever came. She would have him locked up.

"You would not harm an old mother of France!"

I told her she wasn't French, but German, of which I had had suspicions all along. She then spat at us and told us to do our worst, but the old man merely stood there and scowled, and as he stood upright, with folded arms, we judged he was not as old by twenty years as he appeared, though his make-up was perfect. We marched them through the village under the curious eyes of many of our own comrades, but the eager gesticulations of the French people, and the fierce blaze of rage in the eyes of the women showed us that they had no friends among the neighbours, and revealed to us the smouldering fires of hate that the French people have for the brutal invader. I fancy the dastardly pair were glad of our protection for all their looks of defiance. They knew that a spy would meet short shrift at the hands of these French women whose untamed spirit was the same as that of the Margots of the Parisian gutters in the Reign of Terror.

Chapter 26

Bapaume and "a Blighty"

How many weeks I lay under the shadow of the church-tower of Bapaume I know not. But every morning as the mist lifted the church-tower would reappear through the trees, and now and again the flash of a glass would show that it was an observation-post of the enemy, and frequently well-placed shells on our trenches and dumps would show to what devilish uses our enemies were putting the house of God as they directed their shell-fire from a seat just under the cross on the tower.

This is a very old, historic town of France, and the sentiment of the French people would not have it shelled. So we lay these weeks within *cooee* of a nest of our enemies, who were permitted the safety and comfort of a peaceful home almost within our lines. There are other places along the line where we are under the same disadvantage. There is the city of Lille with its million or more of French inhabitants lying within five miles of our lines (such easy range), for over three years, and not a shell fired into it. How the Germans smile as their bases of operation lie in such security, for, of course, sentiment has been erased from the German character forever.

The French made the mistake again in regard to Bapaume of crediting the Germans with human feelings—they vainly hoped that the Germans would respect historic monuments when they gained no military advantage by destroying them. But every day that the war is prolonged is but adding to the evidence already so colossal that the German is a beast who wantonly destroys and takes sheer joy in slaying, burning, and smashing, destroying for destruction's sake, and killing for the sight of blood. When we drove the Germans from Bapaume they left it in ruins as utter as though we had bombarded it, but so much more systematic was their destruction! In the market square there is a hole large enough to hold a cathedral, made by the mine they exploded as they left, which was so senseless as almost to make it seem that, like children, they wanted to hear how big a bang they could make. But their devilish lack of humour is more plainly shown in the system with which they destroyed the orchards in the country further back. Every tree was cut at exactly the same height from the ground, and carefully laid in the selfsame way. Not one of them deviated a hair's breadth in its position on the ground from the angle made by its neighbour. They must have spent hours in obtaining such hellish regularity. Wed System to Lust, and you have an alliance of Satan with the hag Sycorax, and their offspring is the German Empire, the Caliban of nations.

The highest point of the church-tower, however, before the days of our advance, was its cross, and in our misery we could always see this symbol of hope and salvation; but it was a reminder too of pain and suffering endured that man's spirit might be free, and as we also were suffering and enduring in freedom's cause, we knew that our strife was religion and our accomplishment would be salvation.

And what we endured in that bitter cold has scarred our memories and added to our bodies the aging of years. In the chronic agony of cold the pain of wounds was an alleviation, and I have seen men who had just had their arms blown off wave the jagged stump and laugh as they called out—"Got a *blighty* at last, sir!"

We were standing up to our waists in liquid mud by day, into which we would freeze at night. I have gone along the trench and kicked and punched my boys into sensibility, and said:

"Is there anything I can do for you, boys? Can't I get you anything?"

"Oh, no sir. We're all right, but don't we envy old Nick and his imps tonight!"

Who is there that is not abashed in the presence of a spirit like that? And had you been there and these your men, wouldn't you love them as I do? Never did the spirit of man rise more glorious to the demand of hard occasion, than when those boys of Australia laughed and joked in the tortures of hell. Eighty per cent of them had never known a temperature lower than thirty above zero, and here was a cold more biting than they had ever dreamed of and they were without protection, living in a filthy ditch, never dry, their clothing unable to keep out wet or cold. Back in camp every man had a complaint, where it is the province of the soldier to grumble. In those days the orderly officer would go round with his question of "Any complaints?"

"Yes, look here, sir. What do you think of that?"

"Why, dear me, man, it seems very good soup!"

"Yes, sir, but it is supposed to be stew!"

Why, if the Australian soldier did not complain, you might well suspect a mutiny brewing! Too much marmalade, and not enough plum! etc. I never thought there was as much marmalade in the world as I myself have consumed on active service! Those days when we were well off, and did not know it, with dry beds and a clean tent, with good warm food, and plenty to eat and drink, the boys were always kicking about something or other, but now when things were hellish bad under conditions when wounds were a luxury and death a release you never heard a complaint. There were days too when an enemy barrage cut off our supplies and prevented relief, and we were compelled to live on dry biscuits and cold water, taking our water from the shell-holes where the dead were rotting. I remember when I was wounded and being carried out of the trench my brother officers saying to me: "Oh, Knyvett, you lucky dog!"

And I was lucky, and knew it, though I had twenty wounds and trench feet. Why, when I arrived at the hospital and lay in a real bed, with real sheets, and warm blankets, with a roof over my head that didn't leak, and a fire in the room, with the nurse now and again to come along and smile on me, I tell you heaven had no extra attractions to offer me. The man who got wounded in those days was a lucky dog, all right; in fact, he mostly is at all times, and about the silliest thing the War Office ever did was to issue an honour stripe for wounds. The man deserving of the greatest credit is not the man who gets wounded, but the man who stays on in the trenches week after week, and month after month enduring the nervous strain and unnatural conditions, living like a rat in a hole in the ground. There are none who have been there for any length of time who do not welcome the sharp pain of a wound as a relief.

The Germans opposite us in their trenches at Bapaume were, of course, in as bad a plight as we were. When I scouted down their trenches at night I found equipment and stores lying on top of the parapet. Evidently, the mud in the bottom of their trenches was as bad as in ours, and anything dropped had to be fished for. Perhaps there were no deep dugouts just there. We would not allow our men to use these deep dugouts as nothing so conduces to bad morale. Once men get deep down out of range of the shells they are very, very reluctant to leave their "funk-holes." A man has to be hardened to shell-fire before he is of any value as a fighter, and these deep dugouts take men out of reach of most of the shells, and when they come in the open again they have to be hardened anew.

It is not generally a wise plan to occupy the old German trench, as he has the range of it very accurately, and anyway it is in most cases so badly battered about after our artillery has done with it as not to be at all superior as a residence to the shell-holes in front of it, and it is mostly full of dead Germans which are unearthed by the shells as often as we bury them. God knows the smell of a live German is not a pleasant thing to live near, but as for dead ones! ... Our method was to construct a new trench about fifty yards in advance by linking up a chain of shell-holes, and we felt the labour to be worthwhile when we saw the shells falling behind us, and it was not much harder than if we had had to clean out the old German trench.

On our right flank there was a gap of a hundred yards that we patrolled two or three times a night, and in our net we sometimes caught some Germans who were lost. On one occasion a German with a string of water-bottles round his neck, and a grunt that may have been a password, stepped down into our trench. He had evidently been out to get water for himself and comrades from their nearest supply, and taken the wrong turning! He made an attempt at a grin when he found where he was, and evidently thought the change could not be for the worse. He was so thick in the head, however—I have known cows with more intelligence—that I wonder any other German being fool enough to trust him with such a valuable article as a water-bottle.

We were planning to take a portion of the trench opposite to straighten our line, and I had scouted down a hundred yards of it from behind, and got a good idea of the strength with which it was held, taking bearings of its position. The next night, as the attack was to take place at daybreak, I thought I had better go over and make sure that I had made no mistakes. I crossed over the first trench without any difficulty. There did not seem to be any one on guard. I then went toward their support lines where there seemed to be more men, mostly working parties. I passed these and with unpardonable carelessness stood up to have a look round, thinking that it was too dark for me to be seen. But I got a shock to find there was a sentry almost beside me—though he was, if anything, more scared than myself. He pulled the trigger without taking aim and naturally missed me, but if he had been wide-awake he could with ease have punctured me with his bayonet. I did not stop to pass the time of day with him, for the place seemed suddenly alive with Huns as he called "Heinz, Heinz!"—probably the name of his corporal—but I dived into a shell-hole and flattened myself as much as possible.

As I was lost to sight and to memory too dear to be allowed to escape they began to cover the ground with bombs. These all went well beyond me, and had it not been for *butter-fingers* I might have escaped. But a bomb slipped from his hand, rolling into the hole in front of him. He jumped back into the safety of the trench, and did not know that the bomb had fallen on me as it exploded. But *I* knew it—my left leg was broken in three places, twelve wounds in my right, and others on my back, twenty that afterward had to be dressed, not counting some other scratches. Then they came out to look for me, my *friend* almost stepping on me, but after half an hour's fruitless search they gave up. About two hours later I started home on my long, painful crawl. It took me about twenty minutes to pass the sentry near where I was lying, but after that there was no danger of discovery—the front line still appearing almost unoccupied; but I was getting dizzy and not sure of my direction. I knew, however, where there was a derelict aeroplane in No Man's Land, and made toward it. When I sighted this I was overcome with relief, and laid my face in the mud for a while to recover. I had now crawled about six hundred yards dragging my useless legs. And my elbows were skinned through, being used as grapples that I dug in the ground ahead, in that way dragging myself a few inches at a time. I knew our trenches were still about two hundred yards away, and the sweat of fear broke out on me as I remembered the two machine-guns in front of me that would fire on anything seen moving out there, no one expecting me to return that way. So I crawled higher up the line, where it was safer to enter, and a few yards from our trenches gave our scouting call. Several of my boys came running out and tenderly picked me up. I was all in and could not move a muscle. My own boys would not allow the stretcher-bearers to touch me, but six of them put me on a stretcher and carried me over the top just as day was breaking. They would not go down into the communication-trench or shell-holes because they thought it would be too rough on me, and so carried me over the exposed ground; and when they got me to the dressing-station they said: "You will come back to us, sir, won't you?"

I said: "Yes, boys, you bet I will!" And you may bet that I shall, as soon as ever I am passed as fit again.

The pain of my wounds was soon altogether forgotten, for each medical officer that examined me finished up with the liquid melody of the phrase: "Blighty for you!" My leave was long past due, and the very next day I was to report for transfer to the Australian wing of the Royal Flying Corps, which would have meant several weeks' training in England, but "the best laid schemes o' mice an' men gang aft a-gley!"—and there's a science shapes our ends, rough-hack them though Huns may!

PART 5
Hospital Life

CHAPTER 27

In France

My hospital experiences in France were a procession of five nights with intermissions of days spent in travel. From the advance dressing-station I was slid over the mud for three miles in a sledge drawn by the Methuselah of horses borrowed from some French farmhouse. His antiquarian gait suited me, and this was the smoothest of the many torturous forms of travel I endured before I was able once again to move up-rightly on my feet as a man should.

At Trones Wood I was swung into a horse ambulance and thereafter swung and swayed for a couple of hours until, closing my eyes, I could fancy I was once again at sea. This was rougher than the sledge, but endurable and certainly the most comfortable of all the wheeled vehicles in which I travelled. I bless the inventor of the springs that kept it swaying gently on a road all ruts and holes.

I was deposited on the table of the operating-theatre in the field-ambulance, while a surgeon overhauled me to see if there was any injury necessitating an immediate operation. Satisfied that I was merely broken and punctured, I was transferred to a cot and so began my *first hospital night*. I was known personally to all the doctors in our field-ambulance. I had on several occasions messed with them, and they were always very keenly interested in my yarns of No Man's Land, so when the news spread that I had been brought in wounded I soon had a group round my bed, some of them in pyjamas being roused from their sleep to hear the news. One of them very gleefully said:

"Hullo, Knyvett, old man—I've just won five pounds on you. We had a bet that you would not last out another month. You know you've had a pretty good innings and mighty lucky only to get wounded."

But at that moment I was not in the mood to appreciate this form of humour, until one of them, seeing I was pretty uncomfortable, gave me an injection of *morphia*. But I was very glad to be resting there and felt I could hardly have endured a longer journey without a spell. I was given here the first good hot meal I had had for weeks, though I had been given a drink of steaming-hot coffee in the ambulance. There was not much sleep to be got, as a constant stream of men were being brought in and taken away, and now and again shells would fall quite close, but the ground thereabouts was very soft, and I counted fifteen shells that fell close by with a *wouf* and a *squelch*, but did not explode. This hospital was all under canvas, just three or four big marquees and a score or so of tents for the medical officers and orderlies, and any inclination that I had to complain was taken away by the sight of walking cases strolling in with an arm gone, or a hole in the cheek, or their jaw smashed, many far worse than I was, who would sit there waiting their turn to be examined, and then walk out again to the ambulance that carried them on to the next hospital.

Next morning I was carried out to a motor-ambulance and started on the most painful trip of my life. The driver took reasonable care, but could not go too slow, for another load was waiting for him as soon as he could return, but I am sure that I felt every stone in that road. I got the attendant to wedge me in with pillows, but only by holding myself off from the wall with both my hands could I ease the bump, and then I would wait with dread for the next one. I don't know if the other three fellows lying in the ambulance with me were as sore as I was, but I picture today the hours that those ambulances travel with wounded men as being added together and totalling a century of pain. Perhaps after the war is ended, when it is too late, someone may invent a motor ambulance on easy springs that will not multiply unnecessarily the pain of torn flesh and the grating edges of bones.

Now comes the night in the casualty clearing-station at Heilly. Straight on to another operating-table, but one in a sea of many—ten operations going on at once. Then began the probing for pieces of metal in my wounds.

"Good God!" remarked the surgeon, "the best thing we can do is to run a magnet over you. We'll never find them all otherwise."

Nor did they, for I carry some of them still in my body as permanent souvenirs of the few words I had with Fritz. There was a nurse in the theatre with smiling face, laughing blue eyes, and tumbled curls falling beneath her cap, and a brief acquaintance of one day was formed on the spot. She was attending another case, and a wink and a smile served for introduction. She came and visited me in the ward that night and we chatted a brief hour, then she was gone, and I know not even her name. So ships meet, dip their flag, and pass into the night.

In the bed opposite me in this hospital there was a German officer and he bellowed like a bull all night. We got pretty sick of his noise and told the medical officer in charge of the ward when he came on his rounds in the morning that if he did not chloroform or do something to silence the hound, we would. I suggested that he go and tell him that if he did not shut up he would be sent into the ward with his own privates. He did so and there was not another squeak from him.

After breakfast warm sweaters, helmets, scarves, and mitts were issued to each of us and we were wrapped in warm blankets and carried out to a hospital-train nearby. Before I left, however, I wrote out the report of my reconnaissance of the German trenches and despatched it by orderly to G. H. Q. All my possessions I carried in my hand in a small bag not nearly as big as a lady's knitting-bag. My kit was somewhere in France and my uniform had been cut off me and was probably ascending as incense from some incinerator, in a ritual that was an appropriate end after much service. Everything was supposed to be taken out of my pockets (which I have no doubt happened) and sent to me (which certainly did not happen). I have no sympathy with the old sanitary sergeant who superintended the last rites in the passing of my much-lived-in clothes when he was slightly wounded by a bullet from a cartridge that somehow or other dropped into the fire at the same time. These incinerators frequently very nearly caused shell-shock to the sanitary squad, and they might just as well have been in the actual trenches, for in the gathering up of rubbish around the camp cartridges would frequently be thrown with it into the fire and explosions would ensue like the firing of a machine-gun, and bullets would whizz in all directions. Once a mule got shot, but it's a wonder that other flesh less valuable was not occasionally punctured, for these incinerators were just on the edge of the camp and generally had a group round them of those who preferred being fire-tenders to ramrod-shovers.

The hospital-train bore us with many interruptions and frequent side-trackings toward the Channel and Blighty. In England hospital-trains take precedence over all other traffic, but here in France there were many other things more important for the winning of the war than wounded men, so hospital-trains had to step aside and give the right of way to the shells, guns, cartridges, and food for the men still facing the foe. So my third night was spent on the rails lying snugly in a car wrapped in many blankets, and only disturbed by having to "smoke" a thermometer every two or three hours, and by the nurse rousing me at six *ack emma* (a.m.) to have my face and hands washed, which is a mania that afflicts all nurses. A nurse has only one fear, that of displeasing the doctor, and though all should perish, everything must be spotless when he makes his rounds. A doctor is the only man who can awe a woman and obtain perfect obedience. Of course I am referring to them professionally, and not in their domestic relations. I knew a nurse in a military hospital who woke up a patient, who was enjoying his first sound sleep for weeks, to administer a sleeping-draft. When she was remonstrated with she said "the doctor ordered it."

In France there has been since the war much coal-saving, and had it not been that I had been careful to have with me emergency rations of blankets, I would have perished with the cold. I was told that the engine-drivers were given a commission on what coal they saved, so all the steam we got through the warming-pipes hardly took the frost off them. Only the men in the bottom cots were able to see the scenery we passed through, and we up-stairs could have murdered them with pleasure as they kept calling out:

"By George! You should see this!"

"That's the funniest sight I've seen in my life!"

"Isn't that a lovely sight!"

But journeys, even on French railways, come to an end eventually, though it only be second-class traffic, and with much joy did we welcome the news that we were running into Rouen.

In the small hours of the morning with the mist still trailing through the streets we were driven to the Infirmary for Aged Women (which they had vacated), and where was housed Number Eight General Hospital. After our labels had been examined and checked with our wounds, and it was quite evident that we were *les hommes blesses* and not baggage, we were carried upstairs and allotted to our wards according to the part of the body in which we were wounded. They had some difficulty in my case, and as I feared that they might be carrying me from ward to ward all day and night I asked them to look on the other side of my tag to see if it was not marked in red: "Fragile, With Care." There was in the ward where I eventually anchored a V. A. D. (Voluntary Aid Detachment) nurse who will ever live in my memory as the gentlest and most attentive of all that I have known. You could not raise your hand or turn in your sleep without her gliding noiselessly to your bedside to see if you wanted anything. A hundred times would she straighten the pillows, if you fancied you would get extra comfort another way, and she ever had ready a hot glass of milk to make you sleep the better. She was a Canadian, and if there are many more like her among the Canadian women, then the men of Canada are thrice blessed. Thus passed my fourth night in French hospitals.

In the morning I saw through an open door in another ward a friend of mine whom I had parted with on landing in Egypt. I called an orderly to carry me through to an empty bed alongside him so that we might renew our friendship. He was badly wounded in the arm and face, but it was pleasant to meet again after many months. That was many months ago and the other day I met him again in New York. We have only been a short time together on each occasion, yet have continued our acquaintance on four continents, many months intervening between each meeting. There was a great hullabaloo in my ward when the matron came in and found my bed empty. When she discovered where I was, she said:

"Who gave you permission to come in here?"

I replied: "No one said I was not to!"

And anyway the pleasure was worth the commission of the crime! That morning I was again picked up as a bundle and carried I knew not whither, leaving my friend behind.

I was carried on board a British hospital-ship and lowered about three decks down. As placards glared in one's eyes on every side about what to do in case of submarine attack, I did not like very much the idea of going down so far, for I always like to be able to depend upon myself in an emergency, and I was now as helpless as a log. They put me in a swinging cot, which was a great idea to prevent seasickness. We went slowly out the harbour to sea with our prow pointing toward Blighty, the El Dorado of the wounded Tommy. 'Twas little I saw of river, harbour, or sea from my berth in the nethermost depths of that vessel's hold. I was told we went across with all lights out. The days had passed when, in our folly, we painted our hospital-ships white with a green band and marked them with a red cross, or at night circled them with a row of green lights illuminating a huge red cross near the funnel, for we had found that we were only making them conspicuous as targets for the *human shark of the sea*. There have been more hospital-ships sunk than troop-ships, for the troop-ship is armed and convoyed, but the hospital-ship is an easy victim. The English port we entered was shrouded in fog, and wharf buildings never at any time look inviting, but we could nevertheless understand the excitement of our English companions, for it was Home to them, and to us *dear old England*, the brave heart of the freest empire this earth has seen, and after all where is the Britisher who does not thrill with pride at landing on the soil of those little islands which have produced a race so great, and foot for foot of soil there is no land on the earth that has produced so much wealth. We could smile with appreciation and not much surprise at the Tommy who remarked: "Say, Bill, don't the gas-works smell lovely!"

CHAPTER 28

In London

By hospital-train, the most comfortable ever devised, did we run into Waterloo Station—doors were opened, and men in gorgeous uniforms—much gold braid and silver buttons—came aboard. We thought that they were admirals and field-marshals at the very least, but it turned out they were only members of the Volunteer Ambulance Corps, men unfit for military service, who had provided their own cars and received not a penny of pay. With the tenderness of women they put us on stretchers and carried us out to their luxurious ambulances. With each four men went a lady to attend to all their wants. Like a mother she hovered over us and you could see her heart was bursting with love for us far-out sons of empire. Through cheering crowds we drove and our Australian hearts leaped as we heard many *cooees*, which made us feel that we were not far from Home, for twelve thousand miles were bridged in thought by these homelike sounds and the knowledge that we were in the land from which our parents came and where we had many kinsfolk. I was assigned to the Third London General Hospital and out to Wandsworth Common was I taken, where alongside Queen Victoria's school for officers' orphans had been built rows of comfortable huts linked up with seven miles of corridors, while the old orphanage itself contained the administrative headquarters. I was allotted to G ward, but did not know for days what a distinction that was, for the sister in charge was none other than the late Queen of Portugal, and among the V. A. D.'s were several ladies and honourables. They were camouflaged, however, under the titles of "sister" and "nurse," and we had become too intimate to need ceremony before we discovered who they were in social life. In dressing our wounds, washing us, cleaning and scrubbing the floors they were as adept as if to the manner born, but you could not fail to see that they sprung from generations of refinement. On one side of me was an Australian who had been hit on the side of the head by a shell, having therefrom a stiff neck. On the other side was an Irish padre, chaplain to an Australian battalion, and, of course, the life of the ward, and he had a greater fund of good stories than any other man, not excepting other priests, I have known. In an opposite bed was a Welshman with one leg who of necessity answered to the name of Taffy, while next to him was a Londoner who had a leg that he would have been better without, for it had borne fourteen operations. In London we had the world's specialists for every bodily ill, and some of us who had complications were in the hands of ten doctors at the one time. There were skin specialists and bone specialists, nerve specialists and brain specialists, separate authorities on the eye, ear, nose, and throat, and it is a pity that a man is tied up in one bag, otherwise they might all have operated at the selfsame moment in separate rooms on the same man.

There was one sister whom we all loved—I don't think; but she was only in our ward occasionally. Her real name was unknown to most of us, but she will be remembered for long as Gentle Annie. She was so gentle that I have known only a few mules rougher, and never, after the first occasion, would I allow her to touch the dressings on my wounds. With so many to be done it was a painful performance even under kindly, sympathetic hands. We expressed our feelings toward her by giving her left-right every time she came into the ward and she would get mad at the second step. One day she called the matron, so we left-righted her as well. Then the doctor was brought in and we left-righted him, but he enjoyed the joke, perhaps realizing his helplessness, for you can't very well punish wounded men lying in bed except by depriving them of food, and we were most of us on diets anyway! The fact that we were Australians was held to be accountable for our misbehaviour.

There was a little nurse, mostly on night duty, who was dubbed Choom, for she came from Yorkshire and had a rich brogue. But her heart was big enough for one twice her size, and she would always tuck us in and attempt to supply all our wants, however unreasonable.

After an operation which I tell about in another chapter I was able to sit up and propel myself in a wheel-chair, and soon was having races with the champion chair-speeders of the other wards. There was a long inclined plane that was the cause of many accidents, for there was a sharp turn at the bottom and our chariots would get out of control. I have more than once turned a double somersault and it is a wonder I did not break my head, and several candid friends said it was cracked anyway. We had concerts in the hall every night, and as it was a couple of miles from our ward, we cripples who brought our own chairs with us would wait in the corridor for one of the blind to propel us along while we would do the guiding ourselves, giving directions to our steeds in nautical terms, such as:

"Starboard a little!"
"Steady, steady, you idiot!"
"Hard aport!"
"Quick!"
"Now, you darned fool, you jolly nearly smashed that window!"

When we got to the door of the hall, we would be piloted into the area reserved for carriages, and so tightly were we jammed that it took about twenty minutes to empty the hall, or twice as long if we tried to get out by ourselves. However, the concerts were worthwhile, and when Clara Butt or some other world-famed artist came along, we did not mind being late for dinner, the dishes of which were never a surprise if you remembered the day of the week.

In our ward there were mostly leg injuries, and in the one next door arm cases, and hot and fast flew the arguments as to which it were worse to lose. We demonstrated our superiority one night by raiding them for their milk, all the attackers being on crutches, and they were unable to recover it; so we decided to our own satisfaction that we were the most useful members of society, though had we not drunk it so fast they might have got it.

We had some very high talent in the hospital and our monthly gazette was a very creditable production. We had as one of the orderlies a *Punch* artist and he was always caricaturing some of us. The patients contributed drawings, poems, and articles, and I imagine that in years to come these little papers will be of some value, containing the works of renowned artists and authors from many parts of the world.

A good number from our ward were able to take taxi-rides into the city and would return at late hours, sometimes the merrier for the excursion. I have in my memory as I write, recollections of waking suddenly out of slumber to behold Taffy and a mad Australian waltzing to the strains of a gramophone, each with only one leg, and then old Piddington would persist in rousing the ward that we might sing as a roundelay:

And when I die,
Don't bury me at all—
Just pickle my bones
In alcohol.
Put a bottle of RUM— (much emphasis here)
At my head and feet,
And then I know
My bones will keep!

My brothers are in different regiments. We enlisted from different states—one is in an English regiment—yet we all met on Good Friday in this hospital ward. They had seen in the paper my name among the casualties and, inquiring, had found out where I was and there we met, not having seen each other for many years.

One day, like a bolt from the blue, came the intimation that I was to be sent back to Australia in two days as being unfit for further service. I argued the point, went before the Medical Board, and gave each one separately a testimonial that would be no advertisement, but it was of no avail, and I realized that like a worn-out horse I was to be sent out of the fun. But to add injury to insult, I had had no opportunity to see London. What! Go home to Australia and tell them I had been in London and not seen St. Paul's, or the Abbey, or anything? So when I realized appeal was useless I got dressed and called a taxicab and went to see the sights of London. Never was a tourist trip conducted more systematically. On crutches I hobbled round St. Paul's and through the Abbey. I saw the Tower, the Albert Memorial, and all the sights that I could remember or the taxi-driver think of sufficient importance to need a visit. I even went down Petticoat Lane. But most of all I did the theatres, four in one day, returning to the hospital at 1.30 a.m. Next day I repeated and enlarged the dose, returning a little later, but the following morning I was summoned before the O. C. He said:

"It is reported to me that you have been returning after hours. Why?"

I said: "So would you, sir, if you were returning to Australia in two days and had not viewed London!"

He said: "Well, it won't occur again, I hope."

To which I replied: "Only tonight, sir!"

But the boat was delayed, and I had two more days of strenuous existence in the metropolis of the world.

Once again I entered a hospital-train, but this time I would have no mussing round me as if I were a helpless child, but went upright, as a man should, though on crutches.

When we journeyed to the port there was one of our good old Australian coasters waiting to bear us back again—Home. The old A. U. S. N. steamer that I had so often travelled on from Brisbane to Sydney was now under command of the Australian navy and had the proud designation of His Majesty's Australian Hospital-Ship.

Chapter 29

The Hospital-Ship

Some people think that they have made a sea journey when they cross the English Channel, and Dover to Calais holds for many the memory of an age of misery. I don't suppose the provisions on these Channel steamers have very great inroads made upon them by the passengers. The soldiers have a song that well expresses experiences on this narrow stretch of water.

Sea, sea, why are you angry with me?
Ever since I left Dover,
I thought the ship would go over —— *(etc.)*

But on the longer journey across the Atlantic from England to America there is more time to get one's sea-legs, and on the last day or two passengers begin to enjoy the sea journey. But this is quite enough of the sea for anyone but an amphibian. The three weeks journey from America to Australia gets decidedly monotonous, and long before sighting Sydney Heads and entering the world's *pearl of ports* everyone has had his fill of the sea. But lengthen that journey by three and you have had enough sea travel for a lifetime.

Well, we left England and for an eternity sailed south, seeing land only on one day and smelling it for a week. Then we clung to the end of Africa for seven days and then sailed east for a decade till Australia got in our way, and as it could not be passed without a long detour, we were deposited on its soil. In nine weeks we only called at two ports, Freetown on the west coast of Africa, and Durban on the east coast. Freetown has the usual strong combination smell of nigger, cinnamon, and decaying vegetation, in an atmosphere of heavy steam, that characterizes all tropical towns inhabited by our *black brother*. We were told that this place had but a few years ago the pleasant subtitle of the White Man's Grave. If you served one year here in the government service you were entitled to retire for life on a pension, but the likelihood was that long before your term was up you would retire to a six-foot-by-two allotment near the beach, in the company of countless predecessors. But science had been at work here, as at Panama, and wire gauze and the kerosene spray had captured the first trenches of yellow fever and malaria, and against these weapons of the medico all counter-attacks have been unavailing. Some strong hand was ruling in this town, for the streets were spotless and the dogs lean. And, oh, how the nigger does hate cleanliness! Evidently this town was free in a real sense because well disciplined. We were told that all the white people lived up on the hill that backed the town and many kind invitations of hospitality were sent to us; so those whose wills were stronger than the enervating hand of the weather-master boarded the toy train and were carried up and up toward the summit of the hills above the steam heat, where the air seemed to be fanned from the very cooling-house of God. I had the pleasure of being entertained by a French priest who had been on the western front in the early days of the war, and he added to our knowledge more first-hand stories of the bestial Huns' ravaging of convents and raping of nuns. The bishop of this protectorate could not do enough for us, and although we were not of his faith, he looked on us as children who were very dear to the heart of God because of our sacrifices of blood and flesh for the right.

We loaded ourselves down with curios, buying tiger-rugs, mats, bead-necklaces, tom-toms, and *assegais*. We strung these chiefly round our necks, as we had to have hands free to manipulate our crutches, and some of us looked more like the *ol' clo' man* than smart army officers. Of course Bertie Gloom had to suggest that we would have to pay more duty on the *old junk* when we got it to Australia even than the price that the dealers had already robbed us of.

At Durban the first thing we saw was a girl in white semaphoring like mad from the rocks. As we spelled out that she was trying to tell us that she was an Australian, we gave her three times three. Our difficulty in reading her message was not through her bad signalling but because of her speed. Doubt if we had a signaller on board so quick! This was not the last of our indebtedness to her, for when we got into the wharf she had a regiment of Kaffirs with sugar-bags full of apples and oranges, and while we were still fifty yards from the wharf she began throwing them through the portholes and into the hands of the men on deck. Not a half of one per cent fell short. She would have made a dandy bomber, and was a dandy all round.

In fact, the people of Durban were the most hospitable and patriotic of any people we had met. A delegation of citizens and ladies came down to the boat to inform us that we were the guests of the city and that everything was free to us. And later on we found them not to have exaggerated in the slightest. No one would accept money from us, though I don't think any of us tried to get diamond rings on these terms, but conductors on tram-cars and trains and motor-drivers and ticket-collectors at theatres one and all told us that our money was no good and gave to us their best seats.

This did not apply to the rickshaws, for they were run by Zulus and charged by the hour. You would climb in, the shafts would go up in the air, until you thought you were going to be tipped out at the back, and a herculean Zulu, decorated with horns and red and white stripes so that he might look like the devil, whom he, in reality, out-devilled, would rest himself on the body of the rick and trot along at a rate of six or seven miles an hour, quite able to keep up the pace all day. As a matter of fact, they never wanted to know where you were going, and even if you told them to take you to the post-office they would go round and round the block, never stopping to let you out unless you gave them a good poke in the ribs with your stick. Somewhere in their brains was an infernal taximeter adding up the dimes, and like their first cousins with the leather caps, they were determined to squeeze from you your last cent.

Apart from the ordinary entertainments we found that fetes and feasts had been arranged for our delectation at the Y. M. C. A. and soldiers' clubs, so that every minute of our stay was crowded enjoyment. Even those of us who preferred quieter pleasures were not without companions, and I know of no more delightful journey in the whole world than a trip by tram-car to the Zoo or out along the Berea. Durban has certainly one of the most picturesque situations of any city in the world, and the art of man has been used with taste to reinforce nature: there are no homes in more delightful surroundings with lovelier shrubbery and gardens than here. The people of Durban have not only an eye for beauty but they are very up to date and have a coaling apparatus that holds the world's record for speed in the coaling of ships.

Besides these two ports we made two other stops on the journey, but these were where there was no land. The first one was wholly involuntary, and not much to our liking, for through a breakdown in our engines we drifted helplessly for two days in the very centre of the danger zone of submarines.

Our next stop had also some connection with these sharks, for we sighted floating in mid-ocean two life-boats and we went close to them but there was no one on board—only oars and water-casks. That's all—just another mystery of the sea—no name, no clue. Another day we sighted a steamer hull down, evidently waterlogged, and we were going to her assistance when a cruiser came along and told us to go about our business and get out of harm's way as quickly as we could. This cruiser was just a little whiff of scented gum; and Australian air to us, for she was one of the best known of the Australian squadron.

There is a lonely island in the mid-Indian Ocean which is the only land for thousands of miles, and it is an unwritten law of the sea that every ship going that way should steam round it and watch carefully for signal-fires or signs of human occupation, for it is the place that shipwrecked sailors make for, and therefore there have been placed on the island several casks of fresh water and a supply of flour, and goats have been turned loose until they now overrun it. If a ship should find any one marooned thereon they are bound to replace all the water and flour that has been used. At one time there was a large fresh-water lake in the extinct crater of a volcano, but the sea has now broken through and made it salt. We steamed very close in, blew the siren, and had there been a pygmy there he would not have been overlooked as hundreds of trained eyes searched the rocks with glasses. We also got some fine photographs of this romantic isle in its waste of waters.

The officers' ward was on the upper deck and our nurse had a twin sister in another ward and there was not a particle of difference between them. If I was lying on the deck and should call out to our nurse as she passed to get me something, she would generally say, "I'll ask my sister," for, of course, it was the wrong one. There was endless confusion, for when we had a little tiff with our nurse, her sister would be sent to Coventry as well, and in a deck golf tournament there was great dispute over who won the ladies' prize, for both sisters claimed it. This matter could not be settled, as the umpire was not sure if he had credited the scores to the right one. The prize was a set of brushes and we told them it would have to do for both, which was all right, as we were sure they wore each other's clothes anyway. They told us they had made a vow when they married not to live in the same town for the husbands' sake!

The routine of the days was deadly monotonous with a break of a concert on Saturday and church on Sunday. Unfortunately, we had on board only two who could sing and one who thought he could recite. And even of those whose performance exceeded their own opinion we got tired before the journey ended. There were others who attempted to entertain us who afflicted us so much that after three performances we gave them the choice of suicide or having their tonsils cut, so the concerts petered out and the audience at the last one did not pay for the moving of the piano.

The shipping company who had transferred the ship to the Admiralty for the duration of the war still kept on the catering, and retained the same bill of fare as on their passenger trade. There was a good deal of variety and we always were able to get enjoyment with wondering what we would have for the next meal. They even helped us out a bit by calling the same dish by different names on different days and the same curry tasted differently under the names of Madras, Bengal, Simla, Ceylon, Indian, and Budgeree, and the cooking would even have satisfied Americans. The nurses were seated at one long table in the saloon and formed an island completely surrounded by officers. The twins were on opposite sides of the table, and of course we always found after dinner that we had been signalling to the wrong one. We observed a good deal of ceremony and always stood to attention until the nurses were seated, but the nurse who came in late and made us interrupt an interesting conversation with a tender chicken got plenty of black looks. When the matron rose we stood to attention again while they filed out and then carried on with the meal.

One morning there was great excitement. Up from the lower decks the electric current of expectancy ran until everyone's steps quickened and those of us who were on wooden legs beat a constant tattoo on the decks. What means this eager, anxious thrill? Tomorrow we would sight Australia! Only 43,200 seconds—720 minutes—or 12 hours, and once again we would view the fairest continent planted by God in the seas. Mind you, the first sight of Australia (going that way) is not very attractive. Rottenest Island, outside Fremantle, is sandy and barren and really not much to boast about, yet had you spread before us a scene from the Garden of Eden it had not charmed us half so much. For this was part of Australia, the land that we all called home. Back of that, for three thousand miles, stretched the country that held our ain folk and love and joy and home and what a man fights for and worships.

Every man had to be up on deck to see this sight. There were men there paralyzed, who had never moved during the whole long journey, but the saddest sight was to see the blind turning their sightless eyes in its direction and smiling with ecstasy, and maybe it looked more fair to these than to us who could see. How those boys cheered and cheered again! What a new spirit pervaded the ship! All day laughter and singing rang out, for there are no more patriotic troops in the world than the Australian soldiers, and, *east, west, home's best*. Like the old King of Ithaca we had wandered for years in many lands, but at last had returned home, and soon would have Penelope in our arms.

But only the Westralians were really home, and some of these had two or three hundred miles to go; for the rest of us there was still a fortnight more in the old ship as we sailed across the base of Australia to the eastern States.

CHAPTER 30

In Australia

When the ship drew in at the Melbourne wharf I made up my mind to escape the fuss and hero-worship, as I was a Queenslander and knew that none of my folks were among the crowd waiting at the gates. I went to the military landing-officer and asked him if I could not go out another way and dodge the procession. He said the orders were that every officer and man was to be driven in special cars to the hospital. I then went down onto the wharf and approached one of the ladies who looked as if she would play the game and I said to her:

"If I ride in your car, will you promise to do me a favour?"

She said: "I would do anything for you."

I then said: "Well, let me out as soon as we get outside the gate."

She demurred a good deal but I reminded her that no Australian girl I knew ever broke a promise. When we got outside I boarded a tram-car, which had not gone far before it had to stop to let the procession pass. Of course, everyone would see that I was a returned soldier, but there was nothing to show that I was *just* returned. I stood up in the tram-car with the rest of the passengers and cheered and threw cigarettes and remarked loudly to all and sundry: "Some more boys come back, eh?"

But my well-laid plans were entirely spoiled as my friends in the automobile called put, "Here, Knyvett, you dog, come out of that! Here's your place!" and I disgracefully subsided with many blushes, and had to endure all the way up to Melbourne the whispers and concentrated gaze of the whole tramful. I also *fell in* in another way, for when I rang up my uncle I found that he and his daughter were looking for me down at the wharf gates.

Two years ago the site of Caulfield Hospital was a wilderness of weeds and sand. Now it is an area of trim lawns and blazing gardens, bowling-greens, croquet-lawns, and tennis-courts, with comfortable huts, the gift of the people of Melbourne to their wounded soldiers, costing several hundred thousand dollars. As I had served with Victorian troops I was assigned to this hospital, although my home was over a thousand miles away in the northern state of Queensland. All who were fit to travel were given fourteen days disembarkation leave to visit their homes, but twelve of these days I had to spend in travel and only had two days at home after such long absence.

My wounds had healed but I was still paralyzed in my left leg, and the only attention I required was daily massage for an hour, and then another hour in the torture-chamber with an electric current grilling me. After this was over, I would go into the city, do the block, have afternoon tea, give an address at the Town Hall recruiting-depot, go to a theatre, and then as there seemed nothing else to be done, would return to the hospital. Such was my programme for ninety days. Sometimes I varied it by visiting the Zoo to commiserate with the wild animals on being caged.

There were many red-letter days when I was entertained by friends; but I am afraid I only squeaked when they expected roars—to be lionized was too unusual not to have stage fright a little.

The women in Australia are well organized and see to it that if a boy has a dull time it's his own fault. All the automobiles of the city were registered with the Volunteer Motor Corps, and each day certain of them were allotted to take wounded soldiers for picnics. We would generally be driven to some pretty suburb and there would be spread before us a feast of good things. At the end of the meal some of us felt like the little boy who said to his mother after the party: "I'm so tired, mummie, carry me up-stairs to bed, but don't bend me!"

There were concerts every night for the stay-at-home, but I only managed to get to one, given by the pupils of Madam Melba, which was a feast of harmony. After the programme refreshments were brought round by V. A. D.'s, whom the boys called, Very Artful Dodgers, but it was not the "Thank you for the cakes and tea!" that they dodged! We had a cricket-match, one-armers versus one-leggers, and we one-leggers were allowed to catch the ball in our hats; but the one-leggers lost as we were nearly all run out. Some of us being half-way down the pitch as the ball was thrown in, would throw one crutch at the wickets, knocking off the bails, when the umpire, who had no legs at all, would give his decision that we were stumped.

A huge Red Cross carnival was held near the hospital which netted about fifty thousand dollars. We were guests of honour, and on this occasion in the enormous crowds found Long John (one of the doctors, who was seven feet tall) very useful. He wondered why he was being followed about by several girls whom he did not know. We explained to him afterward that a good number of us who had *meets* had thought out the ingenious scheme of telling the girl to meet us at Long John, who would be the tallest object on the grounds. We told him that he didn't play the game properly by moving about so much, as our friends complained that they were just worn out following him round.

The carnival was one enormous fair—there were row on row of stalls, decorated in the colours of all the Allied flags, with the girls serving at them dressed in peasant costumes. The goods on the needlework-stalls represented the work of weeks—there were flower-stalls, sweet-stalls, produce-stalls, book-stalls, and in and out of the crowds girls went selling raffle-tickets for everything under the sun—from tray-cloths to automobiles and trips to Sydney. Ballyhoo-men stood at tent-doors, calling the crowd to come and see the performing kangaroo, the wild man from Borneo, or, "Every time you hit him you get a good cigar!" *Him* was a grinning black face stuck obligingly through a hole in a sheet. There were groups of tables and chairs under bright-coloured umbrellas, every here and there, where good things to eat were served all day. The fun lasted well into the night, when there were concerts, and dancing, and even the one-legged men tried to dance.

I don't think I had any other meals at the hospital than breakfast which I always had in bed. There was an orderly officer who was very unpopular as he had been months round the hospital and missed many chances of going to the front. One day the men played a trick on him. When he came into the dining-room to ask if there were any complaints one of them picked up a dish which was steaming hot and said:

"Look here, sir! What do you think of this?"

He picked up a spoon and tasted it. "Why, my man, that's very good soup! You're lucky to get such good food."

"But, sir, it's not soup, it's dish-water!" (Curtain.)

At last the Medical Board sat on my case and their decision left me gasping for breath, for they recommended that I be discharged as permanently unfit for further military service. But nature sometimes plays sorry pranks with medical decisions. Not more than a week after this, movement suddenly returned to my leg and I threw away my crutches and was able to walk almost as well as ever. About ten days after leaving hospital I had sailed back for France via America, but have not at the time of writing been able to get across the Atlantic.

CHAPTER 31

Using an Irishman's Nerve

I have been saving this for a separate chapter; for besides a natural hesitation in admitting that I am not *all there*, I want to have sufficient space in which to express my gratitude to the doctor who performed the operation and to the *unknown* who had his leg amputated, so providing me with a portion of his anatomy that I was in sore need of. Of course, in these days when surgical miracles are happening continually there is nothing outstanding about this operation, and surgeons have wonderful opportunities in a military hospital, where there are so many spare human parts lying about to patch up a man with. I quite believe that from three smashed men they could make a whole one, which, after all, would not be such a marvel when one remembers that they are continually grafting bones and nerves, and I for one would not like to say that in the next war they may not be able to cure a man who has lost his head entirely, and as a matter of fact, one of the San Francisco papers informed its readers (and as in this country the impossible of yesterday happens today, no doubt they believed it to be true) that I had had another man's leg grafted onto me. After such a statement it is an anti-climax to have to inform the public that it was only a portion of nerve that was grafted.

I had been lying in hospital several weeks before I got worried about the fact that I could not move my leg. Then when the great-hearted, plain-faced doctor who was attending to me said, "How's the man of many wounds this morning?"

I asked: "Why is it my leg is dead?"

He said: "We're only waiting for the wounds to heal until we test it."

And sure enough a day or two later I was put in the electric chair for reactions. When the current was put onto my right leg I howled and twisted, but with twice the current on my left leg nothing happened, as I felt nothing. Some days later a great nerve specialist operated on me and when I came back to this workaday world from the land of fancy, whither the ether had borne me, I was informed that a portion of nerve had been grafted in my leg and that in about three months I might be able to use it.

At this time I had no idea from whom the portion of nerve came. I did not like to inquire, for I was afraid that if I met its previous owner I might be prejudiced against it. Every portion of one's body is so closely related to the rest that I was afraid if his face did not suit my fancy I might subconsciously come to resemble him. But whenever I met one-legged men in the corridors or concert-hall I would try to pick out the one I would most like to receive such an intimate gift from. Some of these had a refined, delicate appearance, and I immediately feared that I would grow tender footed, while others looked like pugilists and I immediately imagined my foot was becoming calloused and might become longer than the other.

So purposely I remained in ignorance of the religion and nationality of my new nerve. Once for a whole day I sweat blood lest it might be a German, and then I plucked up courage to ask if there were any Germans in the hospital, and when I learned that there were not I slept like a child for many hours. On Saturdays I felt it might be a Jew or a Seventh-Day Adventist, but then it did not work on other days either, so I thought it must be I. W. W., I Won't Work as they are called in Australia. Then one day I was sure it was from one of the same religion as myself, for that leg was perspiring alone, and in the outback country in Australia, where the temperature reaches one hundred and twenty degrees in the shade, the Presbyterian Church is sometimes called Perspiration. At any rate, I read in a paper that in one town the three churches were Anglican, Roman Catholic, and Perspiration. As to nationality it might be Scotch, as I had to be *verra cautious* in moving it, or English, being so *sensitive* to the touch. It was only after movement returned that I was quite sure it was Irish! For ever since then the Home Rule controversy has been going on in my body, for when I want to place my foot in a certain position, it's bound to try and go some other way. You can see from all this that I don't know much about nerves, and I even wonder sometimes whether, if they put in my leg a nerve from an arm, I might not try to shake hands with it like the armless man in the circus, or, if it happened to belong to the opposite leg, whether or not I would be pigeon-toed.

I sometimes wonder if the donor of this piece of nerve still *feels it* in his own leg, for, months after a man has lost his leg, he still feels it there. There was one man in the hospital who had lost both legs and screamed with pain every night because his toes were twisted, and it was only when they had dug up his feet and straightened out his toes that he got rest.

There are nerves and *nerves*, and I am sure that the grafting in me of this piece from the *nerves* of an Irishman has given to me more *nerve* than I ever had in my life before, else how could I have written this book?

Part 6
Meditations in the Trenches

Chapter 32

The Right Infantry Weapons

I know scores of men who have been months in the trenches and over the top in several attacks who have never fired a shot out of their rifles. In fact, it is very, very rarely that the man in the trenches gets a chance to aim at an enemy at a greater range than a hundred yards. There are thousands of men whom I know who believe that the long-range rifles used in our army today are useless weapons. A much more serviceable gun to repel a counter-attack would be one firing buckshot like a pump-gun. The bullets from our high-velocity rifles frequently pass through the body of a man at a close range and he is not even conscious of having been hit and continues to come on with as great fury as before. The pellets scattering from a shotgun at a range of a hundred yards or less would do him more damage and be far more certain to stop him. In an actual charge our present rifle is more than useless—it is an encumbrance, and when at grips with the enemy in his own trenches it is often a fatal handicap. With a bayonet at the end it is far too long, and in a trench two to four feet wide it cannot be used with much effect. I have known our men repeatedly to unship the bayonet and take it in their hands, throwing the rifle away. Another danger is that men will fire their rifles down an enemy trench and these high-velocity bullets will pass right through the bodies of the one or two of the enemy in front of him and frequently kill his own comrade beyond. Remember, in a fight in a trench friend and foe are mixed up together and many of our men have been unconsciously shot by their fellows. In every regiment a small squad of picked marksmen only should have these long-range rifles, with the addition of telescopic sights. The average man does not take exact aim before firing, and nearly all the shots go high. If it were not for bombs and machine-guns the enemy could always succeed in getting to our trenches with very little loss. It should be remembered, too, how closely, in an attack, we follow our own barrage—it is impossible to see to fire through it.

The system of barrage fighting that we now use has made warfare as much a hand-to-hand business as it was in olden times and we must go back a good deal to old-fashioned weapons, as we have to a great extent to old-fashioned armour. The picked snipers or sharpshooters could be placed in points of vantage to pick off any of the enemy who exposed themselves and a score of them in each company would get very few shots in a day.

Another weapon that infantry should be armed with is a hand-bayonet as there is no advantage whatever in the long reach that our present rifle and bayonet gives. As a matter of fact, many of our men have been killed through driving their bayonet too far into the body of their opponent, not being able to draw it out, thus being helpless when attacked by another of the enemy. It is no use telling men not to drive their bayonet in more than three or four inches, for in the speed and fury of a charge they will always drive it in right up to the hilt, and while we retain this out-of-date weapon we should certainly put a guard on it not further than six inches from the point. I have used a hand-bayonet which sticks out from the fist like a knuckle-duster and is about six inches long. The shock of the blow is taken on the forearm which also has an iron plate running down it on which to receive the thrust of one's opponent. This is the natural weapon for the Anglo-Saxon, as the fist and arm is used exactly as in boxing. If an enemy comes at you with a bayonet it is the natural and easy thing to throw up your arm and ward it off. The iron plate saves your arm being cut; you are in under his guard; seize his rifle with your left hand and punch with your right, driving the knife home the six inches, which is all that is necessary. I have been in and seen a number of bayonet charges and I am quite satisfied that the parries and thrusts that we teach the infantryman are only of value to get him used to handling his rifle. After that it would be a good thing for him to forget them.

There are only two things that it is essential to remember when you go into a bayonet charge. The first is that *the most determined man will win*. I have known champion men-at-arms killed by a bayonet in their first charge and other little fellows who were no good in the practice combats kill their man every time. If you go into a bayonet charge with the idea of disarming your opponent and taking him prisoner you will most certainly be killed. But if you are quite sure in your own mind that you are going to kill every man who comes against you, you will do it. Your determination impresses itself upon the man you attack and he will be beaten before you reach him. The other thing that it is wise to remember is to make your opponent attack you on your left side. If he attacks you on the right you have to parry him and then thrust, but for an attack on the left side the action of parrying will bring the toe of your butt into his jaw or ribs, disabling him, and it is a good thing to use your knee at the same time.

The general-staff officers who decide how an army should be weaponed never do the actual fighting and few junior officers or men feel competent to offer their advice. I am quite confident that a majority of the fighters would agree with the foregoing opinions, and I would like the chance of taking a company armed as I have suggested into action, and would be quite satisfied of their superiority to any troops on the front.

CHAPTER 33

The Forcing-House of Bestiality

The Germans have given to us an illustration, though such was not needed by thinking men to convince them of its truth, of the fact that the beast in humanity only requires encouragement to make us more bestial than any wild thing of the jungle or even the filthy cur of the streets. If any man takes as his guiding principle the devilish doctrine that *the end justified the means* he will soon become a menace to his fellows and any good impulses that he may originally have will pass away. The German Government made savagery, brutality, and bestiality a deliberate policy, and now it is their unconscious impulse. Germany is paying a terrible penalty in the degradation and demoralization of her whole people for having given the direction of the country into the hands of the Devil in exchange for power, and the German army is today a forcing-house for bestiality and there is no atmosphere in the whole world that so conduces to evil. In the beginning of the war letters and statements of prisoners showed that there were then many decent Germans who were horrified at the abominations they had seen and committed at the command of their government. But latterly, you cannot find any trace of this feeling. Now they gloat over it.

There is no one in the world today except those who are of like mind who do not know that the story of the German atrocities is true, for Germany has *admitted* enough crimes to convince any sane man that she would stick at nothing. No action could be too cruel, no deed too beastly, no torture too diabolical, no insult too keen, no impulse too filthy, no disfigurement too hideous, no vandalism too shocking, no destruction too complete, no stooping too low that Germany would hesitate to do where she has opportunity. When Germany boasted of the murder by drowning of women and babes on the high seas she proclaimed to the world that she was a criminal, and we do not need to have any other crimes proven to convince us that, while there is such a thing as justice, she must not go unpunished.

Criminals have been forgiven, but not before they are repentant; *Safety*, as well as *Justice*, demands that the murderer, the assassin, the rapist shall not go free. Germany has not only committed all these crimes, but her theologians and professors have condoned them. The man who counsels forgiveness to Germany adds hypocrisy to the will to commit the same crimes. To forgive, we are told, is divine, but the Divine does not forgive without repentance. Has Germany shown signs of repentance yet? Well, then, the man who talks of forgiveness to Germany before she is on her knees begging for forgiveness is an enemy of peace and a condoner of crime.

It is so easy for those who have not suffered to tell the victims to forgive. *We* do not go in nightly dread lest in the morning we should have to rake among the ruins of our homes for the mangled body of our baby! We do not have to work in daily fear lest we should have to return to an empty house whence wife or daughter have been dragged by brutal hands! *For three years* the people of London and Paris and thousands of other cities have never known but that at any moment their house might be brought down in ruins about their ears, entombing all that they hold dear! *For three years* the men of northern France and Belgium have never known but that while they were working, under compulsion, against the life of their own blood and country in a German munitions factory, some soldiers might not be calling at their homes to take the woman that they love God alone knows where! These very things have happened to tens of thousands. Week after week the human hawks come over London, and ever the toll of civilians and women and babies done to death grows larger! One hundred thousand young girls were taken from Lille and other cities away from knowledge or protection of their kin, and until recently we had no news of any of them, but some have been thrown into Switzerland, of no further use to Germany; used up like sucked lemons, they are cast aside for the Swiss to feed. Germany has in her maw today more than ten millions of slaves.

In America or Australia there are no hospitals where lie thousands of girls too young to become mothers who have been raped. We have not hundreds of boys who will never become men. A young girl said to me: "There is a baby coming; it is a *boche*; when it is born I will cut its throat!"

A woman showed me on an *estaminet* floor the blood-stains of her own baby butchered before her eyes. These were French women, not ours. But what if they had been? Your sister! Your mother! Your wife! And they might have been but for the accident of geography. Would you then have felt as bitter as these people? Or would you still have kindly feelings to Germany and not want to humiliate her. There may be beings who could see daughter violated or brother mutilated without taking personal vengeance, but such should not be permitted to breathe the air with *men*.

The only people who have a right to say what punishment shall be meted out to Germany for her misdeeds, are the women of France, of Belgium, of Poland, of Serbia, of Rumania, of Italy, who have suffered these things; and if any one, King or President, Parliament or Pope, dares stand between these people and their just wrath they deserve to be pilloried in the minds of men as condoners of crime, as accessories after the fact.

The only chance for permanent peace, and guarantee that these abominable crimes shall not be committed again, is that we should so punish Germany that she shall realize that war does not *pay*, and that the whole earth may know that no nation can commit these atrocities and go unpunished.

Chapter 34

The Psychology of Fear

The observation of men in many circumstances of peril has quite convinced me that it is those who are most afraid that do the bravest deeds. I do not mean that the fact that they are afraid increases the difficulty of the doing, because it lessens it. It is fear that drives men to heroism! And many a man attempts the superhuman feat of courage not to show to others that he is no coward, but as evidence in the court of his own judgment, to disprove the accusations of conscience, which asserts he is craven. The old illustration of one soldier who accused another of having no bravery because he had no fear, by saying, "If you were as much afraid as I am you would have run away long ago," is not true to life, for it is the man of dulled feelings that is the first to run, and the "man who is afraid of being afraid" who stays at his post to the last. I have ever found that the best scouts, men who must generally work alone in the dark, are those of highly strung nervous temperaments. I have noticed, too, that our best airmen were of the same type, for if you go into any mess of pilots on the front you will see them always fidgeting, their hands never still, betraying nervousness. I have gone down the trench before a charge and seen the men with teeth chattering and blanched faces, but at the appointed second these men go over the top, none hesitating, every man performing prodigies of valour; not one but was a hero, yet not one that was not afraid.

There must be something wrong with the make-up of a man who under modern artillery-fire is not afraid. There are no nerves that do not break down eventually under the strain, but the man who shrinks from a shadow, and shudders at the touch of cold mud does his job with care and walks unhesitatingly into the mouth of hell. I have seen our signallers mending the telephone-wire under fire; each time it would break they would curse and tremble, but immediately go out and repair it accurately, slowly, no skimped work, repeating the performance again and again. There is in our spirit some reserve force which on occasion the will uses to stiffen resolution—the second wind of determination.

Fear is the *purgative of the soul*! There is nothing so wholesome for a man as to be scared to death! Nothing that so drives out the littlenesses that poison his life and set up the *toxaemia* of selfishness. Many a man that before the war made the acquiring of wealth or the gaining of the plaudits of his friends his chief aim, now finds that these things have no appeal for him. For he has been to the edge of life and looked into the abyss, and fear has stripped from him the rags of self-adornment; and standing naked between the worlds his soul has found that it needs no beautifying but the cleansing of self-forgetfulness.

This war is one of the greatest blessings this world has ever known, for it has brought to us fear of selfish force, fear of the engines of our own construction, fear of isolation in world politics, fear of secret diplomacy, fear of an unguarded peace, fear of an unprepared future, fear of an undisciplined people, fear of an irresponsible government, and, above all *the fear of forgetting*!

But there is another reason why a man in battle, though afraid, does not fail. The fact is that men in a regiment or an army are not under the domination of their own will at all, but of the collective will of the whole. That is why some regiments are so anxious to keep alive their traditions, and emblazon their battles on their colours. That is why we devote so much time in the training of young recruits to the knowledge of the esprit de corps of the regiment. That is why the regulars are always the best fighters. It is not their longer training, for that is a handicap with new methods of warfare. It is not because of their superior discipline, for the territorials have not lacked perfect discipline. But there is an atmosphere in the regular regiments that makes one brother that goes into the regulars a better soldier than the other that enlists in militia. This atmosphere is compounded of pride in past achievements and confidence that the colours that have never been lowered, though shot down on many a field, cannot be shamed today. The victors of many engagements have an enormous advantage in battle. No one expected anything but the most heroic courage from the British regulars who had never failed when called upon, but everyone was not a little anxious how Kitchener's would stand their first ordeal of fire.

Every mass of men has, besides the will and mind of each one of them, a collective will and mind. Every town has this—who has not felt, on entering a town and viewing its shops and people, a certain pushing toward behaviour—some towns tend to make one frivolous, others grave. I know a city which, every time I enter, makes me think when last I was in church, while there is another in which I always want to dance or view the Follies. Have you not seen countrymen in town, whose clothes proclaim that they have never been out later than nine o'clock in a lifetime, trying to be the gay Lothario, drinking wine in a cabaret? Every house has its personality made up of the collective minds of the people who inhabit it. Take your child to one strange house and he will fidget uncomfortably on the edge of his chair; but take him to another, just as strange, and he will romp about without hesitation. Children are like the canaries we use to detect the presence of poisonous gases, most sensitive to atmosphere.

In the same way an army has *one will*, and that is why in battle you will not see one man fail, or there will be panic and all will fail. In every army there are individual men weak in resolution who, left to themselves, would run away; but as the *mind* of the army as a whole is courageous, so they are swept along in spite of themselves. The German army has *one mind* for bestiality, and the Allied army has *one mind* for victory.

CHAPTER 35

The Splendour of the Present Opportunity

To those who are thrilled by the old-time tales of adventurous chivalry or moved by the narrative of high endeavour and heroic achievement for some noble ideal, I bring a conception of the marvellous glory of these present days. We have been wont to sing of the times when thousands left home and comfort on a Holy Crusade, but the Crusaders of these days are numbered in millions.

Never were there such stirring times as these, never since the first tick of time have the hours been so crowded! Never before did so many men live nobly or die bravely. The young knights from many lands are seeking the Holy Grail, and finding it in forgetfulness of self and in sacrifice for their fellows. You and I are living today among the deeds of men that make the deeds of the heroes of past times pale into insignificance. Never were there bred men of such large and heroic mould as the men of today.

Here's a trench—on which a shell falls—and where one shell falls another always follows in the same place;—the shell blows in a dugout and there is little chance that the men sheltering therein shall be alive, yet those on either side, knowing that another shell will fall in a second or so, in utter forgetfulness of self leap in and with their bare fingers scrape away the dirt lest haply there should be some life yet remaining in this quivering, mangled human flesh.

Oh! What chances the men of earth have today to be as God! The highest conception any religion has given us of God is that he is one that would sacrifice himself—"Greater love hath no man than this that he lay down his life for his friends"—and today they're doing it by the million. Every moment is adding names to the honour-roll of heaven of men who follow in His steps.

Have you conceived that the uniting together of the nations that love peace in this struggle will do more to guarantee peace in the future than anything else that has ever happened in world politics,—that it will join France, Britain, and America into a trinity of free peoples who will prevent war, at least for many generations? We are being bound together by the strongest tie that ever tied nation to nation, that ever bound one people to another, not by political treaties that may be torn up, but by the great tie of common bloodshed in a common cause on a common soil. That narrow lane that stretches from Switzerland to the sea is the great international cemetery, and for many generations it will be the Mecca of pilgrimages from all our countries. The wreaths of America will mingle with the immortelles of France and the flowers from Britain and the pilgrims shall there get to know, understand, and love each other as they engage in the holy task of paying a common tribute to their common dead. Shall not the mingling blood of Frenchmen, Britons, and Americans make the flowers of peace to grow? They never had such soil before.

There is being created, also, in all our countries a new aristocracy—the aristocracy of courage. We never had a chance up till now to prove who were our real, our best people, and we have been accustomed to measure our citizens by the false and small standards of wealth, birth, and intellect. Well! There has been given to us today a new standard whereby we can measure ourselves, the standard of courage, sacrifice, and service. Nobody in England cares today whether you are descended from William the Conqueror or not! No one will care in America whether your ancestor came over in the Mayflower, or whether he signed the Declaration of Independence! Every American has a chance today of signing a far greater declaration than that great one of '76—the declaration of personal willingness to sacrifice all on the altar of liberty. In England, in America, in Australia, in all the countries of the world in the days that are to be, men and women will make their boast in this one thing, or have no cause for boasting at all, of the part that they had in this fight, the greatest fight that has ever been waged for liberty, for righteousness, and for the virtue of womanhood.

What a splendid opportunity it is for us to be able to personally pay the price of liberty. How easy to forget that freedom has either to be earned by ourselves or enjoyed because someone else has paid the price for us. Had we not forgotten in our countries that the democracy that we boast of is no credit to us because it was won by the blood of other men? Men died that we might be able to govern ourselves! Women carried heart-ache and loneliness to the grave that we might make our own laws!

Liberty! Such an easy word to mouth, but how precious in the sight of God! Liberty is one of the treasures of heaven and only committed to men at great cost, lest they should undervalue it.

In these great and wonderful times there has been given to us the glorious opportunity to earn our own liberty, to prove our own personal right to citizenship in a free country.

You may not be able to pay in good, red blood, you may not be able to pay much in the coin of the republic, but if each of us does not pay in whatsoever coin we have, there will come soon to us the days in which we shall realize that we are thieves and robbers, enjoying that to which we have no right, won so hardly with the deaths and wounds of men and the salt tears of women. In the New World that shall be born after the birth-pangs of the present days, we shall realize that we have no place, our souls shall shrink and shrivel as we gaze on the honour scars of those who have paid, and we shall be elbowed to the outskirts of the crowd, as the people bow before the men whom the President and people delight to honour—the men sightless, the men limbless, the memory of the men lifeless.

Chapter 36

Not a Fight for Race but for Right

I have no patience with the waterish sentiment that suggests that the lines of the Germans in America and Australia have fallen in hard places because they are called upon to take up arms against their own blood. For this is not a war of race, but of right! It is not a war of Britons, Americans, and French against Germans and Austrians! It is a war of men in all nations against beasts!

There is something in all of us that is stronger than kinship, higher than citizenship—manhood—and everyone who is a man, though he be of German blood will join us in this struggle against the monster that has devoured women and children and many fair lands.

We have in the Australian army one general of German blood, another of Austrian, and hundreds of men of both, but they have been fighting loyally with us, because they were men and could not be held back from striking at tyranny and wrong. Remember, in the Australian army all are volunteers.

Everyone now knows what Germany stands for and the menace she is to the future of the world if her power is not destroyed, and everyone who does not help to defeat her is an ally of the Kaiser and helping him to win the war.

The Judge is today separating the sheep from the goats, not according to nationality, but according to how they stand in this strife for right, for never was there a cause so divinely right as the cause of the Allies, and never a cause so devilishly wrong as that of the Germans.

The great mass of the German people have shown themselves to be on the side of evil, but every German in our own countries is given a chance in the present days to prove himself a man who hates brutality and cruelty and wrong, or by standing aloof from helping us show that he has the will to do these things as his kinsman in France. These should be given the same medicine as the Kaiser's millions over there. We should also root out the Kaiser's secret allies in our midst, some of them not of German blood, who for pay do his dirty work, never forgetting also that the neutral and the lukewarm at this present juncture are also our enemies and have their hands stained with the blood of our kin who die for this cause.

Washington when he called on the English colonists in this country to resist the German mercenaries of the German King of England did not bewail the fate that compelled them to fight against their own country and where their kin dwelt. No! For his cause was just and just-minded men must support it though a sword pierced their own hearts.

Lincoln when he called on the people of the Northern States to free the slaves did not exempt those who had friends or kin down South, but he called on everyone who was free to strike a blow for the freedom of other men, though in so doing they should be cutting off their own right arms.

In this war we are not only fighting to free millions who are held in a far worse slavery than ever the negro was in, but we are fighting for our own liberty and that of our children, which has been directly attacked. Not all Germans are bestial and cruel, with no regard for honour, but just how many of them are not remains for the American and Australian citizens of German descent to prove.

Not all Britishers and Americans and Frenchmen are willing to sacrifice themselves in our righteous cause—there are traitors even here, and these I would rather shoot than the enemy in France.

There never was a more damnable doctrine promulgated on the face of the earth than that of "My country, right or wrong." Free men could never subscribe to such a doctrine. We have no right to call upon people to take up arms because the government has declared war, but because the government was *right* in declaring war. Those who oppose the government in this are not traitors to a party or a majority, but traitors to the country and to right.

The two great camps in which the world is divided today will be known in history as those who loved liberty more than life and those who loved dominion more than right. Maybe the names of the races will be forgotten but the memory of the opposing principles will abide.

CHAPTER 37

Keeping Faith With the Dead

While here and there politicians grow faint-hearted, the army fights on with cheerfulness. It would be a cure for pessimism of the deepest black to go to the trenches for a while. There all is cheery optimism, no doubt at all about the final outcome, and no talk of peace. I have never heard one man in the army talk or hint of peace or dream of it, for they know that it cannot be yet. The only people who shall declare peace will be the army—no politicians, no parliament, or government—for the army today is a citizen army and large enough to change any government that is weak-kneed, and they shall allow parliament to grant peace only when they are ready, and that shall not be until we have gained a certain victory.

Prime Minister Lloyd George gave us three words over a year ago that are still the beacon-lights of the army, and we shall not reach port unless they are our guiding lights. They were *reparation*, *restoration*, and *guarantees*, and anything less would be a betrayal of France and Belgium and an insult to the wounded and a defaming of the dead.

The army and people of the allied countries have already paid too much not to have the goods delivered.

Do you think, for example, that we Australian boys are going back to our country without having gained that for which we came these twelve thousand miles and have fought so long, and lost so much?

Do you think that I am going back to Australia well and sound to face the mothers of my scouts, and when they come and ask me how their boys died, I will have to say; "Well! Here I am, well and strong, still able to put up a fight, and your son lies over there, his bones rotting on a foreign soil, and all in vain. The blood of him who to you was more precious than any prince or king that ever lived has been poured out like water and uselessly"?

Listen! Here is something of what Australia has paid. There has never been a day for three years that hundreds of Australian wives have not been made widows. There has not been a single week that there has not been more than a full page of casualties in our daily papers. Every woman in Australia if she has not seen there the name of her near kin has seen the name of someone that she knows. I know a father and five sons that have all been killed. Within fifty miles of one town that I know there is not a man under fifty years of age. There are ranches and farms that will go back to the primeval wilderness, the fences will rot and fall down, and the rabbits and kangaroos will overrun them again, because the men who were developing them are gone and there are none to take their places. Never was there a country so starved for men, and sixty thousand are gone forever or maimed for life. Tell me, where are we going to replace these men? No country in the world could so ill afford to lose its young men, the future fathers of the race, for we have still our pioneering to do, a continent larger than the United States, with about the population of New York.

Outside our Australian cities there are some large cemeteries, as we mostly have only one for each city, but the largest of our cemeteries does not lie on Australian soil. There are more Australian dead buried in Egypt than in any cemetery in our own country. On Gallipoli, in enemy hands, are the graves of thousands of our sacred dead. There are more of our unburied dead whitening in No Man's Land in France than have ever been laid to rest by reverent hands in a God's acre at home. Think of all that we have paid in blood and tears and heartache. But, perhaps, more than this has been paid in pain and sweat. Many have been in those trenches more than three years. Consider their sufferings! The unnatural life, like rats in a hole, the nerve-strain, the insufficient food, the scanty clothing. What we have paid, Canada has paid, South Africa has paid, but Britain and France, how much more! And Belgium, and Serbia, and Poland, and Rumania, and Italy. What a price to pay for an insecure peace, an enemy still with power to harm.

We might erect to our fallen dead the most magnificent monument that this world has ever seen, we might built it in marble, and stud it with gems, and have the greatest poets and artists decorate it, but it would be a mockery and a sham.

The only monument that we dare erect to our fallen dead, the only monument that would not be a dishonour to them and a shame and eternal disgrace to us is *the monument of victory.*

And the army will never quit until we have sure victory, for we dare not break faith with our dead.

These lines of a Canadian soldier, Colonel McCrae, who has made the last sacrifice are an epitome of the army's spirit:

In Flanders' fields the poppies grow
Between the crosses, row on row,
That mark our place,
While in the sky the larks,
Still bravely singing,
Fly unheard amid the guns.
We are the Dead—
Short days ago we lived, felt dawn, saw sunsets glow,
Loved and were loved—and now we lie
In Flanders' fields——

Take up our quarrel with the foe.
To you from failing hands we throw
The torch—be yours to bear it high—
If ye break faith with us who die,
We shall not sleep though poppies grow
In Flanders' fields.

But a Short Time to Live
By Leslie Coulson, killed in action

Our little hour—how swift it flies
When poppies flare and lilies smile;
How soon the fleeting minute dies,
Leaving us but a little while
To dream our dream, to sing our song
To pick the fruit, to pluck the flower,
The Gods—they do not give us long—
One little hour.

Our little hour—how short it is
When Love with dew-eyed loveliness
Raises her lips for ours to kiss
And dies within our first caress.
Youth flickers out like windblown flame,
Sweets of today tomorrow sour,
For Time and Death, relentless, claim
One little hour.

Our little hour,—how short a time
To wage our wars, to fan our fates,
To take our fill of armoured crime,
To troop our banner, storm the gates.
Blood on the sword, our eyes blood-red,
Blind in our puny reign of power,
Do we forget how soon is sped
One little hour?

Our little hour—how soon it dies;
How short a time to tell our beads,
To chant our feeble Litanies,
To think sweet thoughts, to do good deeds,
The altar lights grow pale and dim,
The bells hang silent in the tower,
So passes with the dying hymn,
Our little hour.

Over the Top With the Third Australian Division

by G. P. Cuttriss

Illustrated by Neil McBeath

Major-General Sir John Monash, K.C.B., V.D.

Contents

Preface	239
Introduction	241
From 'There' to 'Here'	245
Australians—in Various Moods	252
Sunday, Somewhere in France	259
Soldiers' Superstitions	263
On the Eve of Battle	269
Over the Top	272
Shells: a Few Smiles and a Contrast	278
Messines	286
Bill the Bugler	290
A Tragedy of the War	293
Recreation Behind the Lines	298
For the Cause of the Empire	306
Our Heroic Dead	308
The Silver Lining	309

To the fadeless memory of our heroic dead
and to those who have lost
this brief volume of sketch and story is dedicated,
in unstinted admiration,
in affectionate sympathy,
and in the unshakeable belief that

As sure as God's in heaven,
As sure as He stands for right,
As sure as the Hun this wrong hath done,
So surely we'll win this fight.

The Author

Preface

In response to numerous requests from the 'boys,' this brief volume of story and sketch is published. It makes no pretension to literary merit, neither is it intended to serve as a history of the Division. The indulgence of those who may read is earnestly solicited, in view of the work having been prepared amidst the trying and thrilling experiences so common to active service. The fighting history of the Australian Forces is one long series of magnificent achievements, beginning on that day of sacred and glorious memory, April 25, 1915. Ever since that wonderful test of capacity and courage the Australians have advanced from victory to victory, and have won for themselves a splendid reputation. Details of training, raids, engagements, and tactical features have been purposely omitted. The more serious aspect will be written by others. In deference to Mr. Censor, names of places and persons have been suppressed, but such omissions will not detract from the interest of the book. 'Over the Top with the Third Australian Division' is illustrative of that big-hearted, devil-may-care style of the Australians, the men who can see the brighter side of life under the most distracting circumstances and most unpromising conditions. In the pages that follow, some incidents of the life of the men may help to pass away a pleasant hour and serve as a reminder of events, past and gone, but which will ever be fresh to those whose immediate interests attach to the Third Australian Division.

G. P. *Cuttriss*

Introduction

At the outbreak of the World War in August, 1914, the Australian as a soldier was an unknown quantity. It is quite true that in the previous campaigns in the Soudan and in South Africa, Australia had been represented, and that a sprinkling of native-born Australians had taken service in the Imperial armies. The performances of these pioneers of Australia in arms were creditable, and the reputation which they had earned was full of promise. But, viewed in their proper perspective, these contributions to Imperial Defence were no true index of the capacity of the Australian nation to raise and maintain a great army worthy and able in all details to take its place in a world war, beside the armies of the great and historic civilizations of the Old World.

No Australian, nor least of all those among them who had laboured in times of peace to prepare the way for a great national effort, whenever the call to action should come, ever doubted the capacity of the nation worthily to respond; but while the magnitude and quality of the possible effort might well have been doubted by our Imperial authorities and our Allies, and while it was certainly regarded as negligible by our enemies, the result in achievement has exceeded, in a mighty degree, the most optimistic hopes even of those who knew or thought they knew what Australia was capable of.

For, today, Australia has, besides its substantial contribution to the Naval Forces of the Empire, actually in being a land army of five divisions and two mounted divisions, fully officered, fully equipped, and stamped with the seal of brilliantly successful performance; and has created and maintained all the hundred and one national activities upon which such an achievement depends.

We are still too close to the picture to realize the miracle which has been wrought, or to understand in all their breadth the factors on which it has depended; but, fundamentally, and overshadowing all other factors, the result is based upon the character of the Australian people, and upon the personality of the Australian soldier.

It is the latter factor which, to one who has been for so long in intimate daily contact with him, makes the closest appeal. It is from that close association, from the knowledge born of experience of him in every phase of his daily life, that the Australian can be proclaimed as second to none in the world both as a soldier and as a fighting man.

For these things are not synonymous, and the first lesson that every recruit has to learn is that they are not synonymous; that the thing which converts a mere fighting man into a soldier is the sense of discipline. This word 'discipline' is often cruelly misused and misunderstood. Upon it, in its broadest and truest sense, depends the capacity of men, in the aggregate, for successful concerted action.

It is precisely because the Australian is born with and develops in his national life the very instinct of discipline that he has been enabled to prove himself so successful a soldier. He obeys constituted authority because he knows that success depends upon his doing so, whether his activities are devoted to the interests of his football team or his industrial organization or his regiment. He has an infinite capacity for 'team' work. And he brings to bear upon that work a high order of intelligence and understanding. In his other splendid qualities, his self-reliance, his devotion to his cause and his comrades, and his unfailing cheerfulness under hardship and distress, he displays other manifestations of that same instinct of discipline.

Some day cold and formal histories will record the deeds and performances of the Australian soldiery; but it is not to them that we shall turn for an illumination of his true character. It is to stories such as these which follow, of his daily life, of his psychology, of his personality, that we must look. And we shall look not in vain, when, as in the following pages, the tale has been written down by one of themselves, who has lived and worked among them, and who understands them in a spirit of true sympathy and comradeship.

The Author of these sketches is himself true to his type, and an embodiment of all that is most worthy and most admirable in the Australian soldier.
John Monash
Major-General

From 'There' to 'Here'

Towards the end of November, 1916, our hopes of moving out from 'where we then were' to 'where we now are' materialized to the evident satisfaction of all. Few, if any, cared as to our probable destination; the chief interest centred in the fact that we were to start for the Front. The time spent Somewhere in the Motherland was by no means wasted. Due regard had been paid to the training of the men, who reached a standard of efficiency which earned for the Division a reputation second to none. While in England the Third was the subject of scorn and bitter criticism. Older Divisions could not forget, and possibly regretted, the fact that they had had no such prolonged training in mock trenches and in inglorious safety. However, since leaving England the Division has lived down the scorn that was heaped upon it, by upholding the traditions handed down by older and more war-worn units. Recently the Division was referred to by a noted General as one of the best equipped and most efficient units not only amongst the Overseas Divisions but of the whole Army in France.

The arrangements for our moving out were approximately perfect. There was no hitch. The military machine, like the Tanks of recent fame, over-rides or brushes to one side all obstacles. There was manifest among all ranks an eagerness to leave nothing undone that would in any way facilitate entraining and embarkation. The knowledge that we were at last on our way to the 'Dinkum' thing had the effect of leading us to take a more serious view of the situation. It is surprising, however, how soon men become attached to a place; and though the conditions at Lark Hill were in no sense ideal, it had been our home for several months and we were loath to leave. Perhaps the thought that many of us might possibly never return inspired the longing looks that were directed towards the camp as we marched on our way to the station. Who of those who took part in that march will forget the cheers with which we were greeted by the residents of that picturesquely situated village as we trudged along its winding road? We had enjoyed their hospitality, and we appreciated their cordial wishes for success and safety.

The task of entraining a large body of men was expertly accomplished, and after a brief delay we were speeding in the direction of the port of embarkation. The train journey was practically without event. The men were disposed to be quiet. On arrival at the quay parties were detailed to assist in putting mails and equipment aboard the transports. Punctually at the hour advised we trooped aboard the ships that were to convey us across the water. There was very little accommodation for men, but they squeezed in and made the best of the situation. The trip across was not as comfortable as it might have been, but its duration was so brief that the discomfort was scarcely worth serious thought. The transports cast anchor off the harbour early the following morning, but it was not until late in the afternoon that they were berthed alongside the wharf. Scarcely had the transports touched the wharf-side when they commenced to disgorge their living freight.

From the waterside we marched to No. 1 Rest Camp, situated on the summit of a hill on the outskirts of the town. The camp was reached some time after darkness had settled down over the land. The weather was most miserable. The air was charged with icy blasts, and rain fell continuously throughout the night. The least said about our impressions and experiences during our brief stay in that camp the better; suffice to state that one of the most miserable memories that can be recalled in connexion with our experiences on active service is associated with No. 1 Rest Camp.

The following morning we marched to the main railway station and entrained for the Front. The accommodation provided was fairly comfortable, though the carriages had been used more for carrying mules than men. The train journey extended over thirty hours. All along the route there were evidences of military activity

THE TRIP ACROSS WAS NOT AS COMFORTABLE AS IT MIGHT HAVE BEEN

denoting extensive and effective military organization. We noted the continuous stream of traffic on the roads, and were amused with the names chalked on the heavy guns, which were being drawn by a style of tractor quite new to most of us. *No friend of Fritz* was a powerful-looking gun, and greatly impressed us; but the sight of a number of heavier guns thrilled us, and we involuntarily shouted 'Good old England.'

There was not a dull moment during that thirty hours' run. There was much to interest the *freshmen*. Eventually we reached our rail destination, and marched to our quarters, where we arrived late at night. That we were not far from the fighting line was very evident by the close proximity of the artillery, which expressed itself so emphatically that the air reverberated with its deep boom, relieved at intervals by the staccato reports of machine-guns in action.

The troops were quartered in different places. They were as indifferent as they were different, but any place which afforded shelter from the rain and protection from the cold was greatly appreciated. Despite the inconveniences within and the noises without few had difficulty in wooing Morpheus and reposed in his embrace until a late hour next morning.

Opportunity was afforded during the day for having a look round and cultivating an acquaintance with the district. The country round about is fairly level, and, despite the fact that it was just behind the lines and under enemy observation, farming operations and business were carried on in perfect serenity. A cinema afforded entertainment in the evenings. The men were cheerful, and accepted the change from the 'sham' to the real uncomplainingly, and commenced making their billets as comfortable as circumstances would permit. Stoves were greatly in demand, but few were available. The law in France is that nothing shall be removed from a building without permission. Troops were forbidden to enter houses under any pretence whatever; but very occasionally men lost their way, and unwittingly wandered into forbidden places, and when detected by certain officials evinced great surprise on being found therein. The town major on one occasion was walking past a building, the door of which was ajar, and he observed two men struggling with a stove half up the stairway. 'What are you doing with that stove?' he peremptorily asked.

'Putting it back, sir,' was the prompt reply.

It is surprising with what readiness the Australian adapts himself to whatever conditions prevail. He possesses plenty of initiative, which is an invaluable asset on active service. Friendships were quickly formed with the villagers, who were chiefly refugees, and much amusement was caused as the troops sought to make use of the French words which they had endeavoured to learn. There was scarcely any necessity, however to try to speak French, as most of the people understood sufficient of the English language for ordinary business transactions. It was only when love-making was resorted to that a knowledge of French became a vital necessity.

There was a great deal to interest the troops in this district, which for a brief period had been occupied by the enemy. The town was subjected to heavy shell fire almost daily. Evidences of the enemy's brief stay and the effects of their *frightfulness* were not lacking. Since our occupation, the place has been reduced to a heap of ruins by the enemy's artillery, which appears to have paid special attention to church buildings, for many of them have been totally destroyed. Almost immediately upon our arrival in this place certain units of the Division occupied the trenches along the Divisional Front, and very soon proved themselves to be just as capable as the more experienced troops which they had relieved.

When you are perfectly sober, and you imagine you're not

We were located in and about the town for several months, during which time the Third Division won a name for the efficiency and daring of its raids, and silenced for all time the gibes and criticisms of the more war-worn comrades of the older divisions. 'Here' the Division has comported itself precisely as it did over 'there.' In training the men tried to do their duty. In battle they have done their duty, many of them even unto death.

What of the future? Just the same; but with that courage and confidence born of experience, still greater attainments may be expected.

Australians—in Various Moods

The Australian soldier is a peculiar mixture; but for pluck in the face of danger, patience in the grip of pain, and initiative in the presence of the unexpected, he holds a unique place amongst men. He has been subjected to considerable adverse criticism for seeming lack of discipline. Kind things and other kinds of things have been freely said to his detriment; but if every word were true, he is not to blame. The Australian soldier, like any other soldier, is but the product of a system, the standard or inefficiency of which it would not be just to hold him responsible for. The majority frankly admit that soldiering is not in their line. They would never choose it as a profession; yet the man from 'Down Under' has given unmistakable proof that he is as amenable to discipline as any other, and rightly led he, as a fighting force, compares favourably with the best that any nation has produced. His language at times is not too choice. It is said that on occasions the outburst has been so hot that the water carts have been consumed in flames. Be that as it may, his diction in no sense denotes the exact state of his mind or morals. His contagious cheerfulness has established him a firm favourite with the French people, whose admiration and affection he will hold for all time.

An officer belonging to another part of the Empire tells a story against himself. Arriving in a village late at night, he inquired at a cottage as to whether a billet could be provided. Before replying the occupant, a widow, asked whether he was an Australian or a ———. Upon learning his regimental identity, she told him that she had no accommodation. Somewhat vexed, he retorted, 'If I were an Australian you would probably have found room for me.'

'Yes,' was her reply.

'Well,' the officer observed, 'I fail to understand what you see in the Australians; they're savages.'

Before closing the door the occupant said, 'I like savages.'

The following incidents but imperfectly portray the irrepressible humour, unexampled heroism, and splendid initiative so commendably displayed by the Australian under the varying and trying conditions common to modern warfare

Impromptu Wit

The ——th Battalion had been relieved. The men had been in the lines six days. They looked forward to a few days' spell at the back of the trenches. On reaching the back area some of the men were detailed to carry supplies up to the lines. Whilst so engaged they were met by a General, who was in the habit of visiting the trenches unaccompanied. This officer, himself a young man, ever had a cheery word for the 'boys.' One of the men on duty lagged some distance behind the main party. The expression on his face indicated that he was 'fed up.' He was also beginning to feel the weight of the sack which he was carrying. As he passed, the General acknowledged the reluctant turn of his head by way of salute, and then asked, 'Where are you going, my man?'

'In the —— knees, sir,' was the ready and witty reply.

More Curious Than Cautious

A man on duty in the front-line trenches displayed more curiosity than caution and eventually paid the penalty for his mistake. In the endeavour to ascertain what was going on across 'no man's way,' he exposed himself to the keen observation of an enemy sniper, who quickly trained his rifle on him and a bullet penetrated the steel helmet of the over-curious soldier. The bullet traversed the crown of the head and lodged in the nape of the neck. He flung his rifle to one side and did a sprint along the duck-boards. His mates inquired the reason of his haste. Without abating his speed he called out, 'Do you think that I want to drop dead in that blimey mud?'

As he reached the dry duck-boards his strength gave out, and he would have fallen but for the timely assistance from two of his

'WHERE ARE YOU GOING, MY MAN?'
'IN THE KNEES, SIR.'

mates, who lowered him gently, then brought a stretcher on which to carry him to the R.A.P. As they were about to start away with him, he opened his eyes, and they inquired if he were hurt.

'Well, it does give you a bit of a headache, you know,' he replied; 'have you got a fag?'

A cigarette was handed to him, and as they carried him away he smoked his fag.

It's All in the Game

A similar instance of absolute self-forgetfulness and indomitable spirit occurred at another part of the line. A shell burst near to our wire and projected a tangled heap of it forward. A piece of barbed wire encircled a man's neck. The barbs bit into the flesh. The shoulders of his tunic were torn. The blood flowed freely from nasty cuts in his neck and cheeks. Without altering his position he looked out in the direction of the Hun lines and declared that if he ever got hold of the —— Hun who fired that —— shell, he would drive his —— bayonet through him. When the wire was taken from round his neck, his face wreathed in smiles as he remarked, 'Well, I suppose it is all in the game,' then turning to his mates he asked, 'I say, digger, have you got a smoke?'

My Lady Nicotine is certainly a general favourite amongst the boys. They seek her solace during the critical periods of their active service life. Unquestionably one of the most deeply appreciated issues that the men receive is that of tobacco and cigarettes. For this extra 'ration' credit must be given to the A.C.F. and other funds which have expended large sums of money in making available to the troops the pipe of peace and the comfort of the fag.

A Clever Ruse

This incident is related in the strictest confidence, and solely upon the condition that the identity of the individuals concerned will not be disclosed. A certain officer—I dare not mention his rank, as there are so few Generals amongst us that to even mention it would be tantamount to disclosing his identity. Therefore, a certain officer was on a tour of inspection. The utmost effort had been made by the unit holding the line to have everything satisfactory. The trenches must be kept clean and sanitary. Every precaution is adopted to safeguard the health of the men. The officer's visit was timed just after the issue of rum had been made. Rum is not a regular issue by any means, but a little had been made available at that time, and was supposed to be taken much the same as is medicine, *viz.*, on the M.O.'s recommendation. A few minutes before the arrival of the officer of high rank the platoon officer observed one of his men under the influence of drink. He learned on inquiry that the man had secured some rum in addition to what had been issued. To get him out of the way was his first thought. Somebody suggested that he be placed on a stretcher and covered with a blanket. It was no sooner suggested than acted upon. When the officer making the inspection entered the trench two men bore the stretcher with its burden past him. He stood to one side and saluted as he would the dead. Of course the man on the stretcher was dead—*dead drunk*. No questions were asked, therefore no untruths were told. The unit had the satisfaction of learning that their lines were satisfactory; but in a certain company's orderly-room the following morning a certain man had a most unenviable quarter of an hour in the presence of his irate O.C.

Turning the Tables

During a raid made on our lines the enemy succeeded in reaching our trenches, but were quickly ejected. Two of the raiding party were killed, and as many were taken prisoners. One of them met his death in a very tragic manner. A member of the —th battalion was fast asleep in his makeshift of a dug-out the night the Germans entered our lines. He knew nothing of their visit until wakened by a heavy hand being placed on his shoulder. Great was his astonishment on waking to find himself gazing into the face of a Hun, who gurgled and gesticulated, which sounds and signs he interpreted as an invitation to put his hands up. His hands went up as he struggled to his feet. He then discovered that he was about six inches taller than his captor and certainly much heavier. When they got out on the duck-boards, the prisoner suddenly looked down and allowed his gaze to rest on the boards at his feet. The German's curiosity was aroused, and he fell into the trap set for him. He made the fatal mistake of allowing his gaze to be diverted from the prisoner to the duck-boards. By a quick movement the prisoner possessed himself of his captor's rifle. One blow from a tightly-clenched fist sufficed to lay him his length along the boards, and the next moment the would-be captor was breathing his last with his own bayonet through his chest, and the Australian was heard to remark, 'I'll teach the blighter to waken me from my sleep.'

Heroism Unexcelled

It would be invidious to single out one for special mention from the great army of brave men who have upheld the traditions of the Empire on the field of battle. Without mentioning the name of the hero the following incident is cited as illustrative of many which speak eloquently of the bravery of our boys. Our lines were being furiously shelled, and a member of a certain battalion was severely wounded. Assisted by another stretcher-bearer, the hero of this incident endeavoured to convey the wounded man to the A.D.S. The trench along which they were walking was blown in, making it necessary to carry the injured man *over the top*. This was done in full view of the enemy. While so engaged a *Minnie* was observed coming over, and warning was given for all to get under cover. All did except Private ——, who, actuated by an impulse to protect a fallen comrade, and without thought for his own safety, immediately threw himself upon the wounded man to protect him. For this gallant act he was awarded the Military Medal.

A couple of months later this same person was in the trenches when a British 'plane was compelled to land in a very exposed and shell-swept area. Both occupants of the machine rushed for the trenches. The observer reached a place of safety, but the pilot, who was wounded, fell exhausted. Without thought of personal safety, and despite the fact that the Germans were shelling the machine, the stretcher-bearer climbed over the top, in full view of the enemy, and carried the wounded pilot to a shell-hole, where he rendered first-aid and then brought the injured man to the safety of our trenches. For this further act of bravery he was awarded a bar to his M.M.

We Were Pals

A man came to the D.B.O. just after a certain engagement in connexion with which the Australians did splendid work. They secured a great victory. They got to their objectives on time and took quite a large number of prisoners. Every victory has its price, and it was concerning part of the price of victory that the young man had made the visit. He told of his pal, a D.C.M. man, who had been killed, whose body was lying out on the ridge. He wished to know whether arrangements could be made for the body to be brought down to a back area cemetery for burial. Whenever practicable such is done. The D.B.O. made inquiries, and learned that no transport was available. The roads were in a frightful condition, and in view of the incessant enemy shelling of the area, decided that the body would have to be buried in the vicinity of where it had fallen. Arrangements were made for the man to return on the morrow for the purpose of acting as guide to the Padre who would conduct the service. Next day, he came to the Burials Officer. Surprise was evinced at the change in his appearance. His uniform was covered with mud and wet through, and he seemed to be quite exhausted.

'I have come about the burial, sir,' he said. 'Could it be fixed up for this afternoon, I have brought the body down?'

Upon making inquiries as to how he had managed it, he replied that he and another had asked permission to go out and bring the body in. It meant a carry over broken ground of about five miles, under heavy shell fire most of the distance; but these faithful comrades gladly endured the hardship and braved the dangers to ensure the burial of their deceased mate in a cemetery which is one of the few that has not been disturbed by the bursting shell. Thinking that the deceased was a near relative of this brave lad, the question was asked. His eyes filled with tears as he replied: 'No, sir, we were pals.'

Such an incident will surely suffice to erase from the mind the false impression, which, unfortunately a few seem to have gathered, that the Australian is devoid of sentiment.

Sunday, Somewhere in France

The question that leaps to the lips in connexion with the title of this chapter is, Why should the events associated with this particular day be recorded? Are they different from what takes place on any or all of the other days of the week—something special which clearly denotes that one week has ended and another week begun? Is there a temporary cessation of hostilities, during which bells are rung and men may be seen wending their way to some established building for worship, or does that indefinable stillness peculiar to the first day of the week in peaceful places pervade all life?

Apart from the interest and curiosity that many attach thereto, there is no significance in the selection of the day, and there is little if anything associated with the events of Sunday at the Front to distinguish it from any other day. Yet it is strange that though men may frequently confuse the days between Monday and Saturday, they instinctively seem to know when Sunday has come. Whether by chance or convenience, I know not, some of the biggest 'stunts' have been initiated on the Lord's Day. At times the voice of the Padre was scarcely heard above the din and noise of heavy guns as they dispatched their projectiles of destruction and death over the place in which a church parade was being conducted. The recollection of certain events and experiences of some Sundays will undoubtedly tend to make many a man more thoughtful and analytic than the events or experiences entered into on any other day during his active service career.

The disposition of an army is not affected by certain days, but by developments within the area of operations. If Sunday should be considered the opportune time for putting over a barrage, making a raid on the enemy lines, or effecting an advance, no thought of the sacred associations of that day is given serious consideration. The system in vogue provides for units when not in the line to be in reserve or resting. Such units supply working and carrying parties; so that the number of men available for church services on Sunday is no greater than on ordinary days. The war proceeds. Man may worship when opportunity permits.

A summary of the events of one Sunday will suffice to convey an idea of how almost every Sunday is spent at the Front. The weather is seasonable: over the country a dense mist hangs low in the early morn. The sun rises, and the mist flees before it, revealing the face of the earth covered with snow, mud, or in the tight grip of Jack Frost. Aeroplanes glide gracefully overhead. They are out for observation purposes, or to prevent the approach of enemy craft. The artillery, ever alert both day and night, sends out its missiles of death far into the enemy's lines. The enemy guns reply, and thus it might continue through the day. Shells are ugly killers and wounders; but for them there would be little of the slaughter-yard suggestion about a modern battlefield, with its improved system of well-built and cleanly kept trenches and its clean puncturing bayonet thrust or rifle bullet. While the shells shriek and whirr through the air, heaps of humanity are distributed about the trenches, in the dug-outs, or in the reserve lines. The men sit or lie about for the most part, as unconcerned as if on holiday bent. The order to 'stand to' would bring them to their appointed places, from whence they would resist an invasion of their lines by the enemy, or launch an attack, make a raid, or go forth on patrol of No Man's Land.

Back from the lines units are resting or engaged on the lines of communication; from such units men are available for church parades. Men of different units and of different theological views come together in one place and worship God. Buildings are not always available for parade services. Sometimes they are held in the open field, in farm-yards, or in billets; frequently in tents provided by the Y.M.C.A. Attendance at these services is purely voluntary, and a large proportion of men attend whenever opportunity offers. While the service is in progress the war goes on. The men in the trenches catch the strains of band music, and there is carried over the distance intervening the sound of the singing of old familiar

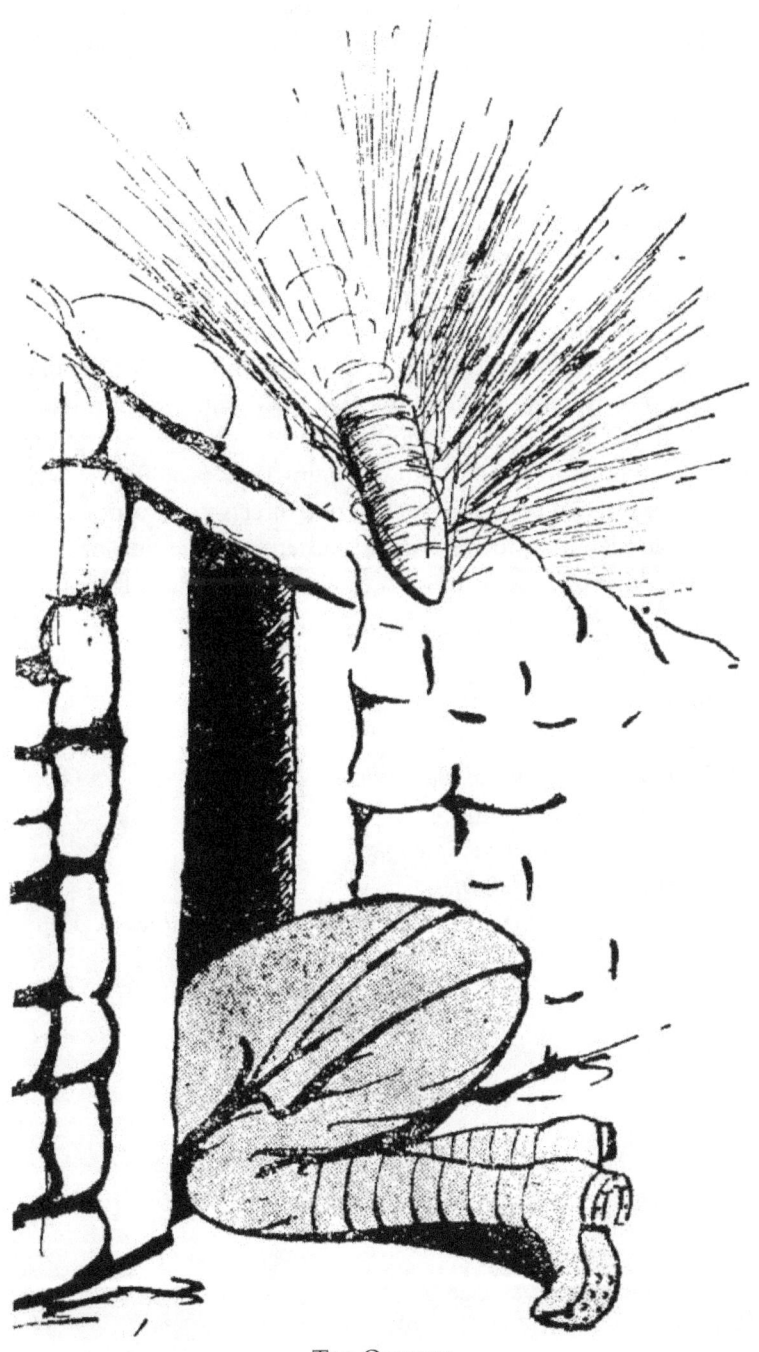

The Ostrich

hymns. It is a privilege to speak to these men who have been in the shell-swept trenches, who have participated in raids, who have taken part in one of the most successful battles of the war, who have seen suffering and even looked into the face of death.

Several parades might be held during the day at hours convenient to those who wish to attend, and in the evening a song-service is conducted, when the men choose the hymns which they would sing. They are reverent in attitude, earnest in attention.

Sundays are no different from other days of the week. They merely mark, as do other days, the passing of time, which will bring either grief or gladness to those who watch and wait for the day of peace, and to us who war a victory crowned with honour. There is no *Sun*-day. The thick, dark cloud of war hides the sun's bright face, but there is hope in the thought that Sun-day is prophetic as well as historic, and insistently in its recurrence directs us to wait patiently for the cloud-bursts out of which shall emerge the Sun of Righteousness, who will proclaim such time to be the Day of the Lord.

For, lo, the days are hastening on
By prophet bard foretold,
When with the ever circling years
Comes round the age of gold.
When peace shall over all the earth
Its ancient splendours fling,
And all the world take up the song
Which angels once did sing:
'Glory to God in the highest, on earth peace, goodwill toward men.'

Soldiers' Superstitions

With the advent of Christmas, arrangements were affected by which officers whose work necessitated their being temporarily separated from the unit could come together for the purpose of observing the special season in the established epicurean style. Every effort was made to make the day as distinct from other days as circumstances would allow. Donations from the officers and small contributions from the men enabled those who had the matter in hand to provide the customary Christmas dinner. Though it was not served up on tables, spread with linen, and the usual impedimenta of the banqueting-table, it was greatly appreciated, and afforded a rare opportunity for reunion. Fresh friendships were formed, acquaintances renewed, brothers and relatives met after months of separation. Toasts were honoured and carols or hymns appropriate to the season were sung. A great deal had been heard or read about our troops fraternizing with the enemy during the Christmas seasons of the previous years of the war, but there was none of that during the Christmas of 1916. There was no cessation of hostilities. The lines were held with the same keenness, and there was considerable aerial and artillery activity throughout the day and night. In fact, Christmas *Somewhere in France* was born to the accompaniment of the boom of guns and the whirr of aeroplanes. The weather conditions were decidedly inclement, and, despite the good wishes from friends in the Homeland, it was difficult to keep warm.

At the back of the lines, in a certain battalion's H.Q. billets, a number of officers had assembled. They had come together by invitation to participate in a reunion dinner. Everything had been done to make it a meal worthy of the occasion.

Despite the good wishes from friends in the Homeland, it was difficult to keep warm

Great taste had been displayed in decorating the table, and the cooks excelled themselves in the quality of the food served. We seated ourselves immediately Grace was said, when somebody remarked that there were thirteen only, and suggested that another be asked in to make fourteen. Little notice was taken of the remark until the same officer ventured to predict that one of them would 'go out' before the year ended. He was teased with being unduly superstitious and attaching too much significance to the supposed unluckiness of the number thirteen. His mind was evidently depressed with the impression which he had gathered, and there was not lacking evidence that the gathering ceased to interest him further.

Exactly a week passed, and another such reunion had been arranged for the purpose of celebrating the passing of the old year and the ushering in of the new. Several jocularly remarked that for G———'s sake we should arrange to have more or less than thirteen present. Late on the afternoon of the last day of the year, advice was received at B.Q.H. that Lieut. G——— had been killed. He had gone down to the trenches to inspect some work which was being done by his platoon, and was on the point of returning when an enemy shell burst and a shrapnel bullet went through his heart. This sad event recalled to us his words at the gathering on Christmas night. His prediction that one would be missing ere the year ended was fulfilled, and he was the one called hence. Arrangements for the evening function were cancelled, and the next day his remains were interred in the military cemetery, and the grave is now marked by a beautiful cross made by a member of his platoon and inscribed by his O.C. He was a fine fellow, full of fun and life, a true comrade, an ideal officer, beloved by all who knew him.

The following pathetic incident speaks of the attachment which springs up between officers and men, and incidentally testifies to the high esteem in which our late comrade was held by one who had exceptional opportunities for knowing him. Duty took me to the cemetery a few days after the burial, and I noticed standing at the graveside with uncovered and bowed head a soldier of the battalion. I could see that the lad was deeply affected, and inquired as to whether he had known Lieut. G———.

'Yes sir,' he replied; 'I was his orderly; and—I miss him so much.'

Superstitions play a large part in the life of the average soldier, and frequently gain the ascendancy over common sense. Though rather reticent about expressing his religious views, he is in many respects intensely religious. He may admit being superstitious and even boast about it, or declare himself to be a fatalist. Fatalism in the vocabulary of the soldier is just another name for Providence.

Few, if any, are afraid of death. They seldom give it a thought. The general belief is that if a man's 'time' has come, nothing can possibly avert it. Under this impression he goes into battle or takes up his position in the lines. He consistently refuses, however, to be a party to anything which is considered at all likely to precipitate the end. For instance, no amount of persuasion would induce him to be one of three to receive a light for his cigarette or pipe from the same match, and owing to the strange coincidences in connexion with the number thirteen, he is prepared to deny himself much.

While soldiers are ever ready to avail themselves of every possible comfort when in the trenches, they hesitate to make use of a field service stretcher. They prefer to make their bed on the ground, under the impression that if they were to lie on stretchers in the trenches they would be carried out from the trenches on stretchers. One of a draft of reinforcements was attached to a platoon which had been detailed to proceed to the lines. On arrival, this man, despite many warnings from the others, took possession of a stretcher and used it as a bed. About eleven o'clock the following morning, the same stretcher was used to carry him back to the R.A.P. While working in the lines he was seriously wounded by a piece of shrapnel. It is hardly necessary to state that this man was completely won over to the belief which only the previous evening he had laughed at.

At the head of a trench in the vicinity of Ploegsteert a rusted revolver which had been found by a working party was suspended from a short pole. It caught the eye of all who passed by on their way up the lines. Nearly every man was seen to touch that useless weapon. Upon making enquiries it was ascertained that a superstition had grown up round that revolver. It was supposed to possess a certain charm, and the men who merely touched it on their way into the line would be protected from all danger. Certainly many

A SILENT TRIBUTE TO THE BRAVE

incidents occurred which tended to support the belief that the mud covered rusted revolver possessed all the remarkable miraculous powers attributed to it.

In course of conversation with a soldier, I questioned the advisability of his proceeding to the trenches. 'Oh,' he declared, 'it is all right; no matter where I may be, if a shell has my number on it, I will have to take delivery, whether I like it or not.' While working in the lines a few days later a shell penetrated the parapet and buried its nose in the clay at the edge of the duck-boards. Allowing sufficient time to elapse to ascertain whether it was 'alive' (it proved to be a 'dud') he then examined the base of the shell, and was astonished to read thereon his regimental number.

Such coincidences tend to strengthen the superstitious tendencies of the soldier, and the effect upon most minds is to lead them to believe that a man's death or deliverance is absolutely due to Fate, which is just another way of saying, 'There's a Divinity which shapes our ends, rough hew them as we may.'

On the Eve of Battle

To the Widows of France

Eyes that have rained tears, lips that have trembled,
Twitching convulsively, torn with their grief.
Now face us bravely with pride undissembled,
Glad to have suffered to show their belief.

Troop upon troop of them, some walking singly,
Weaker ones plodding in pairs for support;
Mates to the spirits of men who were kingly,
Coming from Matins with old men's escort.

Ask them, ye watchers, inquire their elation,
Tell them ye wonder they bear them so brave.
Proudly they'll answer, 'La belle France, our nation,
Requires us to suffer, our country to save.'

To save from the maw of the great avaricious,
The cold scheming brain of a commerce run mad—
A commerce all-grasping and sordid and vicious;
For this are we martyred, for this are we glad.

Then the soul of the Springtime, the great resurrection,
Shines bright in their faces, they wave to the car,
Packed tight with our comrades, a cheery collection,
As we dash thro' the streets to the trenches afar.

TO

THE WIDOWS

OF

FRANCE

And France comes to meet us, to cheer us and greet us,
As we race past the fields to the woods brightly green,
Whose young leaves half rustle with a great show of bustle
When we halt at the fairest of spots ever seen.[1]

Where the old kings of history, now shrouded in myst'ry,
Once hunted the boar, or the feather, or fur.
But we feel this is over as we wade thro' the clover,
No tyrant again in this great wood shall stir.

For France now demands it; however she stands it,
However those brave ones in thousands can smile,
Requires some explaining, so cease all complaining,
And come on and battle and make it worthwhile.

Yes! on to the thunder, tho' it's a blunder,
On to the swish and the whine and the roar;
With the memoried face of one you called 'treasure,'
Above and around and ever before.

Oh! thou in that homeland so wistfully waiting,
Watching and wearing your worries or woe,
So proudly triumphant, consider such women;
Work for them, pray for them, smile as you go.

For into the furnace they've thrown all their 'treasures,'
Knowing that out of the vibrating whole,
Quiveringly molten, pulsating, gleaming,
Europe shall find her immaculate soul—

Soul of the suff'ring, bleeding and dying,
Soul of a freedom unselfish and clean,
Loving the light of a love all around us,
Scorning the actions of men who are mean.

Oh! men who were kingly, mated to martyrs
(Silently, cheerfully, plodding along),
Send all ye can of such great souls to help us,
Make us and keep us triumphant and strong.

G. P. Cuttriss and J. W. Hood

1. Ploegsteert.

Over the Top

From the time of our arrival in France until a week or two prior to the battle of Messines, general dissatisfaction was expressed by the troops because of the seeming slow progress that was being made. The men soon tired of the uneventful trench warfare. They were eager to go over the top. Defensive operations did not appeal to them; they were impatient to assume the offensive. To put it in their own language, they had enlisted not to dig trenches or repair roads, but to fight the Hun. Certainly the monotony was relieved by an occasional raid, for which work they earned for the Division a splendid reputation. The area which the Division occupied was known throughout France as the *nursery*, where men, new to the modern mode of waging war, had opportunity for gaining experience and getting accustomed to shell and machine-gun fire under comparatively safe conditions.

During this period of marking time the men were engaged both day and night on works of importance, without which an offensive would have meant sheer suicide. The elaborate preparations that were being made denoted that a big push was contemplated. In connexion with this work, the pioneers and the engineers did magnificently.

Everything was arranged according to well-conceived plans, and the preliminaries to an unprecedented offensive were completed by June 6. Guns of different calibre were massed at points of vantage, cleverly camouflaged to conceal them from enemy observation. Dumps were replete with the necessary supplies of ammunition, and scrupulous regard was paid to arrangements for keeping the lines of communication clear. Provision was made for the treatment of wounded and their evacuation, and for the burial of the killed. Refreshment stalls were established at convenient points, where the attacking troops and the wounded could receive hot coffee and biscuits. Nothing that could be done for the comfort of the men and to ensure the success of the venture was overlooked.

Only those who are actually at the Front have any conception of the amount of work involved in assuming the aggressive. The staff responsible for perfecting the organization are deserving of the highest praise. There had been numerous rumours in connexion with mines. The air was electric, the men were confident, and all were determined to do their level best to uphold the splendid traditions bequeathed by older Australian units.

During the night preceding the dawn of June 6 the troops who were to take part in the attack marched to their respective assembling points. The march was uneventful up to a certain stage, after which large clouds of gas were encountered, which rendered necessary the wearing of respirators. Despite the sickly sensation produced by the inhalation of gas, the troops advanced. There is much to be written of the latter part of the approach march, but that will be recorded by others. It is sufficient to state that certain unforeseen events threatened to seriously disorganize things, but these were overcome as they were met with.

Almost simultaneously with the first faint streak of the dawn of June 7 the mines at Hill 60 and St. Yves were exploded. The sight was awe-inspiring, and the ground trembled as if in the throes of an agonizing palsy. On the tick of the appointed time our 'boys' went 'over the top.' It was for this experience that they had worked and waited. They advanced immediately behind the barrage so consistently sustained by the artillery, and in the face of a terrific fusillade of machine-gun fire which seemed to leap upon them from almost every angle. Some of the enemy machine-guns were captured by our troops, who used them with deadly effect upon the then retiring foe. All the objectives were obtained with clock-like precision. Again and again the victorious troops were subjected to withering counter-attacks, and shells fell around them like hail. There was no faltering. They held the recovered ground in the face of a merciless tornado of steel and bullets.

As the infantry advanced, the pioneers and engineers followed, digging trenches, extending tramways, and keeping the lines of communication clear. No pen, however facile, could give the true lines to the picture. Ordinary language is inadequate to express all that was achieved, seen, and felt. The men did splendidly. The respective work of the several services was perfectly co-ordinated, so much so that after the 'stunt' it seemed as if a mutual admiration society had been spontaneously organized. The infantry congratulated the Flying Corps, the Flying Corps complimented the Artillery, and both Artillery and Flying Corps were loud in their praise of the dauntless Infantry. All did their part, and the taking of Messines will probably be chronicled as one of the greatest, if not the greatest, of battles in connexion with this world-war.

Prior to this engagement the Third Division had experienced but a sprinkling of fire, but during its progress it received its baptism, and emerged from the battle with a reputation of which any unit might be proud. It was a stupendous task, a severe test for the *baby* Division, but every man rose to the occasion. The wounded were cheerful, the dead died gloriously, and those of us who are alive and remain are proud to have had some part in such an important and eminently successful undertaking.

There were many acts of heroism, some of which have been officially recognized. The Australians have the utmost contempt for the enemy as fighting men. They declare that if the artillery and air-craft were eliminated they would be prepared to give the enemy the benefit of odds in hand-to-hand fighting.

One instance will suffice to illustrate their indomitable spirit. While the push was in progress, a man who, in his own words, had *stopped one*, was carried to an R.A.P. His wounds were numerous and rather serious. Two fingers of the left hand had been blown off, his right arm was shattered, his head and neck were much cut about, and blood oozed from wounds on his chest. This man had got a 'Blighty,' but he did not appear to be at all pleased. It should be stated that the men who receive wounds sufficiently serious to warrant their being sent to hospitals in England are considered, and consider themselves, very fortunate. He was disappointed because he was wounded, not that he complained about his disfigurement or the pain. I expressed my sympathy and wished him a speedy recovery and a happy time in 'Blighty,' and suggested that possibly there would be no need for him to return, for the Hun might soon be driven out from Belgium. He eyed me unflinchingly, and endeavoured to raise himself on his uninjured elbow, and then blurted out, 'It is just as well for the —— Huns that I got wounded.'

These were not the exact words he used. There were many accompanying adjectives, without which the vocabulary of the Australian would be very limited indeed. This big-hearted, whole-souled, hefty Westralian seemed to think that the issue to that particular push depended absolutely upon him.

The men of the Third Division have now had the experience which many had longed for. Going over the top was not quite so romantic as fancy had pictured it to be, and the experience which is common to all who take part in it for the first time defies expression. A peculiar sensation creeps annoyingly slowly along the spinal column, subtly affecting every member of the body. There's a gripping of the heart and a numbing of the brain, and the tongue persistently cleaves to the roof of the mouth, which seems as dry as powdered chalk. A choking sensation accompanies every effort to cough. You may be in the stepping-off trench or lying face-down on the churned-up mud out on No Man's Land, waiting for the signal to go. The seconds tick slowly by, the minutes are leaden-footed in their passing, and seem like eternities. The eyes are almost blinded through the strain of peering into darkness, the imagination runs riot, grotesque shapes are conjured into view, only to be dissipated by a solitary flare or a series of gun-flashes. The fact that it is raining and you are lying in a gradually deepening pool of water occasions no concern. What matters most is that your puttees are frayed or your boots in need of repair, but you console yourself with the thought that after the stunt it will be easy to get a new outfit, and maybe you commence to make plans as to how you will spend your leave. You appear to be quite oblivious to the fact that the next moment may be your last.

Ages roll by; suddenly you are conscious of somebody by your side; you make an attempt to smile, when at the same instant the ground trembles as if in the throes of a tremendous earthquake; flash after flash in quick succession; the air vibrates with noises that deafen; hundreds of shells hurtle overhead. 'That's 'er,' shouts the man by your side. You are pleased that something has happened to divert your mind from its morbid fancyings. This is the Dinkum. The electrical effect upon your mind and body is wonderful. You break from the shackles that fear and fancy have thrown round you. The reports of terrific explosions rend the air, you grip frantically at the soft mud to prevent yourself being hurled through space. Somebody from somewhere makes a sign, and in a moment you are erect and speeding in the direction of the enemy lines. There is but one thought in the mind as you allow your hand to tighten round your rifle—to gain your objective. Heaven help the Hun who attempts to frustrate you. Hurrah! The wire has been smashed to smithereens, and in less time than it takes to describe you are over the top—close up to the enemy line. You stumble forward, onward, without noticing the broken nature of the ground. The sight of the enemy rushing towards you with hands well above their heads, shouting *'Kamerad,'* or fleeing before your advance, excites greater enthusiasm.

You begin to notice other things. Possibly the first thing that dawns upon your mind is that others are taking part in the business—that you are not alone. Then you notice the effect of our shell-fire; this inspires greater confidence, and involuntarily you thank heaven for such splendid artillery. Then you notice little heaps clad in familiar khaki—they are what remain of comrades who have sealed their love of country with their blood. You observe others wandering aimlessly about, suffering from shell-shock; or the gallant stretcher-bearers, regardless of all danger, attending to the wounded and carrying them back for treatment. The sight does not grieve or shock you—only surprise is evinced by a change in facial expression. You just carry on—the shock and grief will come later. You just grit your teeth and take a fresh grip of your rifle and go forward with greater determination to strike a blow in the cause of freedom and honour. Maybe you reach your objective, your clothes sodden with sticky, clammy mud and possibly the red of your own blood showing through.

The whole thing has been like some dream of adventure with wild beasts; but there is firmly embedded in your consciousness the knowledge that you have done the job. Other waves of men pass through the line which you have wrested from the Hun; you cheer them as they pass, and then dig in for all you are worth.

A few days later there appears in the daily papers, under the heading of British Official, that the troops penetrated the enemy's lines to such and such a depth, and have bravely withstood several terrific counter-attacks; and war correspondents will cable the news to our waiting people of the Homeland that the boys magnificently stormed and won additional fame; but if you want it in the every-day language of the man from down under, he merely went over the top.

After the rush there is no time for rest. The recovered ground must be retained. New positions have to be consolidated, fresh gun positions have to be constructed. The lines must be made habitable. The dead have to be buried. The efficient and expeditious manner in which this work was accomplished established the Third Division's right to full participation in the honour and glory of the taking and holding of Messines by the Second Anzacs.

Shells: a Few Smiles and a Contrast

When the guns begin to speak, and shells are hurtling through the air, places of shelter are resorted to. These places are not always shell-proof, but they serve as a protection against splinters. There are few places that would withstand the effects of a direct hit by a heavy shell, but one feels perfectly safe with even a sheet of iron overhead. The effects of an explosion are very local, and the chances of a direct hit are very remote. The first law of nature takes precedence during a bombardment. Precaution is esteemed to be much better than a blanket and burial.

In and about the towns at the back of the lines where the troops are billeted there are a sprinkling of civilians. When these places are being shelled they display no fear. Occasionally elderly people will cover their heads with their hands and seek shelter in the cellars, while the soldier, ostrich-like, is quite contented provided he has some protection for his head, but the majority continue with their work as in normal times. When the civilians were questioned as to whether they were afraid of the enemy breaking through and carrying them off or killing them, they would confidently reply, 'Oh, no! British between.'

They feel perfectly safe, knowing that the British are between them and the Hun.

Many of them have good reason to remember the time when the enemy were in occupation of the town. In some instances the Germans have been highly spoken of. I give credence to every good report. Personally, we bear them no ill-will. We detest the system which has made them what they are, and we are here to crush it, and sincerely hope that the men of the German race who, however, mistaken, are ready to lay down their lives for their country, may emerge from this war and be re-made on the anvil of defeat, and in the days to be redeem to honour the name which today is the synonym for all that is brutal and abhorrent.

That all of them are not filled with implacable hatred towards the British is evidenced in the following incident. We attempted to raid the enemy trenches. The weather was bitterly cold and the night was dark. Our artillery put over a heavy barrage, after which the raiding party went forth; they crept forward over the muddy ground, and entered the German lines. Several casualties were sustained during the operations. When our men returned to their trenches, it was discovered that one of the raiding party was missing. When the noise of the counter-barrage had died down, a cry for help was distinctly heard by our front line troops. It came from No Man's Land. A couple of stretcher-bearers and two men went out in search of the one in distress. While groping about amongst the wire in the darkness, they heard the Germans assuring the man for whom they were searching that he would be all right. Suddenly the enemy turned a trench searchlight on to No Man's Land, and by this light the search party were guided to their wounded comrade. The light was kept on him until he was rescued, and was then used to guide the party back to their own lines. During this time no shot was fired. This was a humane action indeed.

All the Huns, however, are not so humanely disposed. In connexion with another raid on the enemy trenches, our men met with violent opposition, but succeeded in obtaining their objective. When returning, a few of the party were wounded—one very seriously. He was unable to make his way back. The Germans got him, stripped him of his uniform, and left him against the wire. The weather being intensely cold, the man soon died from exposure. These two incidents illustrate the two extremes in the attitude of the Huns towards the British. One was a brutal act of hatred, the other a humane act, which commends itself to both friend and foe.

The Germans have been credited with almost every conceivable atrocity that man is capable of perpetrating. Whether these brutalities are perpetrated with the sanction of the German authorities, or

TO SEE OURSELVES AS OTHERS SEE US

are merely the expression of individual hatred, one is not prepared to state. We have ceased to be angry with or alarmed at their tactics of intimidation. We interpret every act of frightfulness as evidence of desperate conditions. The only effect that such devilish methods have upon the men in the lines is to make them more determined to crush the mad and murderous spirit of militarism which holds the Hun in its merciless grip.

During ordinary trench warfare the enemy appears to concentrate his artillery fire on to the towns and villages at the back of our lines. Villages have been practically eliminated and large towns reduced to a heap of ruins. The destruction of these places is of no military consequence. It is pure vandalism.

Bairnsfather's sketches portraying the humour and coolness that such critical conditions create are in no particular exaggerated. A certain building, prominently situated in a fairly large town, within easy range of the enemy guns, was being used as B.H.Qs. It afforded accommodation for about twelve officers and as many other ranks. The outskirts of the town had been subjected to severe shelling during the day. Towards evening the shelling ceased, but commenced again about midnight; on this occasion the shells were directed more to the centre of the town. Pieces of iron and a hail of shrapnel descended upon the roof of our billet. All were awakened by the noise. From different parts of the building the same query was advanced: 'Are you all right?'

Then a hurried conference was held, and the C.O. decided that discretion was the better part of valour. With the aid of electric torches we collected our blankets, etc., and descended to the cellar. Everybody was cheerful. The report of the guns somewhere along the enemy's lines was heard distinctly, and we would wait for the swish of the shells as they hurtled through the air. Almost simultaneously with the swish would come the crash followed by the sound of breaking glass and falling bricks, and involuntarily we exclaimed in chorus, 'Another one in.'

We thought of the poor devils who may have been in the vicinity where the shell exploded, and various expressions of sympathy escaped from our lips. Almost immediately on reaching the cellar, there was a terrific explosion, and one of the chimneys of the building crashed into the cellar. Gradually we lost interest and became

With the aid of electric torches ... we descended to the cellar

almost indifferent to what was going on. One by one we repaired to our improvised beds on the floor. Sometimes one would have difficulty in wooing the goddess of sleep, and his persistency in asking questions was exceeded only by the annoyance experienced by those to whom the questions were addressed. The usual question of the sleepless individual is 'Where did that one land?' and the answer with some accompanying adjectives is invariably, 'I am more concerned about where the next one will land.'

The enemy generally commences shelling these places at the close of day, and the men have described these operations as 'The Hun's evening hate.' On one occasion a certain village was being strafed. Several men of a certain battalion were on the road at the time. They quickly availed themselves of the shelter of a cellar. The building was hit several times. Shortly after the bombardment commenced a man leading a mule was observed, coming along the road. He was invited to take shelter in the cellar. The invitation was accepted with alacrity. The mule was tethered to the window-sill, and the man was soon in their midst. Shells continued to burst overhead and round about. The newcomer proved to be a blessing. He soon had the men laughing despite the noise and danger. When a shell burst in close proximity to the building, he evinced great concern for the safety of his mule.

'My poor old donk,' he would exclaim; 'there goes his tail.' Another burst: 'There goes his hind-quarters.'

It seemed impossible for the mule to escape injury or death. Turning to his companions he declared that he would carry part of that mule back. If his head were left intact he would gather the harness and wrap it round the head and carry it back to the lines, and if the O.C. transport asked where the 'donk' was, he would say, 'Shot from under me, sir.'

Suddenly the shelling ceased, and they emerged from their shelter. The mule's master was the first outside. He fully expected to see but a blood-stain on the spot where he had left the beast, but to his great surprise and satisfaction he saw the mule serenely nibbling at the grass growing alongside the building. The old 'donk' had not sustained an injury. To say that he was proud to lead a whole mule back to his quarters instead of having to carry only its head, is an altogether inadequate way of describing his actual feelings.

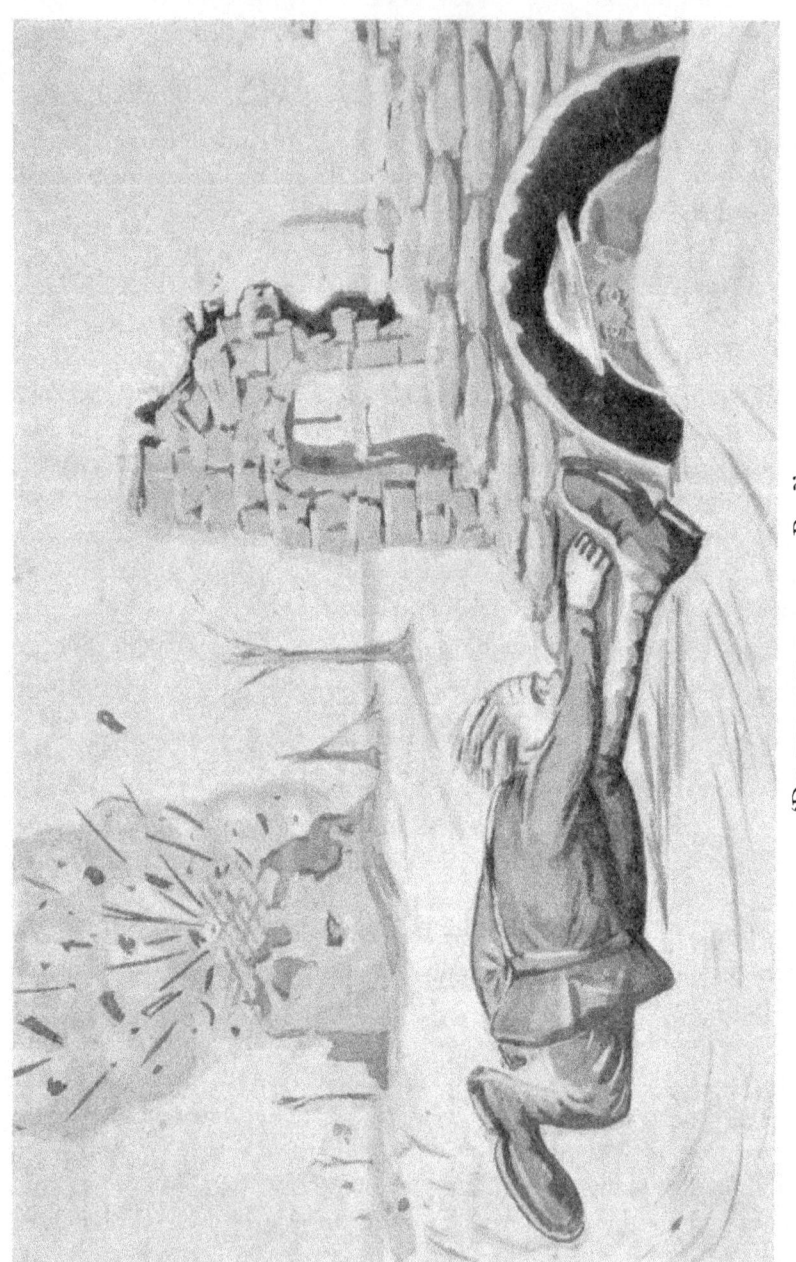

'Did you hear that one, Bill?'

'Did you hear that one, Bill?' asked one man of another who had come along the shell-swept road rather hurriedly.

'Yes,' replied the nearly exhausted man, 'I heard it twice; once when it passed me, and again when I passed it.'

Messines
June 7, 1917

A shell-struck souvenir of hellish war,
A monument of man's stupendous hate!
Can this have been a Paradise before,
Now up-blown, blasted, drear and desolate?
Aye, once with smiling and contented face
She reigned a queen above a charming place.

But soon the sport of leaders and of kings
Transformed her to a resting-place for guns,
Rude scars across her breasts the worker flings,
To shelter countless hordes of hell-born Huns,
The while, upon the next opposing crest,
Our men died gamely as they did their best.

And thus for years, with cold, relentless zeal,
With fiendish science both sides fought and watched,
From loop-holes or from clouds which half conceal,
Or in deep tunnels all their skill was matched.
On sentry in the firebay, or the hov'ring 'plane,
Mining and countermining yet again.

And far behind such scenes, great engineers
Pondered o'er problems without parallel.
And planned with wisdom of a thousand years,
To blow the other to eternal Hell.
Their calculations left no callous scheme untried,
To slaughter hundreds of the other side.

But hush! the whole machinery's complete,
All plans are folded and the great work's done,
The work of building up to cause defeat—
The lever's pulled, and, lo! a new work has begun.
The task of falling on a shattered foe,
And doing things undreamed-of years ago.

Hush! hark! A mighty rumbling roar breaks thro',
And see! Her crest-line leaps into a flame,
The foul disease within her bowels she blew
High into the air to rid her of her shame;
In one huge vomit she now flings her filth,
Far o'er the country in a powdered 'tilth.'

And so the vassals of a fiendish foe
Are scattered far and wide into a dust.
Those who have revelled as they wreaked red woe,
A shattered sample of their own blood-lust.
Whilst from our hill-crest and its catacomb,
A new life comes a-pouring from the tomb.

Eager, and burning with the zeal of youth,
Our Second Anzacs sprang from out the ground,
Bound by their mateships and their love of truth,
The Third Division its new soul has found;
Straight o'er the top amidst a hail of shell
To their objective which they knew so well.

On, on, thro' poison gas and rattling roar,
Past ulc'rous craters, blackened foul and deep,
These comrades 'stuck' as ne'er they had before.
And kept together in their rushing sweep;
Deafened and rattled, hung up in the wire,
Helping each other thro' such fearful fire.

On still until they reached the furthest goal,
There to dig in and hold the new-won line.
By linking up each torn and shattered hole—
By no means easy, but their grit was fine—
They fought and worked like demons till the dawn,
Harried and pestered by the 'Kaiser's spawn.'

And, baffled from his gun-pits far away,
Low-down, well south, an angry foe doth roar,
He opens out again upon another day
And rakes the slope with shrapnel as before.
But only working parties on the top are found,
The rest, save A.M.C., are underground.

Strange sights are seen upon that battle-ground,
But stranger still are unearthed from below;
Here many supermen may now be found,
Just watch those stretcher-bearers where *they* go,
And see those parties bearing food and drink,
Past all those blizzard shells—then stand and think!

But one poor shell-crazed loon roamed far and wide;
Sweat-grimed, wild-eyed, and now bereft of all.
'Me mates? W'ere is my mates?' he plaintive cried,
'They's in that 'ole with ME when IT did fall.'
We took him to three huddled heaps nearby,
But he roamed on as tho' he wished to die.

And as the sun's great light bursts o'er the scene,
La Petit Douve, one-time a sparkling stream,
Now sluggish slides, red-tinted, she has been
Past horrors thro' the night and *did not dream*.
For many days she'll, silent, strive to bear
Such human wreckage down a path once fair.

G. P. Cuttriss and *J. W. Hood*

The Illustrator feeling happy, yet looking 'board.'

Bill the Bugler

I well remember when the subject of this sketch joined up. He was small of stature, and his general appearance was by no means prepossessing. That he had seen a good deal of the world was very evident, even to the most superficial observer. His language was picturesque, though not profane. A few weeks sufficed to lick him into shape, and he presented a fairly tolerable figure in uniform. At spinning yarns he was an adept, and at camp concerts could invariably be depended upon for an item or two, always of a humorous nature.

Bill quickly established himself amongst the boys as a general favourite. This enviable position he still occupies. On account of his duties as bugler requiring him to be one of the first up in the morning, and one of the last to retire at night, he sought a change of duty. He became a bandsman, then a stretcher-bearer, and eventually was detailed to assist in a cook-house—in cook-house terminology an *off-sider*.

Though Bill had as much military experience as most of us, we could not think of him as a soldier. That our opinion of him was justified the following incident will illustrate. A party of officers, including a staff-major, was inspecting cooking and billeting arrangements in our quarters. Bill, who happened to have a couple of hours off that day, was strolling towards the party. He was in cook-house attire—tunicless, his hat well back on his head, shirt-sleeves rolled to the elbow, hands deep in his breeches pockets, a cigarette between his lips. Regardless of the critical eyes which were focused upon him, he sauntered leisurely towards the officers, and when in line with them he nodded and said 'Good-day.'

The officers stopped, and one of them peremptorily inquired, 'Aren't you a soldier?'

'Oh, no,' he replied; 'I'm D Company's cook!'

His reply so amused the officers that he was allowed to continue on his way without being reminded that as a soldier he was required to salute all officers.

After spending a few weeks in the cook-house, he asked permission to go to the trenches when the battalion went into the line. The transfer was effected, and he made a start with real soldiering. No amount of discipline could transform him from the free-from-care, do-as-you-please individual into the polished soldier. One evening he was posted over the gas-alert in the front line trenches, when a shell exploded a few yards in front of him. The explosion caused his hat to disappear and the concussion projected him into a dug-out. Only the solidity of the wall prevented him from going further; as it was, the force with which he was hurled against the side of the dug-out made a deep impression on the damp wall. He lay in a motionless heap in the corner of the dug-out. A N.C.O. rushed along the duck-boards, thrust his head into the dug-out, and anxiously inquired of Bill as to whether he was hurt. Bill by this time had partially recovered from the shock. His small steel-grey eyes gradually opened. The N.C.O. again asked if he were hurt. Bill's eyes rolled, his lips moved, and then he blurted out, 'Oh, no, only my feelings!'

Bill is not a man to make a fuss about anything. He has no time for red-tape in any shape or form, it is true, but whatever work is assigned him is always done satisfactorily. Whether he is any less a soldier or his efficiency as a fighting force impaired because of his failure to meet the rigid requirements of an exacting military regulation is a matter concerning which there might be a difference of opinion; but this at least stands to his credit: he knows no fear, is the life of the unit, and the battalion to which he belongs would sustain a distinct loss by the removal of Bugler Bill, &c.

A Tragedy of the War

From strife they now march back to smiling farms,
Recoiling from the crash and smoke and roar.
Meadows, all verdant, faerie fields, whose charms
Serve for a space to make them as before.
And peaceful pictures of the days of yore,
With thrilling thoughts of those they left behind
Flash thro' the mental vision, and a score
Of letters brightly occupy the mind
Without a care, or woe, or doubt of any kind.

Anon they journey from this place of rest
By night or early dawn back to the brink
Of that volcanic crater where the best
Sit tight, scarce caring if they swim or sink.
Silent they bear it, as they quietly think
The end approaching to their life at last,
And face each other, with a smile or wink
Outwardly stoic, tho' their hearts beat fast
As, thumping down, great shells come racing in and past.

Erase such thoughts from out the o'er-wrought brain,
Think rather of this freshness, and the sight
Of nature in her harvest dress, refrain
From plunging into the eternal night.
Such contrasts seem the only choice by right
Of those who battle for the joy of life.
Out on this troubled spot where Armies fight,

And peasants labour just behind such strife
Shorthandedly, unhelped, save by a child or wife.

So come with me down hedgerows, down the glades,
And thro' the cosy glens, till far away
We come unto a hill-crest—lights and shades,
Bright coloured landscapes far below us lay,
Blue mists and fields of yellow corn and hay,
In rows like soldiers, now the tired eyes see,
And poplars guard the distant dim roadway,
Whilst near the wind sighs thro' the acorn-tree,
Till one feels hushed, serene, contented, almost free.

And here, tucked back behind a leafy lane,
Low in a pocket of some sheltered ground,
An unpretentious farm, so snug and plain,
An invitation in itself; when found,
Only a whining howl like dingoes' sound,
Reminds one that there is a war nearby.
The tools of peace see littered here around,
Weapons by which men learn to live, not die:
A plough, a drill, and there a binder standing nigh.

'*Bon jour, m'sieurs*,' a little hunchback cries;
A wizened, twisted human form divine;
She flashed a look of welcome from her eyes,
From which the soul of ages seem to shine.
'*Entrez*,' she welcomed, and her face looked fine,
As proudly bustling o'er her clean stone floor
She bade us linger, eat, and drink her wine.
Refreshed with food and drink, we loiter more
Within such cool retreat, delaying '*Au revoir*.'

And soon the human tragedy in course
Of progress thro' that little home becomes
Clear to the senses, and to us much worse
Compared with our Australia's peaceful homes.
For, oh, the pity, as one's vision roams

From there to here, and back on wings again;
A rush of feeling and emotion comes,
Whilst hearing this contorted piece of pain,
The stirring times of all their troubled lives explain.

For she to whom Fate seemed at first unkind,
Now lives an angel in a higher sphere.
This pained and twisted cripple seemed to find
Pleasure in living for her kinsfolk dear.
Hard work an honour, in her duty clear
To wives of brothers in the fighting line;
Women and children gather round her here;
For round their hearts her nature did entwine,
Her beaming face proclaimed 'See, Anglaise, they are mine.'

And all around these chubby children play,
Dirty, but happy, fed and cared for well,
With ne'er a troubled thought the live-long day,
For they know little of adjacent hell.
The hunchback warns us we are not to tell
About the 'Allemagne' whilst they are nigh,
Since all have known him in the past too well.
'Let them forget it as we often try.
C'est la guerre,' she said, and quickly brushed her eye.

And then she whispers, as we loiter near,
The story of their young lives years ago,
When, snatched from cradles, with a frenzied fear,
Their mothers hurried on before the foe;
Their men defend and screen them as they go,
And fight a rearguard action with the brute,
Who cares not for their agony or woe,
But only for the blood-streams and the loot.
And now she sees us watching one poor little mute:

'Ah! this one?' and she pointed to the dot
Who sat alone, and smiled to vacant space,
'Waits for her mother; very hard her lot;

"She, smiling, takes the pennies which we lay within her hands...."

For years now has she waited in her place.
"Where is her mother?" I can never trace
Somewhere beyond across "the no man's way."
Someday, perhaps,' she cried, with yearning face.
The tiny mite, tho' happy, could not play,
Except with little restless hands all day.

'Sometimes the shell come here right by,' she said.
'The other day, when I what you call wash,
A big boom quickly pass above my head,
And fall out in the field with a big crash.
But, oh, those children, they so very rash,
They know so little of the dreadful doom.
I come in time to save a fearful crash,
And catch them with the nose-cap in this room—
The nose-cap, unexhausted, from the boom.'

And then we start, inclined to say farewell.
We try to brighten up the little maid
Who sits alone, perhaps in faerie dell;
For she doth seem not in the least afraid.
She, smiling, takes the pennies which we lay
Within her hands, tho' distant is her smile;
And for a space she seemed with them to play,
But drops them ere we're scarcely gone, awhile
We wander back, half dumb, hard, thinking for a mile.

G. P. Cuttriss and *J. W. Hood*

Recreation Behind the Lines

The military authorities have ever recognized the importance and value of recreation in connexion with the training of men. They realize that all work and no play makes Tommy a dull boy; and the provision that has been made for recreation and amusement for the boys commands the deepest appreciation of both rank and file. The Australian is unaccustomed to the rigid restrictions of an inflexible military regime, and a temporary relaxation contributes much towards eliminating that feeling of fed-upness to which he is so susceptible under monotonous and trying conditions, and certainly assists in making him a less dissatisfied soldier.

The sporting instinct is so ingrained in the average Australian that amusement and athletics have become part and parcel of his life, and his efficiency as a fighting force has been increased in consequence. His well-knit, muscular frame, and cheerful, free-from-care disposition, and love for clean sport, have won for him a place in the estimation of those who know and understand him, which is the envy of many. Australia has given to the world champions in almost every branch of sport, and the traditions which have been

Off to the Horse Show

established on the football and cricket fields and in athletic circles in years preceding the war are being upheld and added to by her sons 'somewhere in France.'

A General's task is by no means an easy one. He has to safeguard against dissatisfaction, which invariably is the primary cause of breaches of discipline. He requires to be tactful in the handling of his command, gain the confidence of the men, and enlist their undivided support; yet every consideration must be subordinate to the supreme task of winning the war. His methods must be such as will exact prompt obedience and beget respect, without imposing undue hardships and punishment.

The Third Division is exceedingly fortunate in having Major-General John Monash, C.B., V.D., in command. He is a popular and painstaking officer, a born leader, a strict disciplinarian, possessed of tireless energy. He has not spared himself in his efforts to establish and maintain a high standard of efficiency amongst all ranks. The G.O.C. set himself to put his men right and succeeded. He has a wonderfully comprehensive grip over every branch of activity, and woe betide the officer or man who is indifferent to or negligent of the duties entrusted to him. Any proposition calculated to benefit the men has always been favourably considered, and he has frequently been an interested spectator of various games that have been played just behind the lines. As a result there is little if any disaffection among the men of the Division. Major-General Monash has encouraged by approval and assistance various forms of recreation and entertainment. The splendid fighting record of the Third speaks eloquently of his capable leadership and the rousing and prolonged cheering which greets him when presiding over or addressing an assembly of his men leaves no doubt in the mind as to his popularity.

For a few months after our arrival in France, a cinema afforded nightly entertainment. It was well patronized by the troops. The building used had seating accommodation for about seven hundred, and generally long before the hour of opening a queue of soldiers would assemble. There was no pushing or scrambling for tickets. The Australian good-humouredly submitted to the queue system, and patiently waited his turn. Mr. Frank Beaurepeare, of swimming fame, successfully managed the picture show,

'Sweet and Low' by the quartette party always brought forth rounds of applause.

'Try it a little softer.'
Taff Williams, Musical Director

and eventually got together a few vocalists and comedians, who were organized into a *pierrot* group. These men were relieved from other duties during the comparatively quiet periods. Eventually a couple of talented Tommies were added to the group, which came to be designated the Coo-ees, under the direction of Mr. Dixon, the capable and energetic successor to Mr. F. B. Beaurepeare. In addition to performing every evening, the Coo-ees frequently gave out-door concerts during the day or in the men's billets, after the evening entertainment. A nominal charge for admission was made, and the proceeds were used to augment the Divisional Funds, which are used for the benefit of the men. These entertainments were given within easy range of the enemy guns. On several occasions shells fell in the vicinity of the hall, but few casualties were reported.

In addition to affording amusement, the Coo-ees did invaluable work during engagements. They either acted as stretcher-bearers or dispensed refreshments to the troops as they went forward to or returned from the trenches. They were located at dressing-stations or at R.A.Ps. It is generally hoped that the party as at present constituted will be available after the war for the purpose of giving entertainments in Australia such as they gave to the tired war-hardened troops *somewhere in France*.

Costumes were procured, and the programmes submitted were highly creditable and greatly appreciated. The quartette party was exceedingly popular, and never failed to please the boys.

Periodically horse shows and sports were arranged by D.H.Q. Substantial prizes and valuable trophies were awarded the successful competitors. The day's proceedings would be enlivened by band music. Impersonations of the world's mirth maker, Charlie Chaplin, and Australian sundowners, were decidedly clever and afforded much amusement. Horse shows always attract large attendances, and any vehicle going in the direction of the show grounds was practically commandeered by the tired but interested troops. They have a partiality, however, for M.T. lorries. For weeks prior to the event, men would spend every available minute polishing chains, cleaning harness, painting vehicles, and grooming horses. Every unit has its admirers and supporters, and all events were keenly contested.

Sir Douglas Haig, G.C.B., G.C.V.O., and Sir A.J. Godley, K.C.B., K.C.M.G., at the 2nd Anzac Horse Show

In addition to horse shows and sports organized by D.H.Q., the brigades and battalions within the Division arrange for fête days whenever opportunity offers. The manner in which these are carried out reflects the highest credit upon those responsible for their organization, and they have materially helped to bring about a better understanding between officers and men. Games appropriate to the season are played at the back of the lines. The ground selected for football or cricket may be shell-marked, and the materials used roughly made and incomplete. Football matches between different units have been as keenly contested on the muddy and broken fields of Belgium and France as those that have been played on the specially prepared grounds of the Homeland. The Australians have held their own against other units in both cricket and football.

For those who find such games too strenuous, indoor games are provided by the Australian Comforts Fund, the Y.M.C.A., or the League of Loyal Women of Australia. A circulating library is usually connected with the Y.M.C.A. or Church Army huts, so that practically every taste is catered for. An institution is justified in its existence by what it produces. Judged according to this canon, the various organizations which cater for the amusement and recreation of our fighting men have infallibly demonstrated their right to be, and should command the practical support of all who are interested in the well-being of our fighting men.

For the Cause of the Empire

Irrespective of the state which sent us forth, and despite our denominational and political differences, we are undivided in our admiration of those who, in the enthusiasm of deathless devotion, have made the supreme sacrifice for King and country. Words are inadequate to express the tribute which we would pay to the memory of our brave dead. We are beginning to value heroism more truly, and have not been blind to the valour of those who have fallen in the effort to uphold the honour and flag of the Empire. The story of their deeds makes the heart beat faster. Many have discovered that the most glorious use to which life could be put was to give it away. When the smoke has lifted and the noise died down, the confession made and the true history of this war written, then we shall see their heroism in the right light, and more fully appreciate their sacrifice in the interests of justice and honour. It matters not where they died—in hospital, on troopship, or on the battlefield; their presence in the Army was sufficient evidence of their willingness to bear their share of the cost in sacrifice that had to be made before the end could be achieved. They died as few men get the opportunity to die, fighting for all that is most worthwhile—for God, and right, and liberty—which is just another way of stating that they gave their lives for the glorious cause of the Empire.

The general impression is that the Empire consists of an aggregation of people, in possession of vast territories and enormous wealth: that it consists of Great Britain, Canada, India, South Africa, Australia, New Zealand, &c. Many cannot think of the Empire but in terms of territory, money, and men. The British Empire, like the Kingdom of God, is invisible. These material things are but the practical expression of great forces and unalterable principles such as freedom, democracy, justice, and faith, which lie at the very base of our national life. It is for the retention and general enjoyment of these things that we are fighting. We are not fighting for France, Belgium, nor even for the Empire, as it is generally regarded, but for the enforcement of those standards of justice and honour which have made us the greatest nation in the world. It is not a war of retaliation nor aggression, but a war to redress wrong, to succour the weak and downtrodden. There is not lacking evidence that beneath the material aspects of this conflict there is a tremendous spiritual battle in progress, the issue of which will determine the value of these national assets. We cannot think that our comrades have given their lives merely to enlarge our borders or to increase our wealth. They have died for the cause of the Empire, and the cause of the Empire is synonymous with the cause of humanity, democracy, freedom, civilization—of Christianity.

The cause of the Empire is the cause of God. The highest standard of civilization finds expression in the readiness to make sacrifice that others might benefit. This standard has been splendidly exemplified by the 'boys' from Australia. This is the standard of the Empire as against that of *Kultur*, which is the suppression of the weak, the slaughter of the innocent, and the elimination of the small. The sacrifice has certainly been considerable, the price involved very great, but not too great. We are prepared to pay even a higher price rather than lose our heritage or forfeit our right to the enjoyment of the priceless privileges of freedom and justice. We cannot help the dead, but we can honour them, and we can best honour them by taking up the arms which they have laid down, filling the gaps which their death has made, and resting not until peace with honour shall have been established on firm and enduring foundations.

War is certainly an ugly business; it is hell; but better by far than the loss of liberty and civilization under the heel of Prussian militarism; and we would pay our humble tribute to the memory of our brave comrades who have freely given their lives for the cause of the Empire.

To those who have lost—the wives, mothers, and sweethearts—we extend our deepest sympathy, and trust that their deep sorrow will be tinged with pride in the knowledge that their dear ones died the noblest death that men may die.

Our Heroic Dead

Our heroic dead, though war hath laid you low,
And cruelly robbed you of this earthly life,
You did your best against the fiendish foe,
And gave your all to put an end to strife.

Our comrades still, sleep on; your names will live
Long after this terrific war hath ceased.
No cannon's roar, no hurtling shell, no bomb
Can harm thee or disturb your long last sleep.

Down in your soldiers' graves you rest from toil,
Without the knowledge of the Hun's fierce hate.
The shell-struck, blood-stained clods of Belgian soil
Will open to your souls the Pearly Gate.

There is no place on this earth's troubled face
So sacred as the ground which shields your heads,
Fit resting-place for those so true and brave,
Who for *the cause* the fullest price have paid.

Australia's sons the sacrifice supreme
For honour, truth, and freedom gladly made;
And though the price as high again had been,
We'd have paid it, bravely, for the Nation's sake.

Comrades, sleep on, till God's great Spirit comes
To clothe you with the life which never ends;
And o'er this shell-swept, bruised, and bleeding land
Victorious and enduring peace descends.

The Silver Lining

War in itself is not a blessing—neither is the surgeon's knife. If it were a choice between a slow, painful death from a malignant cancer, or an operation, which would give pain for the time being, but which ultimately would bring relief and complete recovery—invariably the choice would be in favour of the operation.

War is hell, but its prosecution as an effective means in arresting the development of the cancer of mad militarism was as essential as the use of the surgeon's knife to remove a malignant growth.

War is an ugly business—it is carnage and horror. The thought of man butchered by his brother, the thought of both sea and land stained with human blood, spilled by human hands, is too horrible for contemplation. Yet peace at the price we were asked to pay would have been, in its effects, considerably worse than war.

There are accruing to us individually, and to the Empire, blessings which possibly no other event (certainly not undisturbed tranquillity) than this unprecedented conflict could have created. There are compensations that are apt to be overlooked. To realize appreciably the compensatory effects in connexion with this conflict, it is necessary that we turn from the purely sordid and sad aspect to its spiritual and constructive side. The question, Has this war produced anything that would approximately counterbalance the arrest of industry and progress, waste of life at its prime, the desolation of hearts and homes, the devastation of property, and the incalculable measures of sorrow and suffering?—is permissible, and we forget not the atrocities on both land and sea, the deliberate violation of individual and international laws, and the fact that there is hardly a street without a loss, and scarce a heart without anxiety.

Throw this immeasurable pile of war-waste and colossal suffering into the scales of thoughtful contemplation, then heap into it as a counter-weight the blessings that have accrued, and the effect upon our minds must necessarily be to lead us to become more hopeful and less ungrateful.

The Empire has awakened out of her sleep—she is purging away the dross that has accumulated round her life, and at last as a nation we have found our soul.

The war found us in a muddle, both from a military and moral view-point, but out of that muddle a miracle has been fashioned. In addition, the Empire, even to its remotest outposts, has been consolidated, and the people over whom King George reigns are bound together in indissoluble bonds sealed with blood. Russia is now freed from the shackles of tyrannical oppression and autocratic domination; and the right to existence of the smaller nations has been powerfully endorsed.

There are other factors than those stated above which contribute no inconsiderable weight towards counter-balancing the load of hardship and heartaches that this war has heaped upon us. Such will be the theme of many writers when the smoke has lifted and the peoples of this earth again repose in the embrace of world-peace.

We have, so far, only briefly considered the beneficial effects of this war upon the Empire. When we come to consider what the war has done for the individual, particularly those who are actively engaged at the battle fronts, the difference between the weight of suffering and the weight of blessing will be very palpable, even to the most superficial mind.

Perhaps the blessing of most permanent importance that this war has brought to the majority of us is a strengthened faith in immortality. We cannot penetrate the veil that screens the mysteries of the future from our vision. Faith and the inner consciousness are the basis of our belief that there is a future. One cannot be at the Front very long before he is compelled to examine his thoughts in regard to immortality. Death is brought home very closely. The grim spectre points his finger at a man—perhaps in the first flush of manhood—who has just commenced to appreciate the joy of living. Death challenges, and with no shadow of faltering, but perhaps with a smile, the challenge is accepted, and the lad goes under. It is no triumph for death. It is the soul of a man that has gained a glorious victory. One feels convinced that it is but the body that has terminated existence. The physical presence is no more, but the personality—the soul—has been translated and passed beyond us. Freed from the limitations of this earthly life, it has passed into the infinite to be with others who have gone before.

Many scenes have been witnessed the memory of which, even now, fills the eyes with tears. Men waiting the advance of death—resolutely, fearless, hopeful.

The war has done in a few months what years of preaching apparently failed to effect. It has produced a revival of religion amongst men, and consequently a slump in ritualism. Christianity has always had its enemies, and any opportunity for adversely criticizing the system has been laid hold of by some with amazing alacrity. The report that the nearer men get to the firing line the less mindful they become of the claims of Christ is entirely false, and could only have been circulated by people who desired to depreciate the men whose character and courage command the admiration of all who know and understand them. Those responsible for the rise and spread of such a libel are neither the friends of the Church nor of the soldiers.

All soldiers are not saints; all may not be gentlemen. Such claim has never been made by them, nor has it ever been their well-wishers' boast. Yet there are many soldiers whose lives are clean and sweet, who are entitled to be described saints if ever man was. As for what constitutes a gentleman, a difference of opinion exists; but judged by the standard raised since the outset of this terrific conflict amongst the nations, I have no hesitation in affirming that the vast majority of them are Nature's own.

Certainly there are some who are careless and callous, who are not and never were amenable to the claims of Christ, who daily grow more forgetful of home-ties and become slaves to ignoble appetites; but such are few, very few, indeed; and the like are to be seen not only in military but also in civil life, and generally are not unfamiliar with orderly or court-room proceedings. Is it right that all should be condemned because of the capricious behaviour of an infinitesimal section? Is it Christ-like to condemn those whose actions are called into question? Even they are not beyond the pale of reformation and redemption—for such Christ tasted death.

Then there are a few whose knowledge of the world and its wickedness is limited, who are separated from the restraints of home life, and who stray as sheep and sin in ignorance. Are all so strong that they can dispense with guidance, or so pure that sin ceases to allure? *Let him who is without sin throw the first stone.*

The men in the main are better since they joined up, and evidence is not lacking that from the date of enlistment they appreciably realized the seriousness of the work to which they so willingly devoted themselves.

As they get nearer to, and while they are at, the Front, they become more reverent and less disposed to frivolity. All church parades are voluntary, and the chaplains have no occasion to complain about poor attendances. The men crowd the buildings used for gospel meetings, and large numbers of them have publicly acknowledged their acceptance of the Christian faith.

In proportion to the number of services conducted and the opportunities for attending them, more soldiers are present at religious meetings at the Front than civilians at home. In the ranks and amongst both N.C.Os and officers there are splendid Christian men. These men are a tower of strength to the chaplains, and their influence for good amongst their comrades is incalculable.

It has been whispered that the war has completely shattered the foundations of Christianity; but from close observation I am inclined to the opinion that it has exposed the instability and inadequacy of human creeds, and will eventually accomplish what the Churches have so lamentably failed to do.

The war is an indictment against divided Christendom. If Christians the world over had been united in 'the faith' and 'of one mind in the Lord,' this war would have been both impracticable and impossible.

Men on active service have grown indifferent not to Christ and His Church, but to human creeds and *our* brand of Christianity. Both have been proved impotent during the progress of this war.

We have heard much about Christian union; no evidence of such is noticeable at the Front—at least amongst the accredited representatives of the various religious organizations. Emphasis is placed upon denominationalism, and more heart-burnings have been caused amongst the men in consequence of the divisions amongst the Churches than amongst the home folks at the fancied increasing irreverence and indifference of the men regarding the things that are esteemed sacred. The men give evidence of being disposed to stand outside of all *human* creeds. Their query is not 'Are you a member of a certain religious organization?' but 'Are you a member of *The Church*?' Their views of Christianity are as simple as they are scriptural. The soldiers are beginning to realize that what matters most is not whether a man is a member of a certain Church, but *is he a Christian?* Just as the people of Russia have freed themselves of the yoke of autocratic government, so I predict that the most potent contribution towards bringing about Christian union will come not from the recognized leaders of the Churches, but from the soldiers on active service who have been impressed with the impotence of the existing system to bring about that condition which represents the ideal of Christianity, and the answer to our Lord's prayer, 'that all may be one in Him.'

If the Allies were to strive for peace and the overthrow of evil in the same manner as the Churches are seeking the overthrow of evil and the effecting of Christian union, they might well give up the conflict. Prolongation of the war and ultimate defeat could be the only issue.

Many have learned to know themselves better. They have been made cognizant of their weaknesses and their strength—what they are capable of and where they fall short.

Life at the Front affords unique opportunities for studying men. One is brought into such close contact with them. Everyone is different, each having his own characteristics, his own eccentricities—each a distinct and separate personality. A man sees why this one succeeds and why that one fails—he succeeds himself, and learns to have confidence.

Perhaps he fails and learns humility, and, maybe, because he has failed at one job he is given another, and he finds that he can 'make good.' Few, if any, ever dreamed that they were capable of performing the tasks which are daily assumed by or assigned to them.

Following upon a man getting to know himself, he acquires a knowledge of others. This tends to bridge the gulf that society has created between men. Class distinction is virtually eliminated after a few months of camp and active service life. Classification is made on the basis of character rather than on that of social status. This turn of events cannot help but materially contribute to the solution of those problems which arise out of the vexed question of social inequalities.

Another effect which this war has produced, and which will prove an inestimable blessing, is that the home associations and the little joys of home life have become for all time our priceless possessions such as they never could otherwise.

Our loved ones are enshrined in our hearts as never before. We feel that their personalities are with us, helping us every day. We have become capable of greater love for them. We live for them. We fight for them. Yea, we would willingly die for them! And for many of us our thoughts, our deeds, our daily living is the result of a constant endeavour to be as they would have us.

So I feel that the world will be better because of this war. Dark as is the cloud that hovers over all, it has its silver lining, and the majority of soldiers subscribe to the sentiments of the Apostle Paul, who declared that the sufferings of this present time are not worthy to be compared with the glory which shall be revealed in us. 'For our light affliction, which is but for a moment, worketh for us a far more exceeding and eternal weight of glory.'

I feel that Australia will be a better land because of the experiences that so many of her sons have gone through. They have learned what their loved ones and what their homes mean to them. They have learned to appreciate the things most worthwhile, and will return with hearts full of love and thankfulness, more ready than ever before to devote their lives to the happiness of those who with bursting hearts watched them go; and ever prayed for their return.

'*They also serve who only stand and wait.*'

How true that is, and how we have realized it since we have been out here! We know that the wives, the mothers, the sweethearts, have had a harder time than any of us. We realize the long anxious time of waiting they have gone through, and know the magnificent part they have played in this world-wide war.

However dark things may appear now, the future is radiant with hope, and Australia's sons will return to their beloved land bigger and better men than when they left; and our country will be a nobler one because so many of her sons heard the call of the Motherland, and responded gloriously.

ALSO FROM LEONAUR
AVAILABLE IN SOFTCOVER OR HARDCOVER WITH DUST JACKET

DOING OUR 'BIT' by *Ian Hay*—Two Classic Accounts of the Men of Kitchener's 'New Army' During the Great War including *The First 100,000* & *All In It*.

AN EYE IN THE STORM by *Arthur Ruhl*—An American War Correspondent's Experiences of the First World War from the Western Front to Gallipoli and Beyond.

STAND & FALL by *Joe Cassells*—A Soldier's Recollections of the 'Contemptible Little Army' and the Retreat from Mons to the Marne, 1914.

RIFLEMAN MACGILL'S WAR by *Patrick MacGill*—A Soldier of the London Irish During the Great War in Europe including *The Amateur Army, The Red Horizon* & *The Great Push*.

WITH THE GUNS by *C. A. Rose & Hugh Dalton*—Two First Hand Accounts of British Gunners at War in Europe During World War 1- Three Years in France with the Guns and With the British Guns in Italy.

EAGLES OVER THE TRENCHES by *James R. McConnell & William B. Perry*—Two First Hand Accounts of the American Escadrille at War in the Air During World War 1-Flying For France: With the American Escadrille at Verdun and Our Pilots in the Air.

THE BUSH WAR DOCTOR by *Robert V. Dolbey*—The Experiences of a British Army Doctor During the East African Campaign of the First World War.

THE 9TH—THE KING'S (LIVERPOOL REGIMENT) IN THE GREAT WAR 1914 - 1918 by *Enos H. G. Roberts*—Like many large cities, Liverpool raised a number of battalions in the Great War. Notable among them were the Pals, the Liverpool Irish and Scottish, but this book concerns the wartime history of the 9th Battalion – The Kings.

THE GAMBARDIER by *Mark Severn*—The experiences of a battery of Heavy artillery on the Western Front during the First World War.

FROM MESSINES TO THIRD YPRES by *Thomas Floyd*—A personal account of the First World War on the Western front by a 2/5th Lancashire Fusilier.

THE IRISH GUARDS IN THE GREAT WAR - VOLUME 1 by *Rudyard Kipling*—Edited and Compiled from Their Diaries and Papers Volume 1 The First Battalion.

THE IRISH GUARDS IN THE GREAT WAR - VOLUME 2 by *Rudyard Kipling*—Edited and Compiled from Their Diaries and Papers Volume 2 The Second Battalion.

AVAILABLE ONLINE AT
www.leonaur.com
AND OTHER GOOD BOOK STORES

ALSO FROM LEONAUR
AVAILABLE IN SOFTCOVER OR HARDCOVER WITH DUST JACKET

ARMOURED CARS IN EDEN by *K. Roosevelt*—An American President's son serving in Rolls Royce armoured cars with the British in Mesopatamia & with the American Artillery in France during the First World War.

CHASSEUR OF 1914 by *Marcel Dupont*—Experiences of the twilight of the French Light Cavalry by a young officer during the early battles of the great war in Europe.

TROOP HORSE & TRENCH by *R.A. Lloyd*—The experiences of a British Lifeguardsman of the household cavalry fighting on the western front during the First World War 1914-18.

THE LONG PATROL by *George Berrie*—A Novel of Light Horsemen from Gallipoli to the Palestine campaign of the First World War.

THE EAST AFRICAN MOUNTED RIFLES by *C.J. Wilson*—Experiences of the campaign in the East African bush during the First World War

THE FIGHTING CAMELIERS by *Frank Reid*—The exploits of the Imperial Camel Corps in the desert and Palestine campaigns of the First World War.

WITH THE IMPERIAL CAMEL CORPS IN THE GREAT WAR by *Geoffrey Inchbald*—The story of a serving officer with the British 2nd battalion against the Senussi and during the Palestine campaign.

STEEL CHARIOTS IN THE DESERT by *S.C.Rolls*—The first world war experiences of a Rolls Royce armoured car driver with the Duke of Westminster in Libya and in Arabia with T.E. Lawrence.

INFANTRY BRIGADE: 1914 by *Edward Gleichen*—The Diary of a Commander of the 15th Infantry Brigade, 5th Division, British Army, During the Retreat from Mons

HEARTS & DRAGONS by *Charles R. M. F. Crutwell*—The 4th Royal Berkshire Regiment in France and Italy During the Great War, 1914-1918.

TIGERS ALONG THE TIGRIS by *E. J. Thompson*—The Leicestershire Regiment in Mesopotamia During the First World War.

DESPATCH RIDER by *W. H. L. Watson*—The Experiences of a British Army Motorcycle Despatch Rider During the Opening Battles of the Great War in Europe.

ALSO FROM LEONAUR
AVAILABLE IN SOFTCOVER OR HARDCOVER WITH DUST JACKET

WAR BEYOND THE DRAGON PAGODA by *J. J. Snodgrass*—A Personal Narrative of the First Anglo-Burmese War 1824 - 1826.

ALL FOR A SHILLING A DAY by *Donald F. Featherstone*—The story of H.M. 16th, the Queen's Lancers During the first Sikh War 1845-1846.

AT THEM WITH THE BAYONET by *Donald F. Featherstone*—The first Anglo-Sikh War 1845-1846.

A LEONAUR ORIGINAL

THE HERO OF ALIWAL by *James Humphries*—The days when young Harry Smith wore the green jacket of the 95th-Wellington's famous riflemen-campaigning in Spain against Napoleon's French with his beautiful young bride Juana have long gone. Now, Sir Harry Smith is in his fifties approaching the end of a long career. His position in the Cape colony ends with an appointment as Deputy Adjutant-General to the army in India. There he joins the staff of Sir Hugh Gough to experience an Indian battlefield in the Gwalior War of 1843 as the power of the Marathas is finally crushed. Smith has little time for his superior's 'bull at a gate' style of battlefield tactics, but independent command is denied him. Little does he realise that the greatest opportunity of his military life is close at hand.

THE GURKHA WAR by *H. T. Prinsep*—The Anglo-Nepalese Conflict in North East India 1814-1816.

SOUND ADVANCE! by *Joseph Anderson*—Experiences of an officer of HM 50th regiment in Australia, Burma & the Gwalior war.

THE CAMPAIGN OF THE INDUS by *Thomas Holdsworth*—Experiences of a British Officer of the 2nd (Queen's Royal) Regiment in the Campaign to Place Shah Shuja on the Throne of Afghanistan 1838 - 1840.

WITH THE MADRAS EUROPEAN REGIMENT IN BURMA by *John Butler*—The Experiences of an Officer of the Honourable East India Company's Army During the First Anglo-Burmese War 1824 - 1826.

BESIEGED IN LUCKNOW by *Martin Richard Gubbins*—The Experiences of the Defender of 'Gubbins Post' before & during the sige of the residency at Lucknow, Indian Mutiny, 1857.

THE STORY OF THE GUIDES by *G.J. Younghusband*—The Exploits of the famous Indian Army Regiment from the northwest frontier 1847 - 1900.

AVAILABLE ONLINE AT
www.leonaur.com
AND OTHER GOOD BOOK STORES

www.ingramcontent.com/pod-product-compliance
Lightning Source LLC
Chambersburg PA
CBHW031616160426
43196CB00006B/149